Facets of Contemporary Event Management

Theory & Practice for Event Success

Edited by

ULRICH WÜNSCH

International University of Applied Sciences
Bad Honnef • Bonn, Germany

Bad Honnefer Schriften zum Dienstleistungsmanagement

Bad Honnef Series on Services Management

SERIES EDITORS

Prof. Dr. Helmut WACHOWIAK

Professor in Tourism Management at the International University of
Applied Sciences Bad Honnef · Bonn – Head of the IUBH Department of
Tourism Management

Prof. Ulrich WÜNSCH, M.A.

Professor in Event Management at the International University of Applied
Sciences Bad Honnef · Bonn – Head of the IUBH Department of Event
Management

PUBLICATION EDITOR

Kai LÜTTGER, M.A.

Librarian at the International University of Applied Sciences
Bad Honnef · Bonn – Head of the IUBH Library Information Services

Bibliografische Information der Deutschen Bibliothek
Die Deutsche Bibliothek verzeichnet diese Publikation in der Deutschen
Nationalbibliografie.
Detaillierte bibliografische Daten sind im Internet über http://dnb.ddb.de
abrufbar

ISBN 978-3-86796-027-4

Contents

List of Figures 7

List of Tables 9

Preface
Ulrich Wünsch 11

Sensational Sensations! – An Excursion to the Early Days of
Corporate Event Communication
Ulrich Wünsch 19

Imagine Your Event – Imagineering for the Event Industry
Moniek Hover 37

Brand Entertainment at Trade Shows: Are You Experienced?
Urs Seiler 63

Selected Issues of Crowd Management: 25th RhEINKULTUR
2007
Sabine Funk 73

Strategic Event Management – The Decisive Step to Success
Ana Maria Zumsteg, Polo Looser 95

TransRockies Inc.: The Effective Use of Stakeholder
Management in Event Projects
Donald Getz, Aaron McConnell 113

Some Ideas on Specifics of Event Evaluation
Ulrich Wünsch 135

Fira de Teatre al Carrer de Tàrrega – A Performing Arts
Market
Mike Ribalta, Francisco Juárez Rubio 153

The Meetings Industry Yesterday, Today and Tomorrow
Tony Carey 171

German Protestant Kirchentag – Sustainability Strategy for a
Large-scale Event
Gabriele Nottelmann, Tilman Henke 183

Contents

IMEX – A Case Study in Launching a Trade Show
Carina Bauer, Simon Naudi, Brian Wiseman 203

Exhibition Events – A Revolutionary Campaign
Tony Erpelding 219

How a Perfect Storm Created Spectacular Success
Joe Goldblatt...................... 229

Rotterdam – Maximizing City Event Partnership
Johan Moerman 247

Stockholm Water Festival: The Phoenix of Festivals
Charlotte J. DeWitt 257

Deni Ute Muster
Tracy Hull, William J. O´Toole 269

Managing the "Unmanageable" – Producing New York's
Greenwich Village Halloween Parade
Lewis Siris 281

Harry Potter is Coming! – Deutsche Post and Weltbild at the
Controls of the Hogwarts Express
Corinna Geimer, Christiane Legler, Carolin Maluck, Julia
Seehausen....................... 293

Communicating a Country – Denmark's HCA Event Viewed
from the PR Side
Lars Blicher-Hansen, Christian Have.......................... 305

TOYOTA – The Cologne City Grand Prix
Kay Dallmann...................... 325

EMBOK: A Theoretical and Practical Model for the Event World
Julia Rutherford Silvers................. 341

Authors....................... 355

List of Figures

Figure 1:   Matrix of event typology.   14

Figure 2:   Coney Island, USA 1904 – Dreamland Walk   26

Figure 3:   "Bibendum" at the Nice Carnival, France 1911   31

Figure 4:   Heinz-Pier in Atlantic City, USA around 1900   32

Figure 5:   "Imi-Men", Germany, 1920s ("Imi" was a popular
            cleansing powder)   34

Figure 6:   Experience model, Gool, Wijngaarden, adapted by
            Hover, 2007   41

Figure 7:   Model of experiential concept   52

Figure 8:   Comparison between the lay-out of a medieval
            town and Magic Kingdom at Walt Disney World   54

Figure 9:   Global events strategy   97

Figure 10: Fit with brand   100

Figure 11: Eventflector, measurement method of MCI   104

Figure 12: The fundamentals   105

Figure 13: Political Market Square for the TransRockies
            Challenge, 2005   126

Figure 14: New partners in the stakeholder network – political
            market square for the TransRockies
            Challenge, 2006   129

Figure 15: Experience processing model   142

Figure 16: Model of return on communication-perspectives   146

Figure 17: Event parameters   147

Figure 18: Model of the event field with its domains and
parameters   150

Figure 19: Volume of contracting of spectacles at the Fira
during the 2004-2005 season   167

Figure 20: Volume of contracting of spectacles at the
Fira by origin   168

Figure 21: The Producer's Eight Rings of Olympic
Achievement model (Goldblatt/Morton)   231

Figure 22: P R I S M   238

Figure 23: Triangulation: cast, company and audience   245

Figure 24: Elements   251

Figure 25: Annual festival growth   272

Figure 26: Consultancy Methodology   278

Figure 27: Timeline until event   330

Figure 28: Key visual   332

Figure 29: International EMBOK model   341

List of Tables

Table 1:	TransRockies Challenge, Expenses	121
Table 2:	Matrix of event related need factors and their domains	149
Table 3:	Evolution in the number of professionals registered	163
Table 4:	Budgets for the past 25 years (in EUR)	169
Table 5:	Phases of event and organizational production	234
Table 6:	Overview on Rotterdam Festivals	250
Table 7:	Ten years of Rotterdam Summer festivals	255
Table 8:	The Toyota Way	326
Table 9:	Budget composition City-Grand-Prix	334
Table 10:	Media Contacts	339
Table 11:	Scope of the international EMBOK model	342
Table 12:	Curriculum model for financial management	345
Table 13:	Planning system for financial management	346

Preface

Ulrich Wünsch

"The reorganization of time and space, plus the disembedding mechanisms, radicalize and globalize pre-established institutional traits of modernity; and they act to transform the context and nature of day-to-day social life."
(Anthony Giddens, Modernity and Self-Identity – Self and Society in the Late Modern Age; 1991)

"One thing is certain: The creative age is a wide-open game. No single country or region has a lock on it."
(Richard Florida, The Rise of the Creative Class; 2002)

"The difficulty of relating events and spaces does not lie on the theoretical level."
(Bernard Tschumi, Event-Cities 2; 2000)

"Is it still a taboo to take Las Vegas seriously?"
(Rem Koolhaas, Content; 2004)

Events and the event industry have come of age. Worldwide statistics on money spent for event marketing show that events within the last fifteen years have risen to a full-grown tool for companies, governments, cities, organizations and more. Their share of marketing and communication budgets as well as of money spent by private individuals does rise.

About thirty years ago events seemed to be a fun thing, seemed to be part of youth and IT-boom culture with their ostensibly never-ending supplies of fresh money. Matured through several crises and a lot of often trial and error practical experiences, event marketing nowadays is a respected communication tool. Modern man and woman do not seem be so different from their ancestors in believing in what they can test or what is recommended in person by somebody reliable. Experiences with products and services do count for the consumer – and who is not a consumer these days? These experiences – within the framework of the individual belief-system – tell what something is worth, tell what somebody is worth.

The steadily growing event management and marketing programs on all levels of public and private education are further proof of event's coming of age. From a three-day course on event specialties via certificates from event industry organizations to BA and Master degree programs; professionalization is the way to go. Main event industry markets can be determined today as North America, Western Europe, India, China and the Middle East. In Canada, a government supported body of experts is trying to establish a profile of what it takes to be and work in the event industry that is both generic (for all cultures and fields of event practice) and specific (dealing with intercultural differences and various job descriptions). The outcome will help the profession to move along, especially in its relation to bordering professions in the tourism, hospitality or a more general leisure industry. Events were seen academically and professionally to be part of those industries for quite a while. Business tourism was the term used to cover the multitude of aspects concerning events. From the perspective of the traveller, rooms, destinations and modes of transport were dominant matters of discussion. Yet more and more the organizational and marketing aspects of event as a communication tool in its own right were observed. This, for example in the UK, led to the recent renaming of the Business Travel or Tourism sector to Business Visits and Events. Events always have formed a strong part of human culture. This discourse was and still is represented in the argument on ritual, celebration, ownership and inclusion. Creativity functions as an essential ingredient for designing, programming, and establishing events. "Creative Industries" has become a catch phrase in describing the prospects of the social and economic development of places. The European Union, for example, has committed itself to fostering this field, and individual countries like Germany or the UK strive to be leaders in competing for resources and budgets. Sponsoring and sports plus destination development via sports and other events have started to play a big role in event practice. Corporations with their differentiated demands in the promotion of goods and services take a direct interest in occupying empty spaces in minds and hearts of buyers via experiential marketing. In short: any objective driven, staged and intentionally or professionally produced happening is now prone to be part of the event industry.

But what to call an event? Glenn Bowdin has written a substantial report on the findings on the event industry, mentioning as well the problems with the classification of events[1]. Bowdin (2006, p. 1) offers the following terms and formats:

- business events/business tourism (conferences/meetings, exhibitions, incentive travel, corporate events/corporate hospitality)
- festivals/fairs/cultural events
- community events
- outdoor events
- entertainment events/live music events/concerts/theatre/shows
- sports events/spectator sports
- charity events/fundraising/voluntary sector
- party planning/wedding planning/social life-cycle events/ special events.

It is rather problematic that lots of these do overlap and no clear distinction can be made. The terminology even within the Anglo-centered cultural sphere differentiates substantially

---

[1] *Identifying and Analyzing Existing Research Undertaken in the Events Industry: a Literature Review for People 1st", Glenn Bowdin et al. on behalf of AEME, March 2006 – download via People 1st:*
http://www.people1st.co.uk/research/themes

between the UK, USA and Australia, to name just a few. The American "festival" then would run under "Markt = a market" in Germany; the "special event" would be not so special somewhere else but rather a "corporate event"; "business events" could be anything from "cultural" to "entertainment" to "sports" to "charity" to "outdoor events".

The following matrix hopes to provide some orientation in asking two structuring questions: "Who pays for the event and who decides?" and "Who is invited, who is allowed to come?" Within this matrix the various event types can be positioned and its characteristics can be described.

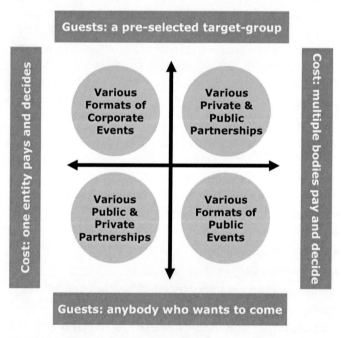

Figure 1: Matrix of event typology

This proposal takes into account the rapid development of cross over, connection, and dependencies of publicly owned and financed as well as privately owned and financed events. In the public domain we do see a rapidly developing take over of the "third place", the space of social encounter apart from home and work, by brand initiated and steered opportunities for encounter and experience. An example might be a format like the "Flight Days" by Red Bull, a Nokia News Years Party around the world, the "X Games" created by NBC, or event-gastronomic efforts like Planet Hollywood. Yet conferences or exhibitions, festivals or community events all can vary due to the degree of their financing or guest profile. The matrix is taken from the heuristics of practical event production.

A range of self-help books and pamphlets has been published on how to create/organize/manage/produce events in all the major event industry markets and countries. Academic study books beyond the fields of the above mentioned hospitality, tourism and leisure fields that concentrate solely on event topics have begun to appear within the last twelve or so years. So far what is missing is a substantial collection of reflected case examples that could provide some material and guidance for delivery on various levels of theory and practice. This publication strives to fill this gap a bit. Yet within the limits of a book not every single event type and event related practice field could be portrayed. Not every culture and main event industry market could be taken into account. The focus of this publication lies on providing experienced and pensive practitioners as well as academics with relevant material for the application of theory plus insights into the background of practicalities. Collecting case examples plus applied/application oriented theory and reflecting on the practice demonstrated, eventually could result in a platform of good or even best practice. I would not define the following case examples as case studies, as a case study in the best sense of the word comprises of dense research, methodological hindsight, a full range of supporting references within practice and theory, and a substantial body of textual evidence to provide an analysis that would function as a benchmark of best practice. This so far cannot be seen in the field of published event studies[2]. Yet substantial case examples as the ones that follow will lead to the formulation of case studies.

---

2 The treasure of BA or MA dissertations written up till now is still to be salvaged and translated. A central collection of titles would be of help.

The case examples presented in this book are not academic in a strict sense of the word and do not follow all rituals of the academic profession. They reflect heuristics that eventually may lead to the formulation of an own academic field of study connected to an accepted set of related theory. The authors do not follow all cherished rituals of academia – such as neutralizing an emotional tone, pretending there is no subject that writes a text, following set steps in the logical definition of terms, providing proof of any thought that might have been thought by somebody before. Nevertheless, reflected heuristics do provide the necessary exploration and rich data of a field for scientific study.

A word or two on the English language used in this book needs to be said. Discussion on English as a global language and mode of communication show that there is a bias between understandability and grammatical correctness. The lingua franca English will globally follow the trend of understandability, this is what I see and believe. A new sort of "Pidgin" of world trade has already evolved. Management looks for practicality, not correctness. The "Standard Oxford Dictionary" is not being followed 100% in this book, as Dutch, Spanish, German, Danish, Swiss, Peruvian, British, and American nationals write their English. This book, being a book on management and marketing focusing on heuristics, follows traditions of managerial book writing.[3] In the true sense of diversity and evolution this book listens to all the languages that exist within English. Only through this will wealth be created.

Contemporary event marketing portrayed, researched, reflected and evaluated in relevant facets; this is what this edition hopefully contains. The examples are somewhat international, taken from North America and Western Europe, yet still a whole world and a lot of event cultures are missing. The examples stem from events that took place in the public realm, that were visible

---

3   Interestingly enough research in international companies on the spoken English word does show that most complaints are being directed against native speakers with strong regional or "class" dialects mainly from England, Scotland, Wales, Ireland, Texas, Alabama, Queensland, Bronx, Soho (to name a few...) as they seem to be hardest to understand for non-native English speakers with a management and business administration background. CNN International, for example employs presenters form non-native English backgrounds to provide an internationally understood "sound".

if not attainable for the common woman and man. The examples provide a look behind the scenes as profound, resourceful and critical as possible. The book deals with various formats of public events and some events produced by corporations within the public sphere and attainable by anyone who wanted. They took and take on the character of festivals. Any exclusion of format is not intended, but caused by personal limits of choice, interest, contacts and horizon.

The editor would like to thank with all his heart the authors of the individual contributions that have undertaken the adventurous and sometimes strenuous journey towards their text and this book. A very special "thank you" goes to the companies, organizations and individuals that supported and helped. This book would not have been possible without the support of the International University of Applied Science Bad Honnef-Bonn and its president Dr. Florian Schütz. Establishing an institutional edition is a noble and daring undertaking that eventually will bear rich fruit in the future.

A very personal thanks goes out to Isabel Weismantel, student of Event Management at IUBH Bad Honnef-Bonn, who untiringly and undauntedly edited, corrected and formatted whatever information technology would allow to be completed. Last but not least: I want to dearly thank my British colleague Philip Sloan who unfalteringly and with all his sensitive British humour pointed me in the right direction in the English academic writing world. Whatever went wrong is my fault, not theirs.

Professor Ulrich Wünsch, M.A. – Hennef-Hanf, May 2008

Sensational Sensations! – An Excursion to the Early Days of Corporate Event Communication

Ulrich Wünsch

Once upon a time there was a place without time. Paradise, an eternal Sunday. Then time and work were "invented" and the eternal Sunday was split into work time and leisure time. Leisure time, at first designated to the realm of the beautiful and unnecessary, later became the domain of recreation. The working day regulated up to the very last detail was created. Thus it might have become a necessity to escape: through play, through entertainment and through travel. The beginning of civil society and the industrialization in the late 18th and early 19th century, with its diverse mass production of objects and later services, initiated the spread of leisure time and a leisure industry set apart from rational production and reproduction. Based on ritual and art, on utopia and dream, on desire and fulfillment, the very return to paradise is being pursued.

The following text will try to provide data and insights on the beginnings of corporate event communication and marketing. The text shall not repeat the history of leisure activity and its industry. Rather, some commercial leisure formats will be exemplified and described for the area of events used consciously and purposely by the industry for brand marketing. As a basis for this, the up to now little researched corner of early modern commercial communication scenarios should serve as an outline for the first appearance of an event industry in the leisure culture of the 19th century. Connecting lines with today are easy to recognize now, however, they, to my knowledge, have not been further researched. Examples will be drawn from major industrialized countries in Europe plus the US, as well as major companies that are still around and have not lost their memory. Company archives try to stop this loss, but it should not be overlooked that some companies are also lost. Especially in the case of fusions, the memories are thrown overboard and the archive is often sent down to the basement. Indeed thankworthy are the efforts of those companies that can look back at a rich marketing history and who do not shy away from admitting to an age of over one hundred years.

1. The Extraordinary in the Ordinary

Events have always been an exceptional part of the leisure industry. Within a modern (from the beginning of industrialization) context, events are often part of promotions, attracting interest and enchantment attached to a commercial background. The history of the industry specific and commercially utilized events is the history of sensations on behalf of sales, image and reputation gain. And yet, before mass media and its two-dimensional advertising (reduced to the flat magazine-page or the flat TV-screen), there was the three-dimensional corporate or special event. The electrification of mass media with its use of radio and television made live-communication step back. But only up to the early 80s in the 20th century, when the marketing departments became aware (again) that a face-to-face contact, or better yet an experience and an adventure, would stand out from the white noise of the multitude of advertising messages. For Germany, as well as other countries, the first Camel Trophy Promotion in 1980, the introduction of the Macintosh computer in 1984 by Steven P. Jobs from Apple and the privately financed Summer Olympics of Los Angeles in the same year may be considered the starting shot.

Initially, joyous discoveries and sensational experiences in short, something out of the ordinary, were the starting point for commercial attractions. They were quite similar to a visit in a baroque curiosity cabinet or happenings at a medieval market. This encounter with uplifting settings should put objects into favorable situations, so the theory goes. At the same time the basic commodities and the experiences that come with objects (aka consumer goods) and their consumptions are fleeting. The deeper meaning of things as consumer goods is disappearance, their dissolution for new consumption.

In connection with the historical research of early forms of event communication and marketing, it is interesting to consider the first signs of globalization in the era of colonization. Certain structures and topics of industrial amusement then are similar throughout the world. A suggestion for the first division of the history of industrial live communication might look like this: Phase One would be up to the turn of the twentieth century, Phase Two would deal with the prevailing electrification and mass propaganda from World War One to the beginning of World War Two, Phase Three would be up to around 1980 and Phase Four would lead up to now. However, the parameters could also be described for events with sensation (in terms of increased sensations and perceptions to become extraordinary events) and illusions (in terms of deluded images and transcendental daily reality). This has only changed a bit in the further development that has taken place up to now – and may be able to tell us something about our future.

2. En Route to Industrially Manufactured Sensations

In the 17th century in Vienna a first leisure time destination emerged at the "Praterauen", the open fields outside of the city. On May 1, 1603, "Taffern-Michel", the owner, opened a wine tavern with a bowling alley at the end of the local district "Jaegerzeile". In 1608 the wooden hut was transformed into a stone building and the amusement business had made its first profits. In addition to the bowling alley, a marionette theatre was added. In 1651, after the death of the first owner, swings and other amusement rides were added.

Scores of puppet theatres for children performed ribald pieces around the main character "Hanswurst" (a dumb clown-like character). Up to the end of the 19th century the collection of attractions grew; by then the imperial hunting ground had already been opened up for the public in 1766 without any revolutionary pressure. In England Vauxhall Gardens set the starting point. Around 1660 they were established in the open fields of Kensington at the banks of the river Thames. The proprietors charged an admission fee and made money by selling food and drink. The entertainment consisted of pleasure walks, fountains, a looking glass and statues.

In France, starting in 1789, the Revolution created a public spectacle by using the guillotine in a mechanically perfectly operated display of higher justice whose sensational value found mass reception. Both in Paris and in the province modern festivities were created for the new state structure, such as those of the "Higher Entity" that were celebrated on the Field of Mars. Another example is the National Industry Exhibition, which was a connection of festivities and industrial display meant to amuse the citizens and workers with a celebration of emancipation. The first was held in Paris in 1798. In England, the economic leading nation of the time, a national commercial exhibition had already been arranged in 1761 under the control of the Society of Arts. However, the first eleven French Industry Displays up to 1851 can be primarily seen as a precursor for the professional amusement industry: the World's Fair, which was formative for the event industry, and for staged leisure time. Soon it was time for the ultimate special event kick-off. On May 1 in London "The Great Exhibition of the Works of Industry of all Nations" opened its doors at the Crystal Palace, the central location for its presentations. More than six million curious onlookers had visited the World's Fair by October 11 of the same year. The architect Joseph Paxton had fabricated an engineering masterpiece with his gigantic greenhouse, whose airiness and lightness were unequalled to at that time – and the organizers were able to close with a profit. (What was not granted to too many World's Fairs until now.) According to the official report, it was about "uniting the industrial products of all cultured nations of the world in a comparative compilation" in order to present "the standpoint of the industrial and artistic development of all humanity by samples of their products". The news headlines of these days read "Exhibition" and the amazement never ended because of all the spectacles provided. An iron turnstile enabled the first mechanical visitor count to be made. The rush was so enormous that the visitors could only move forward slowly. With entrance fees, security, sanitary facilities, temporary concessions and media coverage, this was the first professionally planned commercial mass event – yet one did not have any experience in the arrangement of such novel happenings. This can surely be termed the beginning of international commercial event communication and marketing of goods and services. Also the operation of the venue – likewise totally new – was unusual: the organizational committee decided without further ado that the accommodation capacity of the buildings was reached at 25,000 people. After seeing the rather empty halls a decision was made to increase the capacity and to allow a maximum of 60,000 visitors. Logistics of a certain magnitude were up to then a theoretical and practical area that was essentially reserved for the military, at best the transportation of goods. Now 40,000 people who came to London had to be moved daily. The result was congestion and visitor guidance was needed. Posters on the continent advertising the event offered train and boat trips to London at a reduced price. Mass tourism was born under the sign of organized curiosity. The Englishman Thomas Cook clearly profited with his new travel business from the event; he brought 165,000 tourists to the World's Fair.

Everything from this world should have been collected in London; this was the theme of the huge exhibition. Like a story out of "1001 Arabian Nights", exhibits were displayed in all their glory and enchantment. The number was so big that it was calculated that a visitor who spent three minutes per exhibit would need four years for the complete World's Fair. Additional side events such as the celebrated opening and closing, entertainment at night and during the day accompanied this special gathering of objects and people.

Right away, the professionals among the then marketers slowly became aware that an attraction needs a theme and a story, and the event producers likewise noticed this. How to stand out and attract attention among all the sensations? Statically presented objects were not really noticed; but promotions fit the taste of the visitors. A machine producer showed a fully automatic machine that assembled envelopes. This machine worked continually, giving every passer-by an envelope printed with the address of the producer. Another exhibitor enhanced the water of a decorative fountain with perfume and the female visitors moistened their handkerchiefs in it. Over 1,000 liters of perfume were used during the exhibition. Lastly, colonial cultures and their traditions were also on display. Along with the industrial productions, the encounter with the exotic and the strange were true crowd pullers. How close the first wave of globalization was connected to the electrification of communication and media can be seen by events which promptly followed the World's Fair. Paul Julius Reuter founded his international news agency of the same name in London in 1851. And after multiple attempts, the laying of the first transatlantic cable succeeded in 1857/1858, which enabled the rapid transmission of telegraphic news.

3.　Artificial Paradise Revisited

Already in 1852, riding on the success of the "Great Exhibition", the Victoria and Albert Museum was founded in London, to house the things of this world at a permanent place. That the world of commodities not only needed a home in a museum, but also a congregation of things that could be directly bought and consumed, soon became clear. In 1865 the opulent department store "Printemps" opened its doors in Paris. Around 1822 a likewise covered collection of buyable goods appeared next to the Paris Arcades. This collection however was more committed to rare luxury goods than the completion of the bourgeois consumer goods. However, goods wanted to be seen and sold all over and in mass quantities and thus, rummage and low-cost goods were born in 1879. In the same year Frank Woolworth opened his first "Five & Dime Store". This name stemmed from the "Dime Novels" that became popular in the mid 19th century after the success of the serialized novels in newspapers. In 1872 the obliging customer could shop at "Printemps" by catalogue and mail order. In that same year on the other side of the Atlantic, Montgomery Ward organized the first American mail order shop and the well-known Sears opened in 1886.

Around the middle of the 19th century the universe of things was already well ordered, goods were widely available providing illusions of various kinds. Paris, the capital of the 19th century (Walter Benjamin), is the picture book of this time. Here it is where advanced technology (in the daguerreotype photographic art of Daguerre) and advanced luxury consumption (in the indulgence of the Flaneur and Dandy) met. At the beginnings of mechanization machines had already been animated (i.e. mechanical chess player, mechanical ghosts,) and the appetite for horror as well as the sensationalism had been described in its ambivalence. Shortly after that the novel "Frankenstein" appeared in England depicting an artificially created monster of the Industrial Age, molded from the "Golem" of Jewish tradition.

The audience (always) wanted to personally experience live staged terror (public hanging, Roman Circus,) and the exotic with a touch of horror. Hagenbeck's human zoo (exhibiting natives from various continents) satisfied a need to dive into an artificial paradise. In 1874 the animal merchant and zoo director from Hamburg, Carl Hagenbeck, displayed the first of his approximately 60 human zoos. Initially, the privilege of viewing the exotics from other continents or the curiosity cabinets was granted to only a few from the European royal courts, but it became popular pedagogical entertainment for lots of people to marvel at strange people and their customs in the 19th century. Boomerang throwing Aborigines, drum communicating Duala from Cameroon, wild riding Oglala-Sioux from the Pine Ridge Reservation – all of these traveled through the world. Some even found a home in an overseas museum, like the one in Bremen that was opened in 1872. William F. Cody, also known as "Buffalo Bill", traveled from the USA to Europe. In 1883 he produced "Buffalo Bill's Wild West" show for the first time with living pictures, re-enactment of dramatic scenes, Indian attacks, Pony Express coaches and also General Custer's Last Stand. This mixture of a circus and a history lesson toured around the world until 1913. Mr. Cody credits his nickname to the dime novel from Ned Buntline (aka E.Z.C. Judson), who put together the artificial character of Buffalo Bill out of occurrences from Cody's life.

Figure 2: Coney Island, USA 1904 – Dreamland Walk

These attractive entertainment worlds needed special locations. Permanent amusement sites where the visitor knew what to expect (best entertainment!) were erected. The goal of these then so-called amusement parks was to make those sites suitable for families. Amusement so far had been connected to ill reputed neighborhoods. The forerunners of Disneyland, which can already be considered as a brand, were the already mentioned Vienna Prater and Atlantic City or Coney Island near New York. In 1879 the first horseracing track opened on Coney Island, and the iron pier for steamships arriving every twenty minutes during summer from New York was opened in 1880. Lamarcus Thompson erected the world's first commercial roller coaster, which was called "Switchback Railroad" and only 600 feet long, in 1884. The passengers rolled down a hill and up a second, and then down the second again. This cost ten cents and brought in $700 on a good day, not a bad deal with building costs of $1,600. The amusement industry starts to pay off. In the same year the "Elephant Hotel" opened, an initial centerpiece of entertainment architecture, as it should be perfected in Las Vegas or Disneyland. The "Elephant Hotel", shaped and built like an elephant, accommodated along with rooms, a shop with a view in its stomach, a cigar shop in its leg as well as a diorama and the necessary steps to reach an upstairs platform. In 1894 the first Ferris wheel with twelve cabins, each with room for eighteen people, was opened. In 1895 Capitan Paul Boyton trod on the beach and placed the "Sea Lion Park" east of Surf Avenue. The first amusement park defined and secured by a wall had been established. It showed a sea lion dressage and pleased the paying guests with a water slide and the "Old Mill Ride". The visitors could also admire the captain in his inflatable rubber suit in which he had crossed the English Channel as well as diverse rivers. The year 1897 brought the gambling house "Streets of Cairo", one of the world's first theme oriented casinos with minarets, belly dancing and camel rides. At this time in Vienna things were quieter, although the Prater definitely could offer some strange things. Freak shows aroused the desire for horror with midgets, people with werewolf syndrome, Siamese twins and other freaks, like the monstrously fat "Prater Mitzi" or the crippled and limbless man named Kobelkoff. Leisure time amusement for the general public was offered via fireworks and balloon rides along with the popular merry-go-round and the train carousel that was built in 1844. In 1895 the big Ferris wheel with originally thirty cabins was erected at the Wurstelprater, one year later than on Coney Island. The fenced in illusionary architectural display "Venice in Vienna", a rebuilt city within a water-park, made money like its counterpart across the Atlantic. Finally electrification triumphed and the electric fairy tale train replaced the steam driven carousel in 1898. The goods of the planet were to be shown in especially bright light and electricity made it possible. In 1888 the crystal dome of the "Printemps" shone in electric light, even before the city of Paris could afford electric streetlights.

These showcase examples show the first developments of amusement worlds towards brand worlds (stores or other permanent architecture dedicated to one brand and operated by the relevant company). They show the connection of products and services to amusement, leisure time and special experience worlds that are so much wanted by the present day brand communication and marketing departments. So what do the early efforts of product or brand staging in a customer oriented experience context look like?

4.   First Industrial Brand Experiences: "Bibendum" Meets the "White Lady"

The development of brands is closely interrelated with the acceleration of industrialization in the 19th century. Up to that point production and consumption were so closely joined that image and placement were not necessary. But due to mass production of new and different products and brands intermediators like advertising were necessary to draw attention. Catchy brand names were found, advertising figures were invented, slogans were shaped and illustrations were painted. Photography and film had not yet appeared on the horizon of promotional happenings, live communication was in full bloom. Advertisements and activities in public – the forerunner of live communication – balanced each other when it was about bringing the brand closer to the public. Marketing pioneers like the Frenchman André Michelin, the Swiss Julius Maggi, the Germans Karl August Lingner and Fritz Henkel as well as the Americans Henry Heinz or Asa Griggs Candler show that original communication doesn't collect dust. That their activities contributed to sales, image building and customer retention should be satisfactorily proven by the continuing existence of their brands.

Surely there was already brand marketing before this, when bread and games had been an essential motivational instrument, when the French Revolution and its festivals on the Mars Field contemporarily explored the ritual of mass belief, when the World's Fairs were locations of industrial entertainment, when artists had always known the use of staging and design; however the orderly and planned application of methods and formats for the popularization of products by the manufacturing companies began around 1870.

Johnny Walker is coming. As early as 1820 the three dimensionally used advertising figure "Johnny Walker" had been created in order to give the drink a place in the public as well as in the public awareness of the USA. This date marks one of the essential onsets of promotional activities. However, nothing in commercial brand build-up followed for a long time, nothing that has established itself up to today. Finally, in 1886 the accountant Frank Robinson wrote the name "Coca Cola" in his stylized handwriting on a piece of paper. A trademark worth billions was born plus a corporate identity that has yet to find an equal. Asa Griggs Candler bought the company in 1891 for $2,300 and started to provide the pharmacists – at that time the brown soda was only sold in pharmacies – with branded articles like scales, clocks, calendars and more, such as coupons for a free glass of coke. In 1893 the name and logotype were trademarked as a brand. "Bibendum", the Michelin Tire Man, followed in 1898. Since then the rotund symbol has been personified by performers in many actions on the street and is found at events, both public and corporate. At the same time unmistakable packaging was discovered as a brand symbol: in Germany the Maggi bottle (liquid seasoning) dates from 1887, the Idol bottle (mouthwash) was patented in 1906 and in the US the Cola bottle was copyrighted in 1916. To not only present the product but also to also present the specifically designed packaging with its over-dimensional brand signets was a new idea for the industry. The era of the operetta and huge revues provided the initial spark. In 1924, to mark an exhibition on hygienic issues, Idol bottle cabs trotted through the streets of Leipzig; at the same time Ata-boxes (dish washing powder) wandered through the city centers on two legs for Henkel; boys earned a few extra cents as paste package boys and "IMI-Men", the neatly costumed representatives of a detergent, were the amusement of the bobbed ladies. Starting in 1922, lovers made appointments under the "Persil Clock" – tower clocks that were centrally located in inner cities and displayed the likeness of the washing detergent Persil's central figure, the "White Lady". Promotion actions of the white umbrella men from Persil around these clocks created further sensation.

As early as 1911 Michelins "Bibendum" appeared on his own car at the Nice carnival. Parades or processions especially served Michelin as an instrument for getting attention: new products were presented worldwide with street parades that were led by "Bibendum". In addition to this, the advertising figure appeared at bicycle races, car races and other mobility activities for a good cause, the popularization of pneumatic tires. In 1924 André Michelin succeeded in creating the first integrated communication of the known advertising history: he contrived the so-called "pig campaign". The following problem needed to be solved: public transportation in France used solid rubber tires that really shook up the people inside busses, but Michelin sold air filled tires that promised gentle gliding. The public transportation services did not agree; the solid tire lobby was mean and strong. André Michelin focused on provocation and scandal. He placarded the following motive: a herd of pigs in a truck with pneumatic tires and next to it people in a bus with solid tires. The caption read: "Parisians! A scandal! Demand the same rights for all!" on huge 60 square meter big placards. At the same time postcards with the same motive were distributed to the people, a petition was started and a truck loaded with pigs was driven in front of the National Assembly. Workers and pigs delivered the collected signatures together. The press was enthusiastic and so were the passer-bys. A short time later, one could ride in air suspended local public transportation in France. These arrangements were planned and executed with military precision, furthermore supplied with effectiveness control measurements. The true visionary streak hit with the founding of the "Guide Michelin", a restaurant and hotel guide. Produced for the first time in 1900, this brand building informational manual with a circulation of 3,000 pieces was published for the then 2,897 French motorists. Food, accommodation and leisure simply belong together.

Figure 3: "Bibendum" at the Nice Carnival, France 1911

Of course successful new formats and possibilities of live communication had also been found on the other side of the pond. Henry Heinz, the future ketchup king, bought a whole pier in Atlantic City, New Jersey in 1898. He renamed it "Heinz Ocean Pier" and used it as a promotional vehicle for his products. The attractions were a sun deck, a test kitchen with product tests and a museum for Mr. Heinz's art collection. A 23-meter highlighted sign that advertised the Steak Sauce 57 over a long distance soon crowned the construction in the popular holiday resort. Next door, on the "Garden Pier" the Underwood Company displayed a gigantic typewriter, the world's largest. And Chesterfield illuminated its Atlantic City cigarette advertisement with 27,000 light bulbs.

Figure 4: Heinz-Pier in Atlantic City, USA around 1900

Next to this, at the "Million Dollar Pier", the world famous escape artist and magician Harry Houdini plummeted spectacularly and promotionally effectively into the ocean. The seaside resort with its then massive visitor numbers embodied the ideal location for every type of promotion with its considerable number of visitors. At an exhibition it had become clear to Heinz that reaching out to the masses was important. Product sampling and live tests had been the center of his live communication actions early on; however his true greatness was reached with the Pickle Pin give away. Due to the extremely unfavorable position of his stand at an exhibition he committed a horde of boys to tell everyone at the exhibition that there was a gift at Heinz's stand (the Pickle Pin) that could be personalized with the name of the wearer. Thousands visited the stand of Henry Heinz – the power of the gratuitous is unbowed up to today.

The use of public events for advertising purposes or even for arrangement or sponsoring proved itself early on. In 1887 Julius Maggi substantially and clearly supported one of the first exhibitions for cooking and nutrition and Karl August Lingner bet on his own traveling exhibition "Common Diseases and Treatment" for Idol in 1903. These were the first hours of infotainment. The first International Hygiene Exhibition in Dresden in 1911 arose from this and was visited by five million people over five months. Lingner was the main sponsor and the initiator. The German Hygiene Museum, a monument for Odol, was founded from this exhibition. In 1926 the laundry detergent producer Henkel got involved with the Henkel House on the GeSoLei – an exhibition in Dusseldorf dealing with health care, social aid and physical exercise that was visited by seven million people. Laundry demonstrations that were already touring through cities showed inquisitive women the way to a true white. What could be more convincing than experiencing the product on-site in an entertaining environment?

Male company choirs and sport clubs dominated corporate events at that time. The first corporate song on German soil can be credited to Maggi. In 1907 the male choir of the Maggi factory in Singen composed and wrote the Maggi March that was from then on presented at internal festivals and meetings as well as public celebrations. Corporate identity at its very best. Sport clubs, allotment gardens, company housing and vacation lodges for employees as well as art and leisure centers were the motivational instruments of the industrial revolution. Dynasty patriarchs rather than clever managers arranged company anniversaries. However the content and format have stayed similar: an even more golden future based on a golden past is envisioned accompanied by an attack of multi-sensuous stimulation (i.e. food and music).

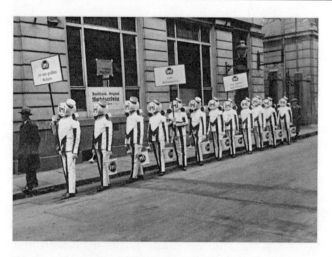

Figure 5: "Imi-Men", Germany, 1920s ("Imi" was a popular clean-
sing powder)

The conquest of public space by moving advertisements continued through the beginning of the twenties with the deployment of branded blimps; Persil and Idol were the leaders
in Germany. Henkel went one step further: in 1926 the first
airplane took off and wrote the brand name Persil in the blue
sky with let off gasoline clouds. Company vehicles, either
branded or stylized as product packaging, roared through the
streets. The conquest of the night commenced at the beginning of the century and peaked with a first glamour in the
twenties. In 1925 André Citroën illuminated the Paris Eifel
Tower with his brand name, in 1929 Idol radiated in neon
lights over Berlin's Potsdamer Platz and New York's Times
Square shone in the brightest light starting in 1904. The
heavily illuminated boat "Persil" chugged up and down German rivers from 1932 at night and brightly projected the
brand name using a spotlight.

It is difficult to determine what companies of that time did
at their special or corporate events that were held behind
closed doors. Motivation was not an urgent concern of the
then management. Caring company founders and owners

turned their attention to company housing, libraries and sport and culture clubs. Industrial conferences for the purpose of exchanging of ideas, gaining information and networking were subject to strict rituals that were mainly formed by diplomatic protocol. Nevertheless it is peculiar how close congress and pleasure were to each other. In 1814 the benchmark "Vienna Congress" was held in the Prater and the calciferous saying "the congress dances" is taken from this diplomatic event.

The art of spoken persuasion, or rhetoric, was taught at higher schools, as opposed to today's skills in dealing with media. The traveling salesperson, the eternal showman who had to be a natural because hardly any training existed, went from door to door or from company to company. Incentives as a planned tool of company motivational encouragement were rare, bigger trips served as an incentive of a later time.

5.   Keeping the Ephemeral

Considering the history of event communication and marketing in the context of the leisure industry, the fundamental problem areas in staging products and services resonate: selecting a topic, providing logistics, controlling and evaluation, staging, integration in further communicational measures, context determination, teeming, story telling, persuasion efforts, creating awareness, customer retention and management of a comprehensive customer experience – to say the least. At the same time, extensive areas on which the industrial staging efforts are based on – such as religion, theater, games, rituals and rules of daily communication – are not taken into consideration here. Surely here and in further research and examination of certain periods of the 20th century, (political staging of fascist and communist totalitarian systems in connection to new technical developments would be worth a whole chapter) more insight in the function of event communication remains hidden. An interesting field of research would be to further determine what procedural steps and rule observances the staging of product experiences in a virtual environment such as "Second Life" does follow. Or what virtual real-time events will emerge from combining these entities. Neither can possibilities and limitations of city marketing as a stage for consumption in the post-industrial society be viewed here. In any case, the idea and vision of the artificial paradise is one of the most important paradigms for the planning of experience oriented and marketing focused destinations from Dubai to Shanghai.

Trying to hold and to fixate the ephemeral, the fleeting, the enchanting moment of a one-time live meeting, to capture a true moment in its highest pleasure and even still to reproduce it effectively and to make it accessible and sustainable as a product, is work, skill and art at the same time. To solidify these ephemeras for scientific description and analysis will be dour, as witnesses and photographs hardly refer to advertising, companies do not often supply the necessary means and interest and public collections suffer from reduced budgets. A wide field has opened here. It is essential to find methods and sources to research events as communication in the context of a social-cultural phenomenon. Yet one thing is certain: artificial paradises will always be received with immense popularity. Even if they are sometimes called "brand marketing".

Literature

Kretschmer, Winfried (1999), Geschichte der Weltausstellungen, Campus Verlag, Frankfurt Main, New York
as well as archives and internet pages from the individual companies, brands and locations.

Copyright photos

Henkel Konzernarchiv
Michelin Reifenwerke KGaA
Deutsches-Hygiene Museum Dresden, Bildstelle
Library of Congress Washington
US Historical Archive

Imagine Your Event – Imagineering for the Event Industry

Moniek Hover

Events are in principle unique. In actual practice, however, it is highly evident that events are not that distinctive *where* the actual experience is concerned. It is becoming increasingly more difficult to affect people emotionally. Events, therefore, do not reach their full potential.

From the importance attached to events, the basis, i.e. the development of the event concept from the perspective of experience, deserves greater attention. This chapter will do justice to this subject and will provide tools for the event manager/developer for developing fully experiential events or for innovating existing events, through the application of imagineering.

In this chapter the following subjects will be dealt with: Section 1: imagineering's background; Section 2: an insight into the difference between the staged and the lived experience; Section 3: imagineering, a tool to create meaningful experiences, with subjects as the imagineering process, experiential concept, physical surroundings and experiential instruments.

1. Background of Imagineering

Imagineering came into existence in the last century in the United States. It is a compound of imagination and engineering, two concepts that at first sight would appear to be at odds with each other. Within the Disney concern imagineering has boomed since Walt Disney started applying it in his company in the initial years. In the early 50s, Walt Disney surrounded himself with an interdisciplinary team for conceiving, creating and realizing Disneyland. Imagineering is the way in which, within the team, the right part of the brain (which stands for creativity) is brought together with the left part (which stands for analysis). The Disney imagineering teams are always multidisciplinary, from creative people (such as storytellers and designers) to analysts (such as engineers, project managers and financial people). It is precisely in the implementation of this diversity from the very first step, that its strength lies.

The Disney case consists of far more dimensions than can be assumed at first sight. Disney is conspicuous in creative concept and product development, in the perfect realization of leisure experiences, but also in managing and communicating the experiential concept, both internally and externally. In this chapter, Disney will often be quoted as an example. The danger of quoting from Disney lies in the associations the brand name often conjures up in Europe: too American, too commercial, experience as in "superficial" fun and entertainment. However, experience is much more than this.

In 2002 in their book 'Imagineering', Diane Nijs and Frank Peters have interpreted the subject in terms of the European situation. Imagineering can serve as creative input for engineers, designers, developers of commercial concepts and communicators. In this way, imagineering stands for the integral approach to designing worlds of experience, which continue to fascinate (Nijs/Peters, 2002). In a broader perspective, Imagineering stands for: Value creation and value innovation from an experience perspective (Nijs, 2006). Experience is a crucial term within imagineering. In the following section we will describe what experience is and which factors play a role in experience coming into existence.

2. The Staged versus the Lived Experience

Some years ago one of my students did a graduation project connected to a show by André Rieu. After having performed abroad for several years, André Rieu was back in Holland, or rather, in his home province of Limburg, for an open-air concert. My student gave me three complimentary tickets. Although I personally did not like André Rieu's music very much (as a university lecturer in leisure I regarded it as quite superficial entertainment), I decided to invite my parents to come along, because I knew they liked his music very much and they always watched his shows on television.

My father had been very ill that year and driving over to the venue I realized it was the first time in a long, long time, my parents went for an evening out.

During the concert I was very impressed by the atmosphere André Rieu managed to create in interaction with the audience. People were waltzing between the aisles. To my parents this brought back memories of when they were young and they used to go dancing together: the waltz had always been their favorite. They shared these memories with each other and with me and I was touched by seeing them in their late seventies still so very much in love.

At one point during the concert André Rieu was there on stage with his violin, just him in the spotlight, and he started to play the anthem of the province of Limburg. I will never forget what happened: people in the audience sang to the music, some of them moved to tears by this shared emotion. It was an experience that changed my view of staged experiences completely: what is generally regarded as superficial entertainment can cause deep emotions, and can even bring about transformation in people.

Two years later my father died, very unexpectedly. Ever since, I cherish our last evening out together even more as a wonderful memory. Whenever I can, I watch André Rieu on television. Although I do not feel the exact same emotion I felt then, it still touches me because I feel my father is watching too, smiling down on me from heaven.

Some years ago one of my students did a graduation project connected to a show by André Rieu. After having performed abroad for several years, André Rieu was back in Holland, or rather, in his home province of Limburg, for an open-air concert. My student gave me three complimentary tickets. Although I personally did not like André Rieu's music very much (as a university lecturer in leisure I regarded it as quite superficial entertainment), I decided to invite my parents to come along, because I knew they liked his music very much and they always watched his shows on television.

My father had been very ill that year and driving over to the venue I realized it was the first time in a long, long time, my parents went for an evening out.

During the concert I was very impressed by the atmosphere André Rieu managed to create in interaction with the audience. People were waltzing between the aisles. To my parents this brought back memories of when they were young and they used to go dancing together: the waltz had always been their favorite. They shared these memories with each other and with me and I was touched by seeing them in their late seventies still so very much in love.

At one point during the concert André Rieu was there on stage with his violin, just him in the spotlight, and he started to play the anthem of the province of Limburg. I will never forget what happened: people in the audience sang to the music, some of them moved to tears by this shared emotion. It was an experience that changed my view on staged experiences completely: what is generally regarded as superficial entertainment can cause deep emotions, and can even bring about transformation in people.

Apparently, the same event can cause totally different experiences from one person to the next. Also two similar events can cause two totally different experiences within the same person.

Many suppliers within the leisure industry focus on "the creation of experiences". However, there is an obvious difference between the stimulus (the "staged" experience, in this case the event) and the response (the actual, lived experience within the individual: the emotional, personal reaction to the stimulus). The experience that takes place within the individual guest or visitor depends on the terms of the frame of reference of that individual, on the particular moment (of the experience).

2.1 Experience Model

The model below shows the many different aspects involved in the process of (leisure) experiences taking place.

We will first discuss briefly the psychosocial framework and the lived experience. In section 3 we will discuss the different aspects and tools of the staged experience.

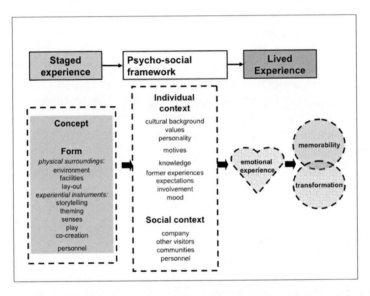

Figure 6: Experience model, Gool, Wijngaarden, adapted by Hover, 2007

2.2 Psycho-Social Framework and the Lived Experience

No matter how carefully staged, the experience is non-existent as long as people aren't there to experience it. Each and every visitor will take himself along to the staged experience or the event, with his own personal framework which includes non-situational aspects like cultural background or personal values, but also situational aspects like specific motives, former experiences and related expectations and a level of involvement with what he is about to undertake. Last but not least, he will most likely go there with other people. Visiting an event with colleagues can be totally different on the level of experience than when people do this with their own family. In addition, how people personally experience the other visitors is also influential: what one person experiences as "enjoyable", maybe for another be "irritatingly busy". In terms of the social context personnel is crucial in the experience. Research in a theme park based on "gardens of the world" showed that what a visitor remembered most strongly was the fact that a maintenance man had not stepped aside on a narrow bridge when she wanted to cross. (Hesselmans, 2005) Personnel appear to be able to make or break the experience. Personnel can also be used as an experiential instrument. This however will not be discussed in this chapter.

The social context reaches further than the time boundaries of the experience. Through virtual communities new social contexts exist which influence the experience in the pre-exposure and post-exposure phases that is the time before and after the actual event.

All of this will lead to a lived, personal experience, which includes emotions and which may range from relaxed detachment to intense involvement. (Kleiber, 1999), the optimum involvement being flow, which is a state of 'intense immersion'. Flow is linked to an enriched perception, a pleasant, enjoyable feeling and a strong personal involvement in the situation. (Nibs/Peters, 2002)

An emotional experience is more likely to be remembered more intensely. If the memory brings back emotions then this may strongly influence expectations and decisions in future experiences. In the context of the experience economy transformation is often mentioned. Transformation is seen as a durable change in attitude or behavior as a consequence of one or several experiences.

The psychosocial framework is essentially a 'black box': nobody can argue with certainty which factors are crucial for a specific experience to take place. In this chapter we will limit ourselves to discussing values because, within the context of Imagineering, the focus on values is crucial.

Values are here understood as an individual's approach concerning what is desired or good. Values are strongly anchored ideas about what is meaningful in life, something to strive for, a sort of ideal. Rokeach was one of the first to conduct research into consumer values (in: Boom and Weber, 1994). He distinguishes between two sorts of values: final values (concerning a person's desired "final" objectives in life, like freedom, self-respect and peace) and instrumental values (concerning the means of achieving final values, like ambition, compassion and honesty). We believe that in order to create meaningful experiences, appealing to people's values is more effective. Values are more stable than wants and (material) needs. Furthermore, they are rooted deeper within a person. By appealing to values, people are more likely to be touched on an emotional level and have a memorable experience.

3. Imagineering: Creating Meaningful Experiences

As mentioned in the introduction we regard Imagineering as: Creating value and innovating value from an experience perspective.[4]
Imagineering concerns creating and managing worlds of experience, based in internal values (DNA) on the one hand and/or values of the target groups on the other, with the objective of creating the emotional involvement of all stakeholders.

In other words, not only the external target groups, but also that all those concerned internally also feel involved.

---

4   Nijs, 2006

The example below indicates that internal values may also be a point of departure in creating meaningful experiences. Groups of 'followers' will automatically come to exist who feel attracted to these values.

The Skyway Foundation makes impossible events possible. In 2003 founder Ronald Ligtenberg organized the first music event for young deaf people called Deaf Valley. The event was so successful that it was renamed Sencity. Thousands of people from all over the world come to visit the Sencity events. They take place all over Europe: from Spain to Finland, but also in Miami, Mexico and Jamaica.

The focus on stimulations of all senses makes them attractive for deaf as well as for hearing people. Through aroma jockeys, vibrating floors, video projections, taste sensations, dancers, light effects, sign interpreters and massages, the emotion behind the music gets translated so that it becomes accessible for everyone.

All the people within the organization have their own goals to achieve; yet they share the same values, which are deeply implemented in the way they work. Skyway wants to inspire people, inside and outside the organization, with its vision and the related concept: If you go for it, you can achieve way more that you ever thought – you can make the impossible possible!

At present, the Skyway foundation is also involved in photography projects for blind people worldwide.
www.stichtingskyway.nl

In the imagineering process a central role is set aside for the creative development of an *experiential concept* which links supply and demand. It is precisely through linking the experience in an innovative way to shared values that it becomes meaningful for all involved.

3.1 Competences of the Imagineer

The imagineer thinks and acts in worlds of experience. Designing experiential concepts demands an integral, concept-oriented and creative approach. It is important for an imagineer that he/she can apply competences such as fantasy, imaginative power and empathy, both in the analysis phase as well as in the creation phase.

In November 2006 lecturers from NHTV Academy for Leisure organized a two-day workshop at Kaospilots in Aarhus, Denmark. The students had to come up with an experiential concept for an event, which would involve people into the Pasa la Voz project for street children in Peru, in which these children make and sell their own (street) magazine on the streets of Cusco. An important first step in the Imagineering process was to get the students emotionally involved with the assignment. Therefore, we sent them into the Aarhus streets where they were supposed to sell the Spanish (street) magazine to Danish people. This way they could experience the same rejection or indifference that these children are often faced with. Also see: www.pasalavoz.nl

An imagineer needs passion: an enthusiastic drive for creating extraordinary experiences. The most essential competence is however creativity.

3.2 Creativity

Developing new experiential concepts in a purely analytical way will not lead to results. Although knowledge and analysis are essential, creativity is the indispensable ingredient for the concept development process. Creativity is concerned with innovation: thinking of solutions, which other people have not thought of. It may then concern developing completely new ideas, but also the skilful combination of various fields of knowledge.

Creativity is also concerned with 'looking beyond the usual boundaries': applying knowledge and ideas from other subject areas often leads to a completely new view of the matter.

Creativity does not necessarily have to take place in one person; it can just as well take place within an imagineering team, providing they are all passionate about what they are doing.

3.3   What Does the Imagineering Process Look Like?

The imagineering process always begins at the heart. If the heart does not beat, then everything would be at a standstill. It is a question of thinking with the heart, allowing the heart to speak and doing things with heart and soul. From the heart you go to the head:

Left part of the brain

This is where the phase of the acquisition of knowledge begins. An analysis is made of the problem or idea, which forms the cause. Look at the problem from different angles, bring the problem up for discussion, and raise as many unexpected connections as possible. Analyze the existing internal and external supply, possible networks, trends and developments, target groups.

Target groups are analyzed on the level of values. Existing experiences can also be analyzed. Both values as well as experiences are difficult to chart in a hard, quantitative way. In research into values and experiences, it is mostly a matter of carrying out qualitative research in which methods are used such as in-depth interviews, group discussions, and participant observations. In this, various creative techniques are often used such as laddering, storytelling, visualizations (e.g. mood boards). The analysis of values and experience is however insufficient on its own. Use as many sources as possible. Watch films, read stories, visit areas, look at the world around you and become inspired by everything.

In this phase, continual shifts are made back and forth between the left side of the brain and the

Right part of the brain

Dreaming, experiencing, brooding, brainstorming:

The acquisition of knowledge phase gradually turns into a brooding phase. This is a chaotic phase in which hope, frustration and new insights alternate with each other. Dreams are visualized and communicated to each other. In this phase it is absolutely essential that imagineers project themselves into the intended experience. Which emotions does it concern? Which values play a role and how are these values expressed? Which images does the experience conjure up? Which colors and smells? But what is also particularly important: what is "the end", what feeling should the guest be left with at the end of the event?

In this creative phase, creative sessions are an important aid.

Know your end result. Istt could be an image, feeling, or a metaphor. Do research to that end. Find a visual direction that matches the result you want.

When you are faced with a project, relate it to something you know. For example, how would you paint a room that should "feel like the look on a child's face when they receive their first puppy?" You would paint it very differently than if you were simply asked to paint a room.

(Susan Dalin in The Imagineering Workout, Disney Enterprises, 2005)

The stomach: creating a vision and an experiential concept

In this phase it is important to step back and to take stock of everything that has come up in the first phase as far as knowledge and feelings are concerned. A clear, innovative and appropriate vision will be created. A vision is by definition always subjective: it is a personal opinion or a bundle of views, a means of seeing or observing, an inner perception. A vision represents the broad outlook.

In the extension of the vision a meaningful experiential concept is created which captures the essence of everything the imagineer knows and feels. This is to do with a "gut feeling": in order for the concept to be right, it has to feel right.

The development of the concept is the first and most crucial step in the development of the experience. Creative techniques (such as brainstorming) can help in the development of a concept.

3.4 What's in a concept?

What do we understand by concept? In the leisure industry, the notion of *concept* is used in many ways and not univocally. *Concept* sometimes appears to be a meaningless container notion: everything can be labeled concept. The definition for concept that we use is:

A concept (as related to an idea) is the working principle that creates coherence and provides direction to the realization of one or more objectives (Hover/Kops, 2004).

A concept does not cease to exist the moment that the realization of products has taken place. To the contrary, it ensures that the coherence remains.

Under working principle we mean the way in which something works in essence, from what something derives its right to exist, "what makes it tick". The working principle within a concept may be naturally present (such as the cold North Sea on the 1st of January which may or may not invite a dip), but it is only when somebody comes up with the idea to put this working principle into action for realizing an objective that we call it a concept. To continue with the example: the Unox New Year's dive, in which thousands of people in the Netherlands on the 1st of January simultaneously take a dip into the North Sea, is in this sense a concept. The event has a typically Dutch winter atmosphere and is organized by Unox, a typically Dutch brand for typically Dutch soups and winter dishes. That such a successful event strengthens the brand goes without saying.

With regard to a concept, there is thus on the one hand an underlying idea, on the other hand, a concept provides coherence to various components such as themes, products, personnel, communication.

Opera in the Bus: Once in the two years, Yo! Opera Festival attracts a wide audience in Utrecht with an international opera festival for youth. The objectives are: building bridges between opera and a wide/young audience, placing opera in the middle of society and fulfilling a booster role for repertoire development and a new generation of young opera makers.

The concept 'Opera in the Bus' and 'Community Opera' appear to have really hit the mark. It resulted in six splendid operas in moving buses, each of which did something in their own way with the social, historical context of the specific bus routes. From the neighborhood projects, which additionally took place during the festival, the 'Opera Flat' was perhaps the very height. Fifty-four households took a singer into their homes for one day. The audience could ring the door and the singer sang his/her song or aria in the doorway especially for the listener.

The bus operas literally dragged opera out of the ivory towers onto the street. The part of the project 'The Singing City' (with the stream of choirs as its high point) brought amateur singers and children out of the community centres and neighborhood halls to the theatre.

The following special results can be mentioned:

The special bus driver's choir that was set up for this festival continues to exist. The bus drivers meanwhile write their own lyrics.

After the festival, a number of opera buses were invited to perform in other places at home and abroad.

Other cities and festivals have adopted the stream of choirs as a strong concept for performing on a large-scale with local choirs.

More at: www.yo-festival.nl

We make a distinction between functional concepts and experiential concepts. Functional concepts are aimed at functionality. For example the working principle of a transport cafe is the self-service principle. Physical environment, personnel, and activities: all of these are in keeping with the functions 'quick' and 'easy'. In experiential concepts the objective is to realize an experience for the guest. All choices, so the functional aspects too, are connected to the concept and are directing the intended experience.

Experiential concept

A strong experiential concept is satisfactory at the moment that the objective is realized, in this case, that the experience actually takes place. To increase the chance of this as much as possible, an experiential concept must satisfy a number of criteria. Strong concepts:

1. Are meaningful, they consist of a sort of "inner truth". Precisely by basing an experiential concept on relevant values for the target group, its authenticity will be felt. It concerns making a connection with what people experience as important in their lives. It is only then that a concept can bestow meaning.
2. Are distinctive and, in the ideal situation, unique. Today's consumers are spoilt: they have already seen and experienced many things. Uniqueness does not necessarily mean something completely new, but may also consist of a surprising combination of existing elements.
3. Have enduring appeal. A strong experiential concept has appeal for a longer period of time. However, there should also be room for it being regularly renewed or supplemented, without it losing its essential strength.

4. Should be multi-layered. They are subject to more than one interpretation and because of this they are often more exciting and interesting for more than just one target group. In this sense, in essence concepts resemble stories such as fairy tales: these can also be said to have a key message surrounded by various layers. Storytelling is the key for strong experiential concepts.

5. Should be right as far as timing is concerned. A concept may be strong on paper, but if it is not realized at the right moment, it will lose its potential value. For this reason it is very important to keep a sharp eye on trends and developments, not only in an analytical manner but also particularly in an intuitive manner.

A method for developing an experiential concept is by applying storytelling in the concept development phase. In this, you select a 'story' as a working principle within the concept. Via this story, it is then possible to lay down values and emotions in the experience from within. The story can be the one that the guest will experience. In this way, you make a link with the idea that an experience for a consumer often seems to follow a certain 'story line'. Encapsulating a concept in a one-liner is one way of telling the story in its most essential form. This one-liner can also be used as the name/means of communication.

Rock 'n' Roller Coaster: A good example of a powerful experiential concept is the Rock 'n' Roller Coaster at Disney's MGM Studios, Orlando (a somewhat 'leaner' version can be found in Paris). The primary target group for the roller coasters is boys between the ages of eight and 18. Important values for many adolescent boys are 'adventure' and 'pushing back boundaries'. In today's society there is however little room for expressing these values in a responsible and safe way. What is actually tough and exciting nowadays? In what way can you still really push back boundaries? The roller coaster is an answer to this. Imagine the feeling of the young boy who is finally tall enough for the roller coaster: he is no longer a child but he feels he is becoming a young man. Be-

51

cause of this, the first ride in a roller coaster is a sort of initiation ritual. The small, big boy wants to cast off his childhood. Rock music is tough and exciting and is totally in keeping with this experience. From this experience the experiential concept has come into existence and is encapsulated in the name: Rock 'n' Roller Coaster. The name expresses the story of what you will experience: Rock in a Roller Coaster, Aerosmith taking you for a dazzling ride in a 'limo'.

The following model demonstrates how storytelling can constitute the working principle in an experiential concept:

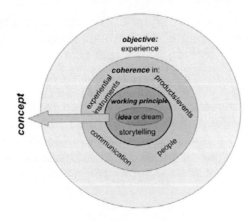

Figure 7: Model of experiential concept

The legs: directing the experience

An experiential concept has to "land" sooner or later; it has to make contact with the earth.

As working principle, the experiential concept gives direction to all the choices that are made; it is as it were, the operating system and the driving force behind the process. All further products, experiential instruments, communication (both during as well as around the experience; through all channels) have to contribute to strengthening the story. It is in this way that the experiential concept provides coherence, which makes the whole stronger than the sum of its individual parts. The objective has to be continually in one's mind: it concerns realizing an experience for people.

In the context of this chapter, we will limit ourselves to staging an event as an experience and the instruments that can be utilized in this.

3.5 Physical Surroundings

The physical surroundings are highly influential for the experience. From research it appears that a location firstly has to meet a number of basic aspects before there can be any talk at all of a positive experience.

1. The environment has to be clean. No matter how beautiful an attraction may be, a dirty toilet or an overfull rubbish bin will be immediately disturbing.

2. Lay out. Cognitive psychology has discovered that people principally try to get an internal idea of a place as fast as possible, painting a so-called cognitive map. They look for specific reference points. European cities whose histories stretch back to medieval times are excellent examples of psychologically styled places. They always have a main axis. The intersections of these axes, the large street crossings, are significant hubs. They lead to central squares emphasized by a mnemonic point – the cathedral, city hall. Axes, hubs, mnemonic points and districts are the four typical features of (Western) cognitive maps.

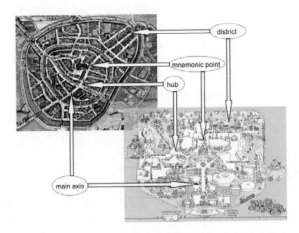

Figure 8: Comparison between the lay-out of a medieval town and
Magic Kingdom at Walt Disney World

Entering modern exhibition halls you often feel overwhelmed by the confusing mass of innumerable visual elements and inundating visitors. This 'visual heap of rubbish' prevents any cognitive map from forming. (Mikunda, 2004) A place should seduce visitors to promenade, mall and stroll. In some respects, a place does have to offer surprises but if wandering around means becoming lost, then the experience is immediately disturbed (Hesselmans, 2005).

3.6 Experiential Instruments

There are various experiential instruments available for directing a leisure experience. In imagineering it is important to continually make all choices from the viewpoint of the experiential concept as a guiding principle. It is to do with the holistic approach in which the instruments reinforce each other in a cohesive, meaningful whole.

Theming

Theming is a much used instrument in the leisure sector. A theme as in experiential instrument we interpret as follows:

A theme is the outward, recognizable, explicit subject, which is carried through in setting, in details and in communication.

Themes have the goal of achieving a change in the consumer's perception of reality, of immersing him/her in another world. In the ideal situation, space, time, material and people (individuals) are integrated in a cohesive whole (Nijs/Peters, 2002).

From research into theming at leisure locations, it appears that it does not always automatically lead to a memorable experience. The lower the degree of involvement with the theme, the less value people place on whether the 'cues' are in keeping with the theme or not.

Experience research into the themed restaurants (Koopman, 2005) shows that when a theme has a "natural connection" to the basic content, then it is more powerful where experience is concerned.

At Pasta e Basta (themed restaurant based on the "Italy dining experience" with singing waiters) people were in general more acquainted with and also more involved with the theme than at a restaurant based on Robin Hood. Italian food has a very good reputation in the Netherlands. The Dutch have quite a clear idea of the look and feel of an Italian dining experience. Guests were more critical where the cues were concerned, for instance if the dishes were really Italian. Personnel at Pasta e Basta plays more of a leading part within the experience. Often enough the singing by the waiters and the personal story by which they were introduced was mentioned as the most memorable element. This personal interaction and storytelling contributed very clearly to the lived experience.

Storytelling

Our understanding of storytelling is: communicating stories. Storytelling is perhaps as old as mankind. It is an outstanding means of communicating values and norms (as is the case for fairy tales), of conveying emotions, of involving people. Storytelling can help people to understand the world. People are looking for frames of reference to give meaning to the world in which they live (Rijnja/ van de Jagt, 2004). It is not facts which are important in stories, but actually the meaning. Stories catch on because they help us to daydream: 'to momentarily abandon your thoughts, without losing your head' (Gabriel, 2000). They activate pride, fantasy and longing (Rijnja, 2004). These are elements that are closely connected to the lived experience.

An important dimension within storytelling is authenticity. In this, the concern is not authenticity in the sense of something really having happened, but it is more about originality, credibility in the sense of real emotion and meaningful values. A fantasy story may also be authentic in this sense. Lord of the Rings is not credible on a factual level, but on an emotional level it is.

In relation to theming, the contextual authenticity in stories plays a role. If the story is "in its original surroundings", it becomes stronger. For example, if a story about Indians is told in a wigwam, this will evoke a stronger experience. Layering is an important dimension of storytelling. Powerful stories have many layers, which can be interpreted, on various levels. Being able to continually discover new elements in a familiar story may perhaps play an important role in the repetition of leisure activities.

In storytelling, explicit storytelling can be used, in other words, a story can be literally told by someone. The storyteller can infuse the story with emotion and can involve the audience in the story by giving them a 'role', or by means of interaction using questions and answers. On the other hand, implicit storytelling also exists. A visual performance or an object can trigger some story in individuals, which they then complete with their own fantasies. It can stir up a nostalgic memory from a personal or collective past. In directing experiences it is highly important to incorporate a connection between instruments such as storytelling and theming on a concept level.

Stimulating the senses

Sensory perceptions lead to emotions (Frijda, 1986) and emotions are the crucial factor in relation to experience. The more the senses are involved, the more intense the experience will be (Pine/Gilmore, 1999). However, this is certainly not always the case. Someone may also have a very intense experience when listening to music or looking at a painting. Stimulating the senses, like using certain colors or smells, can be used to strengthen the experience. From experiments it appears that sight is the most dominant sense, immediately followed by hearing. Processing smells takes place in the limbic system in the brain. In this area, the driving mechanisms for emotions are also located. The importance of the sense of smell is not always recognized, whereas it is precisely smells that bear a strong relation to moods, experience and memory (Dekker, 2006).

Working with the addition of smells is currently being used quite often, also at events, for example by aroma DJs. It is a matter of working subtly. Research into smell as related to the lived experience shows that if in particular taste and smell conflict with each other (you smell cinnamon and taste beer), this can be confusing and it will result in a disturbance of the experience. Too much stimulation at the same time is not recommended. (Boom, 2006). A smell can however be utilized to divert the attention from relative discomfort during an event (such as waiting in a queue). (Dekker, 2006)

Play

There are various sorts of play. Play denotes unorganized, spontaneous playing. This concerns a setting in which pleasure and development are the most important factors. Games are a different discipline. Games have been designed and organized in relation to time and space. Challenges, optimizing the rules and tactics are central in games (Verhagen, 2006). Playing consists of surprise, allows room for creativity and enables the player to develop cognitively, physically or emotionally.

Play, game and sport are closely related. Although in sport – professional and amateur – clear characteristics of playing such as "freedom" and "pleasure" would sometimes seem to be disappearing into the background, for both the practitioners as well as the audience, sport has been since time immemorial a much sought-after form of leisure activity in which the emotions can run high. Playing is often associated with children but playing is also an important element in the leisure activities of adults. Playing is an outstanding means of involving people in an activity, as onlookers or participants. Playing has been used with great success in events and the business world for years: it frees people from ingrained patterns, offers room for interaction (social context) and carries people away in an experience.

Co-creation

Consumers are increasingly becoming better at gaining access to information and are therefore capable of making well-founded decisions. The role of the consumer is changing. There is a growing need for interaction with the organization to arrive at the creation of value proposition, which is meaningful for the individual consumer (Pralahad/Ramaswamy, 2004). Co-creation is the involvement of the consumer in designing the experience, which is most in keeping with the meaning that the individual wishes to give to his/her life. It is the ultimate form of a demand-based approach. Co-creation is often presented as an innovative concept within the new generation of experience economy. For a great part, it is however based on the same principles as play, such as interaction, room for creativity and self-development. (Verhagen, 2006).

It is clear that co-creation can also be used as an experiential instrument. From time immemorial, an event as an experience has often in fact already been interspersed with some form of co-creation. At a rock concert the lived experience really takes place through the contribution of the visitors to the experience. A performer playing to an empty hall is not an experience. The visitors, who applaud, sing along, dance or give expression to their emotions in another way, make this experience what it is. The ways in which the fans from various countries dress up and present themselves during the Football World Cup contribute to their own total experience but also to that of third parties.

It is possible to involve the consumer earlier in the co-creation process by giving him/her a say on the concept and product development level. Digital media such as the Internet offer many possibilities for doing this. This already regularly happens in an event context. Various major festivals give the consumer the possibility of voting for their favorite line-up via their websites.

Unexpected Encounters

The objective of the client's personnel party (Erasmus Medical Centre) reads as follows:

The creation of a feeling of togetherness, amongst other things, through the staff being able to meet each other. The total programme should also consist of enjoyable ingredients for the people who have to stay on the job in the hospital.

'Unexpected encounters' is the central concept: a series of surprise meetings in which there are no obligations.

The ultimate event is part of a communication mix which consists of, amongst other things, posters, family days, a website, a soap series and the event itself.

In this example, we will confine ourselves to the website. The website constitutes the connecting link between all the other components such as the family days and the personnel party. Moreover, this party site creates a virtual meeting place for the members of staff and their supporters. In this way the people who stay on the job are also treated to the festivities.

The site is designed as a virtual hospital consisting of a virtual reception, waiting room, kiosk and the party lift that will take the guests to a choice of festive departments. Various activities and components within the site will ensure that the guests will experience unexpected encounters with other colleagues, professors, and mystery guests.

Soap: In the first weeks hospital soap in photos was realized. The film shots created a great deal of positive commotion in the departments of the medical centre and the personnel themselves unexpectedly played a role in the story. The story of the soap ended with a surprise encounter of the two leading characters at the personnel party.

Radio broadcasting company: Here the guests could vote on their personal evergreens from the fifties right through to 2004. The Erasmus MC top 25 gradually acquired form during the course of the festivities and was played during the event in the disco.

The kitchen: The international seaport city of Rotterdam along with the Erasmus MC is a melting pot of cultures. In the virtual kitchen these cultures came together, which was a guarantee for a varied menu compiled by the guests through sending in personal recipes for tasty dishes. Moreover, people were invited to think of a special party snack for the Erasmus MC party.

It's your party: after the family days and the personnel party, photos would be placed here online. It was also possible for the guests to express their appreciation here. More under: www.planetevent.nl

For the consumer who enters the co-creation process with the provider on this level, it will undoubtedly result in a strong personal experience: he can after all invest in his own creativity, which may be strongly linked to his own experience. Moreover, he will be strongly personally involved before, during and after the process and he can share this involvement with others. The down side of co-creation is, however, that visitors, who have determined their experience in advance, already know what they can expect: there is little room any more for surprise, or for exceeding expectations. In brief: sometimes it is fun to do your own cooking, at other times it is exciting to choose a surprise menu in a restaurant.

3.7 Keep Moving!

The imagineering process does not stop once an experiential concept has been developed and the experience of the event directed. Imagineering means being constantly oriented towards experience, it is a different way of thinking and doing, a way of life that has to be understood and exercised by everyone within an organization. The experiential concept has to be "lived through" and, also outside the boundaries of the event, be disseminated through all channels.

Literature

Blom, A. (2005), De beleving van een verhaal, een onderzoek near storytelling als belevenisinstrument, thesis

Beunders, N., Boers, H. (1997), Exploring Leisure, Toerboek, Leiden

Boom, E.J., en A.A. Weber (1994), Consumentengedrag, Wolters Noordhoff, Groningen

Boom, M., (2006), Op weg met geur, geurbeleving in de vrije tijd, Thesis

Bull, C., Hoose, J., Weed, M. (2002) An introduction to Leisure Studies, Pearson Education Limited, Essex UK

Buuren, R. van (2006), Beleef je eigen verhaal, storytelling in oorlogsmusea, Thesis

Capodagli, B., Jackson, L., (2002), The Disney way, McGraw Hill, New York

Cornelis, J. (2005), De Magie van Fantasie, Thesis

Czikszmentihaly, M. (1999/2001), Flow, Psychologie van de optimale ervaring, Boom, Amsterdam

Dekker, E. (2006), Ik ruik je wel maar ik zie je niet, Belevingsonderzoek near geur als belevenisinstrument, Thesis

Franzen en Holzhauer (1987), Het Merk: Waarden, levensstijlen en merkartikelen, Deventer, Kluwer bedrijfwetenschappelijke uitgaven

Frijda, N. (1986), The Emotions, Cambridge University Press

Gabriel, Y. (2000), Storytelling in Organizations, Facts, Fictions, Fantasies, Oxford University Press

Havitz, M.E., Mannell, R.C. (2005), Enduring Involvement, Situational Involvement, and Flow in Leisure and Non-Leisure activities, Journal of Leisure research Vol.37 No.2, pp 152-177

Hench, J. (2003), Designing Disney, Disney Enterprises/Editions, New York

Hesselmans, K. (2005), Thematisering als belevenisinstrument, onderzoek naar succes- en faalfactoren van thematisering in de attractieparkensector, Thesis

Horsten, P., Hover, M. (2004), Cursushandleiding Instrumentarium voor de regie van de belevenis, interne uitgave NHTV

Hover, M., Kops, C. (2004), What's in a Concept?, interne uitgave, NHTV

Hover, M. (2006), De beleving van storytelling, thema en concept: a 'love story', MMNieuws 3, jaargang 8

Kleiber, D., (1999), Leisure Experience and Human Development, Basic Books, New York

Koopman, W. (2005), De juiste ingredienten voor thematisering, Thesis

Mikunda, C. (2004), Brand Lands, Hot Spots and Cool Spaces, Kogan Page Limited, London

Nijs, D., Peters, F. (2002), Imagineering, het creeren van belevingswerelden die blijven boeien, Boom, Amsterdam

Pine II, Gilmore (1999), The Experience Economy: Work is Theatre & Business Stage, Harvard Business School Press

Pine II (2003), Lecture at International Business Forum Imagineering Academy, NHTV, Breda

Poel, van der H. (1999/2003), Tijd voor vrijheid, inleiding tot studie van de vrijetijd, Boom, Amsterdam

Pralahad, C.K., Ramaswamy, V. (2004), The Future of Competition. Co-creating Unique Value with Customers, Harvard Business School Press, Boston

Rijnja, G., Van der Jagt, R. (2004), Storytelling. De kracht van verhalen in communicatie, Kluwer, Alphen aan de Rijn

Schmitt (1999), Experiential Marketing: How to get Customers to Sense, Feel, Think, Act, and Relate to your Company and Brands, Free Press

Schürmann, E. (2004), Merkenmanagement in de evenementen-branche: een praktijkcase bij Mundial Productions, MMNieuws 4/5, jaargang 6

Snel, A. in Boswijk A., Thijssen, T., Peelen, E. (2005), Een nieuwe kijk op de beleveniseconomie, Pearson Education Benelux

Stok, K. (2006), van Flow naar Betrokkenheid, Thesis

Van Pelt, P. (2005), The Imagineering Workout, Disney Enterprises/Editions, New York

Verhagen, D. (2006), Co-creatie wordt groot! Van toekijken naar meedoen met zelfontplooiing als hoogtepunt, thesis

Brand Entertainment at Trade Shows: Are You Experienced?

Urs Seiler

Are marketing events the new black? Yes, but remember: your customers do not only visit a show or an event in order to explore new products or services. They are looking for a brand experience: one that changes our lives.

Now what is an experience? We share many beliefs with Joe Pine, author of the seminal "The Experience Economy. Work Is Theatre & Every Business is a Stage".

Some people in our industry have an understanding of a customer experience as a one-off show act, designed for a special event. They do not see an experience as a customer interaction with a lasting value. This of course is a false interpretation of Brand Entertainment. In an interview with us Joe Pine argued that companies – theme restaurants, almost any retailer – give away the experience to better sell the goods and services they have on offer. Eventually companies have to align what they charge for with what customers value, and that means charging explicitly for the experience. It is that experience that creates value within customers because goods and services are mere commodities. Joe Pine says: "Even more lasting value can be gained in recognizing that experiences can indeed shape our lives – they can become life-transforming experiences".[5]

---

5   Joe Pine: Authentizität. Neues von der Erlebniswirtschaft. Interview, St. Gallen: Künzler-Bachmann/Expodata 12/2006

1.   Fair Enough

There are people who really believe that fairs exist to exhibit products for, say, 10 days; deliver, unpack, exhibit, dismantle.

But at fairs there is also the issue of demonstrating the growth of production, management and knowledge (in an entertaining way). Fairs are more suitable for demonstrating this complexity than other events or forums. Even in-house fairs can never be a substitute for the pulsating market place of supply and demand. There are numerous examples as to why companies renege on attending fairs....because competitors have withdrawn. This view reminds us of Henry Ford's old chestnut that whoever stops advertising to save money might as well stop his watch to save time.

Attending fairs simply to demonstrate products is however the old way of doing things. Even specialists want to be entertained these days, but in an intelligent and novel way. In attempting to entice the youth of our hedonistic society towards new technological subjects, the image of the sometimes rather derogatorily treated "bag collectors" at fairs must be redefined, as these people are often the customers or engineers of tomorrow. Even if they are wearing trainers today.

2.   Hollywood as an Example

We have always been amazed at the levels of energy, staffing and money in hardware used by exhibitors on their fair stands and how little creativity is used in entertaining their customers. At an emotional level, the customer does not quickly forget an entertaining experience. Emotional entertainment is the greatest potential for real encounters which evades other forms of marketing communication such as advertising, public relations or e-mailings. And the quantitative value of visitors to an event is largely untapped. The average number of visitors to fairs is far larger than any theatre director dare imagine even in his wildest dreams, even though he offers, as a rule, a more professional and emotional act.

The automobile industry is one of those industries which does not only set standards with its products but also in terms of its designs for fairs as the leading industry for brand management. And this is no coincidence as for around a century it has focused on the successful dramatic examples that Hollywood uses for its successful formula dream factories over and over again. One of the world's leading stage managers of fair exhibitions and theme parks, Xavier Bellprat, explains how his customers General Motors and Opel use such Hollywood-style examples. "It is a question of telling an emotive story following all the rules of a drama. There is a type of magic formula, which comes close to the perfect Hollywood story: you must be able to discern the plot within the first seven minutes. The climax comes twelve minutes before everything is wrapped up in a happy ending. This is the typical storytelling format for a blockbuster."[6]

This means that car fairs are nothing more than a place where a story is told, just as in a theatre or cinema. To work out more precisely who is involved in this scenario, the agent has undertaken research to find out exactly who the visitors to car fairs actually are and has come up with nine classic profiles: ranging from "event butterflies" to brand pilgrims.

A theatrical design has to be constructed for these types of visitor. The brand is treated as a person with a soul and character and the different models of car are involved in a family drama as if they were actors in a play. They have to be immersed for a while in another reality, participate in a story that affects them personally and they want to have a happy ending.

---

6   Xavier Bellprat. Imagineering. Interview, St. Gallen: Künzler-Bachmann/Expodata 5/1997

3.   What is Brand Entertainment?

Almost every company has to secure its future market success with a business model that goes beyond the core product because products and services have become exchangeable at their high level of perfection. The so-called "product" is frequently merely the material embodiment of yesterday's business model and needs added value. The added value lies in additional benefits or is tomorrow's "current" business model.

We are convinced that the new business model is brand entertainment. We understand this to mean all different types of dialogue that engage and involve the customer and give him the opportunity to participate actively and creatively in the business process. Being active and involved are the only valid yardsticks for experience marketing, everything else is just chitchat on the subject.

Business entertainment in this philosophy has nothing to do with superimposed, staged events but has more to do with focusing on real customer thinking. We also talk of customer economy. In other words: a company can only be successful in the future if it is not only concerned with its own success and does not just offer its customers "a product" but is also involved with a solution to make it more successful.

4.   A Different Way of Exhibiting

For the research in brand experience, more than 250 trade shows were visited over the last two decades. And guess what: hardly any (but some!) have created a lasting experience.

First and foremost the breathtaking and daring putting on stage of the Chevrolet and Cadillac stand at the Frankfurt Motor Show 1997 by Xavier Bellprat. It has changed our lives since we understood what it looks like if every business is a stage: it looks like the Fifth Avenue project in Frankfurt. Against the skyline of the Big Apple and between steaming drain covers, live performances transported scenes of everyday New York life to Frankfurt. Also included was a genuine New York Yellow Cab, accompanied by a taxi driver and an eccentric shopping queen in conversation.

This performance has transformed our lives because we took up creative storytelling for brand lands instead of exclusively writing articles for trade publications. It was then, when we understood, that Disney is the master of all brand experiences because it takes interaction with its customers, better: it's guests, seriously.

Then the exhibition stands of d'art design. Traditional stand builders or designers are obsessed with roofs, walls, floors (carpets). That it is possible to create different environments has been shown by d'art design over and over again. Not least the putting on stage of their own company. Their exhibition stands at Euroshop in Dusseldorf have neither entries nor exits, let alone roofs, walls or floors. The scenic picture takes you into a world of print, web, film, sound and actions in a poetic collection of bubbles. That's storytelling at its best: no roofs, no – well you know.

Another eye-opener was the change of attitude towards our customers as shown by the board of directors of Deutsche Messe AG, the organizers of Cebit and Hannover Fair and another three of the worlds leading trade shows. The former President, Sepp D. Heckmann stated that trade show organizers will have to go beyond their classic way of rating the success by its hall-size and number of customers, but extend their focus on and support the success of their customer at a show. In the intention to "think and work for the customer of the customer" the Deutsche Messe as a show organizer has created a turnaround from "*Platzanweiser* for m2 to interpreter for customer success."[7] Clever.

Asked for his opinion, Joe Pine fully agreed. In his opinion, the exhibitor is of course responsible for the experience that it stages for its would-be customers – but it's the organizer's

---

7   Urs Seiler (2008), Brand Entertainment. Erlebnismarketing in der Kundenökonomie. Hastings/Zürich: The West Hill Academy

responsibility to provide the stage set and help make the end experience compelling. "Mr. Heckmann's view is akin to what called transformations. If he viewed his role as ensuring that each exhibitor staged a wonderfully engaging experience, then he would start doing things differently to make sure each exhibitor's experiential aspirations were met, including much greater customization to each exhibitor's unique needs. Indeed, I heartily encourage him to take that view! It would propel his venue beyond all others." (Pine 2006)

If we are talking life-changing experiences, we must pay homage to another great. Bob Rogers. His BRC has created some of the most outstanding brand experiences on the planet. We have learned a lot when we asked him what he considers an experienced. Bob said he started with a very big, romantic dream: we must come to understand and solve our big problems if humanity is to survive the 21st century. This was the big dream that all of us were working on. It was truly an inspired goal for behavior modification. The heart of Disney for example is an entertainment company. The heart of Bob Roger Company is about positive behavior modifica-tion. "My personal goal is to enrich the world and leave it a better place than I found it. Marketing on a new way can achieve this: a lot of things are done in marketing that fail to modify behavior. To me it is not enough for the guest to be-come aware of a brand. Instead they must fall in love with it and buy it. If you do marketing you must modify behavior or why would you do it? We must make a real difference. I use the word behavior modification because it is much more spe-cific than marketing. It is also a lot harder to do."[8]

So what can exhibitors at trade shows learn from "the 21st century experiential revolution"?

Bob Rogers shows how the audience has changed, it is not just about the use of new media like Tivo or Bipod or mobile computing. What used to work does not work any more. "For example I read a study about people who do multi-tasking.

8   Bob Rogers: Ein Markenraum muss immer eine Einstellungsänderung bewirken. Interview, St. Gallen: Künzler-Bachmann/Style 2005

The average person my age can do 1.4 things successfully at once. This is why I must never drive while talking on the cell phone. However, the average 15 year old can successfully to 4.9 things at once."

This is not just a lot, this is a different species. Many young people who graduate from a high school go to college and have no idea how to use a public library. They walk in with a lot of books and have no idea what do to. They find and digest information completely differently. I cannot watch TV with my son, because he has the remote control. He is watching three programs, a Basketball-Game and the rerun of *The Simpsons* and a Bruce Willis movie, all at one. How do you communicate to these people? It needs to be faster, be layered and be shorter. We have opened a new project that pioneers a whole new approach with the Abraham Lincoln Museum. It is a huge hit. What we did, we took all of the ideas that we have been developing for brand experience and applied it to a museum. We are telling Abe Lincoln the same way we would sell Ford and it works.

First of all everything is visual first and verbal second. It's visual, you sell it with images and settings first. There is a plaque-copy (i.e. words on a wall). Most museums do it the other way round. You have to read the words to understand the object.

Another one is: we are emotional first and intellectual second. We use both, but the emotions lead. There is one of the scenes about slavery (Abraham Lincoln). The guests come around the corner and discover a slave auction: a mother, a father and a boy are sold in different directions. You do not need any words to explain what happens. It is not statistics about slavery; it grabs you by the ear. It makes some people cry, it is deeply moving. But then, if you look around, there are plenty of words on the wall. The intellectual ideas are definitively there, but it was visual before verbal, emotional before intellectual.

A third idea is that it is very cinematic. Traditional museums are designed by professors. Professors are professors because they love to read. Most young people do not like to read. So the entire museum in Lincoln has plenty of plaque-copy, but if you choose to walk through without reading, you can and you get the idea. Remember: in any brand-land, the guests come in groups of two, three or four. Even if they came on a tour bus, they can experience it in a group. They do it instinctively. They break down immediately. So you are always talking to groups in three or four. In any group of three or four there is always one, who is interested, two are not interested and one does not want to be there. How are you going to capture all four? You must assume the audience is *not* interested. And you must win them. The professor assumes everyone is interested in the subject. The chairman of VW is very interested in cars and assumes everyone else is too. I take the opposite approach. I assume no one is interested in cars and I must work very hard to show them how fascinating VW is (Rogers, 2005).

Then we asked Bob Rogers about BRC's Volkswagens Theme-Park in Dresden "Die Gläserne Manufaktur", what it does for VW (and it's customers) that classical brand-experience cannot supply.

Bob Rogers: "First of all, every brand has a mythology. Volkswagen has a very different mythology in the USA than in Europe. In USA it is the counter-culture. VW is a car that is for independent young people, who think for themselves. They do not go along with their parents. This comes from a brilliant ad campaign from the 1960s. In Europe Volkswagen means great engineering. If this is the mythology, the audience walks into the "Gläserne Manufaktur"; then we must start there and say the other things. You must embrace people where they are and then introduce the new ideas as extensions of the idea they already had. Dresden therefore has a very high-tech texture to its design. But the idea that comes second is that this is technology that serves people and the world. This is a subtler idea. So we start by living the cliché VW is technology and then, because we want to achieve a softer image, we show how this technology is in service to life. The lives of people and the life of the planet. The new mythology follows the old mythology." (Rogers 2005)

5. Authenticity: How to Separate the Wheat from the Chaff

But brand experience is not all about stage experience or experiential marketing. Brands must foremost be honest in order to create lasting experiences and interactions with their customers. Asked about the consumer sensibility and customer expectations Joe Pine argues that it is *because* of the rise of the Experience Economy that we see the rise of authenticity. In a world of paid-for experiences, people increasingly question what is real and what is not. They no longer want to accept the fake from the phoney; they want the real from the genuine. Businesses, therefore, have to render their offerings to be perceived as authentic.

Asked to define authenticity, Joe Pines says: "It's an incredibly amorphous topic difficult to get one's arms (or mind) around. (That's why it's taken us so long to write this next book!) From a consumer's perspective, you can think of authenticity as "conformance to self-image". Consumers now purchase offerings of all stripes based on how well they conform to their own self-image of who they are – or, perhaps even more so, of whom they aspire to be. Does it fit in with who they are and they want to become? Does it match what they desire to say they are? Does any disconnect exist between what this offering is and how it represents itself, and what they are and how they wish to represent themselves? Those economic offerings that conform in both depiction and perception to the self-image – the state of being – of the buyer will be viewed as authentic. Those that do not match to a sufficient degree to generate a "sympathetic vibration" between the offering and the buyer will be viewed as inauthentic. Today, even worse than being commoditized is being perceived as phoney. Don't let that happen to you." (Pine 2006).

It is obvious that the traditional forms of so-called live communication such as fairs or events are intended to meet the customer's needs because of all the marketing tools these allow the highest level of interaction (in terms of dialogue) and customer activation. As traditional stages of live experience, fairs, events, seminars, conferences and road shows have a particular affinity for business entertainment.

Last but not Least: Event Intelligence for the 21st Century

1. Think in communities, not customers
2. Create life-altering experiences, not commodities
3. Think and work for the customer of your customer
4. Use your illusions
5. Create transforming experience for the entertainment-society
6. Visit Disneyland

Selected Issues of Crowd Management:
25th RhEINKULTUR 2007

Sabine Funk

1. Introduction

Crowds occur frequently nowadays – at planned events as well as in everyday situations (e.g. Metro- or railway stations). The sports, music, event and entertainment industry is growing fast – up to 80.000 people in stadiums and up to a few hundred thousands on open-air sites is nothing unusual. While most events occur without any serious problems, we mustn't forget that the more events that take place, the more likely it is for a serious accident among the crowd or even a crowd disaster to happen. Even the most harmless gathering can suddenly become threatening and dangerous, whether due to an incident within the crowd or due to an external impact.

Fortunately, major crowd disasters are rare but crowd related falls and other accidents associated with crowding are relatively common. Therefore, a lot of effort has been put into investigating crowd management, the behavior of crowds and other crowd related topics[9].

To handle crowds properly – regardless if gathered by chance or as a defined audience of an event – one does not only need adequate facilities, venues, staff and infrastructure but organizational structures and an efficient and suitable crowd management plan, as well. To assure a safe and com-

---

9 One of the first and still important reports on crowd management is the so called „Cincinnati Report" from 1980, after the death of eleven people at a concert by "The Who" in Cincinnati, Ohio, USA.

fortable environment for crowds, their management has to be planned. The crowd management plan follows the risk assessment, which is always the first step when planning an event. The risk assessment deals with every possible impact associated with the event.

But not only is the safety of the audience determined by an efficient crowd management, it also has an impact on the quality of the audience's experience. As a promoter is held fully responsibly for any crowd-related accident, he should keep in mind that if he wants the audience to come back next time, he will have to make sure his audience feels safe as well as entertained.

In the following, this essay is going to address some issues and topics of professional crowd management in general and their implementation during the 25th RhEINKULTUR Festival 2007 in particular. The examples given will provide a good insight into the special situation of the festival and into general crowd management issues.

2. RhEINKULTUR – A Short Description of the Festival

The RhEINKULTUR is an annual admission free open-air festival, taking place in a recreation park in Bonn, Germany.

On July 7th, 2007 nearly 200.000 people celebrated the RhEINKULTUR's 25th anniversary on a bright and sunny festival day. With an audience of never less than a hundred thousand people in the last few years, the RhEINKULTUR is one of the biggest open-air festivals in Europe.

The festival site is a green field with almost no infrastructure present. Even basic infrastructure like electric power or water supply has to be brought in. The festival area covers over 360.000 m² including a small lake, lots of trees and small plateaus. The area that is actually usable for the audience measures about 100.000 m².

The festival consists of five stages with different types of music, a sports area, and a special area for children. The program runs from 12:00 am to 12:00 pm.

Even though it is an admission free festival, the festival site is fenced in to prevent people from bringing their own beverages or even dangerous items to the festival ground. For the same reasons visitors get searched for contraband at the ingress. The fence stretches across five kilometres and there are nine entrance points around the festival area, two of them being „main entries".

Only a few steps away from one of the main entries is a station for light rail transit, which serves about 50% of the festival visitors.

Since it is a one-day festival no campsite is offered. People usually arrive in the morning or during the day and leave right after curfew at 12 p.m.

In its 24 years of existence there have been hardly any unpleasant incidents or damages to report. The vibe among the audience is usually very laid-back which is not only due to the audience's diversity in age, social background and culture but also to the broad and green festival site.

As an admission free festival the RhEINKULTUR works with an extremely limited budget with most of the money coming from sponsors and the selling of licenses (beverages & food).

As there are no advanced ticket sales it is difficult to predict the size of the audience. Experience shows that the size of the audience is not only a question of the line-up but especially of the weather. Since the weather forecast isn't reliable until three to five days before the festival, the promoters only have this short time frame to make concise calculations on the expected audience. This makes it very difficult to plan and budget infrastructure, staff and material.

The 25th RhEINKULTUR turned out to present a truly unique challenge. Due to perfect weather conditions as well as an exquisite line-up, the festival had to face its biggest audience ever. The size of the audience combined with its unexpected early arrival caused a lot of serious problems, especially at the main ingresses and the main station.

A lot of lessons could be learned from the problems and incidents that occurred at the 25th RhEINKULTUR regarding the crowd's behaviour and its management. These incidents led to a general re-considering of the festival's risk assessment and crowd management plan.

3.   Risk Assessment

Risk assessment means the anticipating, monitoring and controlling of potential risks.

A proper risk assessment is the first and very crucial step towards solid planning of an event and the setting up of an effective crowd management plan. Even though risk assessment is primarily a management responsibility it should incorporate everyone involved in the event.

On top of being done first of all and early in advance of an event, risk assessment has to be carried out as a fluent analysis and re-evaluation during the whole planning process and during the event itself. As risk assessment in general should be an on-going process, the crowd management plan has to be flexible as well for it has to be able to adjust to changing conditions arising from the risk assessment.

Even if it seems to be "the same procedure as last year" risk assessment has to be carried out anew for each single event. There is a constant change both in society and in the entertainment industry and new and unexpected difficulties, which have to be re-assessed again and again, come up every single day.

Risk assessment deals with everything that could have an impact on the event, such as:

- crowd profile, expected crowd size and behaviour
- staff profile and staff training
- environmental profile

- programme and schedules
- site-layout
- weather forecast
- background information about previous events
- traffic management
- seating types
- roles and responsibilities of parties involved
- door opening policy and contraband searches
- concessions
- communication

RhEINKULTUR: The risk assessment

Based on the particular results of the previous year a first risk analysis is carried out nearly half a year before the up-coming event. These experiences are a good foundation and orientation for the current risk assessment – nonetheless new artists and bands, new people involved and the design of the festival site due to number and character of selling points demand a revision of the former risk analysis every year.

In 2007, once the headliner and other parts of the program were confirmed, it became clear that the festival's "capacity" was going to be a major topic. The billing was much stronger than in the previous years and it was expected to get much more publicity and therefore a lot more visitors.

The "capacity issue" got even more important as a change in the structure of the beverage concessions led to nearly twice as many bars than in the year before. This, of course had an enormous effect on the site layout. During a first planning session, every single position on site was elaborated again. The positions of booths had to be changed, new positions had to be found and new pathways for the audience had to be arranged. Furthermore, infrastructure and material were re-considered as well as the number and the positions of security staff.

These topics were presented insistently in meeting with the authorities, fire brigade and police too, in order for them to take the necessary precautions (as for traffic management or number of staff).

"Capacity" and "capacity extension" turned into fundamental topics of the whole planning and executing process.

Three days before the festival the risk assessment had to be modified again, when it turned out that the day of the event would be the first sunny day after a two-week period of rain. At this time a record attendance was more than likely. This fact demanded a final alignment, especially in regard to number and positions of security staff.

4.   Crowd Management

According to the Cincinnati Report,

"Crowd management is defined as the systematic planning for, and supervision of, the orderly movement and assembly of people. (...) Crowd management involves the assessment of the people handling capabilities of a space prior to use. It includes evaluation of projected levels of occupancy, adequacy of means of ingress and egress,   processing procedures (...) and expected types of activities and group behavior". [10]

The primary crowd management objectives are the avoidance of critical crowd densities and rapid group movement. To reach this target everything that could have an impact on the crowd has to be considered. There is a huge of crowd-related factors, both physical and behavioural, which makes

---

10 *Crowd Management. Report of the Task Force on Crowd Control and Safety. City of Cincinnati, 1980*

crowd management a very complex issue and a massive challenge.

Some of these factors will be described later on, such as:

- size and behavior of the crowd
- site layout (general design, space, ingress and egress)
- communication (to the audience, within the crowd management)
- roles and responsibilities of people involved

RhEINKULTUR: The crowd management

Crowd management holds a special position within the festival's planning process. This is not only due to the complexity of the topic itself but especially due to the festival's size and unique structure.

As the RhEINKULTUR is an admission free festival with a very limited budget, it is difficult to set up a proper crowd management plan. The budget limits a lot of possibilities and requirements such as computerized counting systems, for example, which could compensate the difficulty of forecasting the size of the crowd.

As the important issue "crowd size" remains difficult to estimate, there is an even stronger focus on the other issues, such as site layout, communication or welfare to compensate the above-mentioned planning uncertainties.

4.1 The Crowd

Crowds gather frequently, usually without serious problems. Reasons for gathering are as different as size and group line-up. Therefore, the crowd management plan must be based on a variety of factors and on a wide range of information. This includes an assessment of the size and the nature of the crowd, potential behavior patterns and experiences from similar events.

The promoters of the RhEINKULTUR can hark back to 24 years of experience in organizing this particular festival, which reached an average of 150.000 visitors in the last ten years. They have also started a frequent exchange of experiences and information with other European festivals. For this purpose a platform was established with the European Festival Association, YOUROPE[11].

Size of the crowd

The expected size of the crowd is one of the most important factors for the crowd management plan. Being able to forecast the size of the crowd means being able to react accordingly and knowing what amount of infrastructure, material, bars, toilets and staff is needed. This is quite easy at events with ticket-sales and a predetermined maximum size of the audience. On the contrary it is extremely difficult for events in public places without defined access and the possibilities to count people. To have a chance of properly assessing the size of the audience, festivals without ticket-sales need as much information as possible, from experiences with similar events, the artists playing to the weather forecast. They have to be prepared to face the highest realistic amount of people and have to come up with methods to prevent the festival area or the public place from overcrowding.

RhEINKULTUR: The size of the crowd

Even with a festival site of 360.000 m² the RhEINKULTUR has a limit of manageable people – which is 200. – 220.000 people. The usable space for the audience is approximately

---

11 www.yourope.org

100.000 m² due to the festival seating situation[12] and natural obstacles like trees or even a small lake. Since it is not possible to count the people, the promoter uses a grid pattern to get a realistic idea of how many people are on the festival site. This grid pattern is the result of a long time monitoring of the audience and audience movement on the festival and therefore needs an evaluation of highly experienced users.

Good crowd management deals with both the festival area and external capacities and areas. For the RhEINKULTUR the public transport system and the main stations are the most important external factors. 50% of the people arrive by public transport due to the lack of parking spaces as well as the efforts to make the RhEINKULTUR festival as eco-friendly as possible. This huge amount of people using public transport puts a real strain on the main train and tram station and it easily turns into a bottleneck where dangerous overcrowding can occur. This is a problem that has to be incorporated into the festival's crowd management plan.

Since "capacity" became the most important topic very early on within the risk assessment, discussing it resulted in an improvement of the barrier systems in front of the stages, the re-positioning of bars and merchandise stands, in upgrading the number of security staff and a lot of additional efforts in communicating with the audience.

The last risk assessment that was done after a definite weather forecast three days before the festival led to a new discussion about increasing the number of security staff again and also about the re-alignment of their positions. To actually conduct these changes was very difficult, as expensive site damages caused by the load-in during bad weather had already exhausted the limited budget. Nonetheless, it had become obvious that the rush of visitors to the festival couldn't be stopped and that more staff was definitely

---

12 *Festival seating events simply provide an open area without seats or reserved space. People can wander around, sit or even lay down. Festival seating is reminiscent of picnic style seating.*

needed. Apart from the fact that there wasn't really any money to pay for more staff, it was difficult to say exactly how many more staff members would be needed. The only solution for this situation was to take another very critical look at all other measures and aspects and finally, to employ a special task force to react to any possible incidents and to support the staff when needed without being limited to one position.

Unfortunately, neither the authorities nor the people in charge of the public transport network reacted to the special combination of circumstances. For this reason, the public transport services were quite unprepared and had to deal with the biggest problem they ever had in connection with the festival.

But even with regular risk assessments and a very careful elaboration of the situation the promoters still had to face a lot of problems on the festival day.

In the past there were never more than a few people waiting in front of the entries when the doors opened at 11.30 am. This year, the first visitors turned up so unexpectedly early that security was not yet in place. As more and more people gathered early in front of all entries, it was decided that the staff should already take their positions at 10:30 am instead of 11:30 am. By doing so, the staff could communicate with the visitors and inform them that the gates could not be opened before 11:00 am, as there was still traffic on the site. By communicating with the visitors any possible agitation could be prevented.

These early visitors weren't so much attracted by the first bands, but by the idea of making the most out of a sunny festival day by lying in the grass and hanging out with friends.

The peak-time of arrivals at the festival site always used to be reached at around 5:00pm. This year, the former peak was already reached at 2:00 pm, and supervisory staff at the main station warned of a seemingly never-ending flow of people trying to pass through the station on their way to the festival.

Under these circumstances, at 3:00 pm the decision was made to open the main entries completely and to stop searching people for contraband. Of course this decision posed other potential risks, but after all, it was definitely the lesser of two evils. Letting people wait in front of the gates for an hour or more would have created a bad atmosphere that could have quickly turned into aggression and caused big fights. People with dangerous items on them might have actually started to use them in this kind of atmosphere.

It wasn't until 5:00 pm that the amount of arriving people finally came back to a normal rate that could be managed as usual again.

Behavior of the crowd

The crowd's characteristics, its behavior and its varying vulnerability are another major concern of the crowd management plan.

Due to a varying mix of age range, social, educational and cultural backgrounds within a crowd, the reactions to the same action vary, too. To be able to estimate a crowd's reaction one has to know as much as possible about the vulnerability of the crowd and the effects that different influences have on a crowd and as much about the crowds social make-up and its likes and dislikes. In other words: to manage a crowd it is vital to have certain knowledge of human nature and social structures or: to manage a crowd you have to know your crowd.

"Effective crowd management requires a thorough understanding of crowd behavior and a coordinated effort to plan safe environments to accommodate all kinds of audience at all kinds of events"[13]

---

13 Cincinnati Report, 1980

One of the most difficult topics is the issue of alcohol and drug abuse, which unfortunately is a common problem at festivals. People under the influence of drugs and / or alcohol are a danger to themselves and others around them. This is a very important topic for managing a festival crowd. On the one hand, it often leads to aggressive behavioural patterns, on the other hand, people under the influence of alcohol or other drugs often loose their natural sense of self-protection and find themselves in situations that are very dangerous for their physical and their psychic health.

RhEINKULTUR: The behavior of the crowd

The RhEINKULTUR has hardly any problems with bad crowd behavior on the festival site itself. The atmosphere among the audience is usually very relaxed due to the audience's diversity in age and culture and the spacious festival site, which offers a lot of space beyond the stage areas. Most problems stem from the alcohol and drug abuse within the younger visitors. Over the last few years the alcohol and drug related problems have increased. More and more very young people (who are neither used to drinking nor used to the whole festival environment) arrive at the festival site either already drunk or get drunk very quickly once they are there. Unsurprisingly, they cause the promoters, medical services, the other visitor's and themselves a lot of trouble.

Since the line-up of the main stage was aimed at an older mainstream audience, in 2007, the average audience profile was expected to be a relaxed one. But unexpectedly and quite early on the medical services gave warning signals concerning the increasing amount of very intoxicated young people. To cope with this situation, the security staff was asked to keep a very close eye on these people and to inform the medical services immediately when they recognized people with obviously alcohol-induced problems.

Even more difficult is the people's behavior on their journey to and from the festival site. There are always huge problems with drunken people at the main station who are frustrated because of overcrowded trains and long waiting times. In 2007, serious problems arose when people started pulling the trams' emergency brakes – "just for fun". These actions led to a total loss of seven trams, a temporary collapse of the affected lines as the stopped trams blocked the tram tracks and therefore caused enormous delays. For this reason the main station got dangerously overcrowded as people kept arriving from other directions but couldn't leave to get to the festival. Therefore, the police in accordance with the promoters and the local authorities decided to close the main station because of too many people gathering inside the rather small station. This was also dangerous as the main station is located between two traffic lanes and there also isn't any safe area nearby for the crowd to move to. It took about one hour until the bulk of people inside and outside the station had disbanded and the flow of traffic had gone back to normal.

4.2   Structural Influences on Crowd Management

When talking about structural influences on crowd management, two major points are to be discussed. One point is the critical density of people or the extremely minimized space per person that occurs in uncontrolled crowds, the other one is the site layout and the arrangement of buildings on the festival ground.

Site layout and design affect the flow of the audience through the festival site. A lot of problems arise from bottleneck situations or dangerous pressure points caused by placing objects in the wrong locations. The ingress and egress capacities have to be well calculated and the barrier system has to be well designed and dimensioned too. They have to be chosen according to the expected size of the audience and have to withstand the pressure of the moving crowd. They have to be placed in a way that gives people adequate space to move and allows efficient mass movement.

To prevent dangerous situations or crowding in general, multiple barrier systems, multi-entrances and other measures for adequate queuing and metering have to be of the right dimensions and be well positioned. Every unit on the festival-site, e.g. bars or merchandise units must be set out in a way which allows a direct visitor flow and straight sight lines. Layout and arrangements have to be considered under normal traffic conditions as well as under a worst-case scenario in which principally harmless situations and minor design deficiencies can suddenly become very dangerous.

RhEINKULTUR: The festival site

Even with a festival site of 360.000 m², the promoters have to be very careful when planning and designing the site layout as natural obstacles such as trees, knolls and even a lake within the site have to be considered. One has to find a balance between placing bars, merchandise units and sponsors for maximum presentation and giving the audience as much room as possible for unobstructed movement. This is important especially in front of the stages where there isn't much room anyway due to the multiple barrier systems. Bars are placed either to the left or the right of the stage so that they are outside the line of sight or behind the FOH.

Ingress and egress

The most crowd-related problems arise at the ingress and egress situations at an event. History has shown that more people get killed or injured at the ingress and egress than during the event itself.

To avoid dangerous situations at ingress or egress both architectural and organizational arrangements have to be made. Organizational strategies can be the early opening or the delayed closing of an event. Opening a venue early extends the ingress arrival process. Extending the entertainment program is one possible strategy to lengthen the egress process and to reduce crowding at the egress points and traffic pressures on public transport, the roads and parking facilities.

Instead of a single centralized entrance system, a multiple entrance system with different points to enter or exit the event reduces pressure and avoids bulks of people in front of the ingress or egress. Number and size of ingresses and egresses have to fit the number of people expected. Besides the capacity of the ingress & egress points, external facilities and the capacities of parking or public transport have to be considered. The crowd management has to make sure that the traffic flow must not exceed the capacity of the ingress and egress points. Queuing and metering are strategies to organize an orderly and disciplined process and to keep crowd densities below critical levels. Queuing means lining up people in single files, mostly with the help of barriers or other structural devices. Metering is strategy to control the rate of arrivals and the degree of crowding at a known bottleneck situation, e.g. ingress or egress points, stairs or gates where uncontrolled crowding might cause problems. Metering must be applied with caution since it also produces a further accumulation of waiting people. The waiting area should be big enough for the crowd and big enough to establish formal queues as well.

RhEINKULTUR: Ingress & egress situation

The RhEINKULTUR festival site has nine entries, two of them being multi or "main" entrances. These main entrances are located on opposite sides of the festival area. The single entries are located at different spots around the festival.

All of the gates are used for ingress and egress. Once the amount of people arriving decreases, the ingress points are turned into egress points. There are eight additional emergency exits that are only opened by the security staff in case of an emergency.

One of the main ingresses which is used by about 50% of the visitors is located directly at the tram station. The platform is at a higher level than the festival ground, so that the visitors have to walk down some stairs or down a bevel to reach the site. Within the festival site this area poses the most risks. At certain times there is a disproportion between people arriving by train and people moving through the ingress due to the contraband search. If the crowd density becomes too high the contraband search is accelerated or even stopped and the doors are opened to take the pressure off the entries. In the last few years this action didn't have to be taken very often. Most of the times, the visitor flow and the security check are restored again within a few minutes. In 2007 the doors had to be opened completely for at least two hours before the situation eased up. Even if this was the right decision it was also dangerous because visitors could bring prohibited items to the festival.

Though the RhEINKULTUR is allowed to play music after curfew and even though people are still able to buy drinks on the festival site, most of the visitors move to the tram station right after curfew. At about half an hour after curfew there is always a huge bulk of people waiting in front of the tram station. To avoid overcrowding barriers are set up for queuing and metering. With these barriers the bulk of people is queued in a zigzag line and can proceed in a regulated and steady manner. For the security guards positioned at the foot of the stairs this is much easier to control and regulate the amount of people entering the platform and to maintain a safe occupancy level.

4.3 Communication

A lot of crowd-related problems are base on a lack of communication and information. Therefore, these factors are key points to an effective crowd management plan. This includes all means of communication and information either before or during an event. Information always should be clear and concise, regardless if given by signs, word of mouth or electronically.

Pre-event

There are a lot of possibilities to contact and inform the audience before an event. The most important information tool is the homepage of the promoter/the event itself. Also newspapers, flyers, radio announcements and TV spots are common tools. Even on tickets there is space for information to familiarize with the event and the venue.

Pre-event information must contain site-maps with relevant positions (information tent, emergency exits, toilets etc), the house rules with a description of forbidden things and behavioural patterns on the event. Especially information for people who are attending the first time must be offered. This must be very concrete information and hints about clothing, useful things (such as sun block, raincoats), risk and behaviour.

During an event

All the information given beforehand has to be available during the event, too. There have to be information points with general information and help as well as concrete schedules, meeting points or lost and found units.

The most important communication tools during an event are the PA system, video-screens and megaphones. These systems enable the promoter to immediately communicate with the audience and to quickly defuse a potentially dangerous situation if necessary. Form and wording of the message must be chosen carefully. A misunderstood message, or one that produces a sense of urgency or threat to personal safety, can worsen the situation. Special messages for handling emergency situations as well as general and useful information should be prepared in advance and be included in the crowd management plan. The emergency messages must be handed out prior to the event to all security-relevant acting personnel, groups and institutions. They must be present at all relevant positions in written form and different languages.

In case of a critical situation it is of high importance that people are informed about what is happening. This has to be clear and reliable information from an authority -as the host or even the artists – to prevent people from speculating and reacting to rumours or false information.

Critical situations can arise from harmless developments, e.g. a delayed door opening or changes in schedule or program. If promoters want the audience to accept changes and delays without causing dangerous situations they have to take care that the audience is not only notified, but also informed about the reasons for their discomfort.

RhEINKULTUR: Communication

Communication and information are the most important factors and tools for the RhEINKULTUR's crowd management plan.

The RhEINKULTUR uses all available media like the festival homepage, the program magazine, flyer and press to communicate with the audience. Not just concrete information about the programme or the festival site plan is provided, but also tips for a good time on the festival. This ranges from concrete advice for appropriate clothing, using sun block, to arranging meeting points and meeting times and even drinking enough water. Out of experience the promoter even tries to explain that taking drugs is dangerous in general but especially within an anyway stressful festival situation.

During the festival the hosts of the stages have a central position for the communication with the audience. Each stage has its own host who informs the audience about the schedule, the bands and other relevant topics. They also give good advice as mentioned above. As the RhEINKULTUR has no video-screens, the hosts also have a special task in case of an emergency. They have standardized announcements with clear and concise information for any kind of incident. These announcements and other relevant information are topic of the security briefing with the hosts and other security-relevant acting personnel prior to the event.

In 2007 the host of the Punk and Hardcore stage got a central position before the headliner "Sick of it All" entered the stage. Known for their extreme and "wild" audience and extreme movements, the host informed the audience of what they must expect from this band. All guests were asked to leave the first barrier section if they didn't get the upcoming situation straight. A lot of guest followed the advice and were thankful about not being part of the "wall of death".

Communication also received a central significance after the end of the event as well, when the audience rushed to the egresses and the tram station. Neither the promoter nor the audience knew at this time that the rail traffic almost got disrupted because of an accident 10 kilometres away on one of the central access rails to and from the festival.

Because no trains were leaving or arriving a huge crowd arose at the tram station extremely fast. High alcohol con-sumption and the certain will to leave the festival area caused a high potential of aggression in this crowd. The pro-moter as well as security staff and police were in high alert at this time. An emergency schedule of the public transport ser-vices only allowed trams leaving in a 30 minutes interval. This was even more difficult than no trams leaving at all for people did not leave because they saw or heard trams from time to time and did not believe the announcements of the public transport services at the platforms. For this reason se-curity staff informed the guests individually about the reason of the traffic disruption and asked to pass this information on. The information spread in the crowd, supported by short, additional announcements by police and promoter. Because of the detailed information the expected trouble hold off completely and most of the visitors started to walk towards the city. They understood that this situation wasn't the promoters or the transport services fault and tried to make the best out of it.

4.4 Roles and Responsibilities

A safe event needs the attendance and cooperativeness of all parties involved. Their roles and responsibilities have to be specified, written down and known by all prior to the event. There must be a clear understanding of the chain of command and the duties that each person has to perform as well as their competences to act or react.

Among the parties involved are:

- permission giving authorities
- police
- fire brigade
- promoter
- crowd manager
- stage manager
- head of security
- performers

Especially the performers have a huge influence on the audience and the behaviour of the crowd.

A lot of the performers support the promoter regarding the crowd management, making announcements and giving safety advices, but unfortunately there are still others who encourage fans to move closer or throw souvenirs to the audience. Performers and entertainers must be held fully accountable for their actions and therefore should be informed of their own responsibilities.

Even if a thoughtful and elaborate crowd management plan may be implemented, it can neither be completely effective without patron cooperation, nor can it protect individuals from self-inflicted harm. In a crowd, patrons should always be aware of the possible effect their actions may cause on the safety of the whole group.

RhEINKULTUR: Roles and responsibilities

The promoters of the festival cooperate with the permission giving authorities, police, fire brigade, medical services and public transport services. Besides periodical updates there is a meeting with everyone involved about two months before the festival where strategies are discussed. During the festival there are regular meetings every two or three hours. Due to the special situation during the last RhEINKULTUR these meetings were held hourly.

As part of the contract the artists and bands receive an information sheet with all relevant rules and regulations. Furthermore, the stage manager briefs the artists and their managers about the expected behaviour, the show stop scenario and the "no goes", such as throwing an item into the audience. Fortunately most of the artists understand the reasons for the regulations and follow these instructions. There were no incidents caused by artist or bands during the last years. Most of the bands even support the promoter by explaining things to the audience and keeping them calm.

5.   Outlook

The experiences of the 25th RhEINKULTUR showed that the RhEINKULTUR's risk assessment and the crowd management plan are sufficient but not satisfying. The limited budget remains a major problem even if there are a lot of efforts to compensate this handicap.

2007 showed that communication is of vital influence for a safe event – in this case public transport services ignored the promoter's warnings about the expected crowd and did not inform the promoter about the traffic collapse after the show right in time.

If the public transport services would have informed the promoter and if the host would have been able to announce this to the audience, there would have been a chance for the people to make a decision about this special situation. Not stopping the people from moving to the tram station minimized the possibilities for the crowd management to react.

Crowd management can only play to its strength as a tool for safer events if every party involved as mentioned above understands how to use this tool properly. During the event, communication is one of the main measures to adjust the crowd management planning to the crowd management execution.

One has to be aware that it was not only due to a good information strategy within the crowd management at the tram station but also due to a warm and comfortable night that this situation eased up that easy.

Furthermore, the incidences in the trams and at the main station led to a discussion about the responsibility of the promoter and questions of control and surveillance. Answers and agreements have to be found to the question where the promoter's responsibility starts.

"Some risk to public safety is inherent in any activity in any place. No one can anticipate all of the elements in an event that might lead to danger, but cooperative efforts among and between facility or site owners, event promoters, agents, entertainers, tickets sellers, security, police, government, health and safety personnel etc. can be made to identify and reduce that risk"[14]

References

www.crowddynamics.com
www.crowdsafe.com
www.yourope.org
www.rheinkultur.com

---

14 *Cincinnati Report, 1980*

Strategic Event Management – The Decisive Step to Success

Ana Maria Zumsteg, Polo Looser

Events offer the unique opportunity to address target audiences in a controlled environment; an opportunity to create unique experiences, lasting memories and personal relationships, impacting on brand associations and preference in a manner unparallel to all other marketing tools.

Based on this, the authors of this chapter try to demonstrate how, by adopting a strategic view of events management and aligning event goals and overall event portfolios, to company marketing and business goals, the company organization can increase their brand equity and produce long term shareholder return.

The main focus of this paper is in identifying the key processes and performance indicators relevant to transforming traditional "nice to have" events into marketing tools supporting the achievement of strategic business goals.

1. Introduction

When brands became the talk of town in the late 80s, most people expected it to be one more management fad. Today in 2007 and going into 2008 most companies know that brands are not just a fad but strong brands result in increased equity value and play a role in guaranteeing long term business success.

Traditionally companies and organizations have hosted events for a multitude of reasons: prestige, tradition, and recognition, to name but a few. However with increased competition, new marketing channels such as internet, mobile telephony, etc; increased knowledge and understanding of what really motivates people to buy and what makes them feel identified with a brand, is seeing investment move, more and more, from classical advertising to event related activities, focusing on narrow target audiences and concrete business goals, reverting into business profit and increased brand equity.

However, whether trying to built brand awareness, creating product interest, or increasing customer loyalty, choosing the right activities, identifying the key objectives and keeping the goal in front of the eyes throughout the planning, implementation and follow up of an event are key to business success and the Return on Investment (ROI).

2. Basic Facts and Figures about Events

Advantages of events over other marketing media:
Cost of traditional advertising continues to increase whilst ratings and readership decline, events cost less and successfully reach targeted audiences

- Increasing need for two-way communication. Events allow companies to "deepen" their relationship with customers/distributors and learn about their expectations
- Lack of tangible differences amongst products makes emotional logic the single most important business driver, events can create this differentiation
- Events provide an opportunity to narrowcast target markets, provide an incentive to distributors and establish relationships going beyond products and services
- They can effectively combat larger ad budgets from competitors
- They provide an opportunity to reach various objectives at the same time.

Events reach a smaller audience but give "hands-on" experience of the brand and have the potential to speak to your customer's aspirations. Successful brands are not any more centred in product innovation but in customer transformation, the kind of transformation that makes the customer your biggest fan.

Through Strategic Thinking and Integration of events to overall business programs we can turn "events" into smart marketing. The most important, single factor however, remains in the decision to host the right events for the right audiences at the right time and place.

3. Prerequisite to the Strategic Management of Events

Whilst the facts reviewed above provide an understanding of the potential role that events may play in building brand equity and increasing business, the question on how to actually do this, remains open and unanswered in most corporations.

For a company to be able to use events in their strategic dimension, management needs to get a clear understanding of the company business goals, the concrete strategies, products, services and customer segments, all of which are a key to developing a company wide strategy for hosted activities supporting the achievement of business goals, and strategic event portfolio.

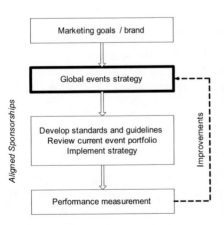

Global Strategy
Provide a clear global events strategy and governance structure with clear focus on the achievement of business and brand goals.

Guidelines
Introduce clear guidelines to facilitate standardization and compliance.

Organization
Streamline planning, implementation and evaluation of all company hosted activities through the marketing function.

Process
Introduce consistent processes to plan, execute, measure and report events. These processes will allow for transparency on events investment and financial benefit.

Procurement
Work only with preferred partners ensuring that they understand your brand and your business objectives

Tools
Improve information systems to facilitate management decision making. Develop and Implement other tools to support strategy. i.e. Event Aesthetic material, templates, training.

Figure 9: Global events strategy

97

However, having the perfect event mix and clear business goals alone cannot revert in brand value unless the brand identity, the values and the tone of voice are embedded in all activities and communications in a standardized and coherent manner throughout the organization, going beyond audio and visual elements to involve executives' behaviour. This requires the development of clear brand aesthetic guidelines governing the type of venues, the look and feel of invitations and other collateral event material and all other elements impacting on participants experience, and on the creation of long term brand associations leading to purchase and brand loyalty.

Integrating and aligning all these elements to other marketing tools is imperative to creating a strong identity. Making these elements known to all employees, making them easily available and choosing the right procurement partners are necessary aspects of success

Last but not least, management buy-in, from the very top, is absolutely necessary to ensure success. Changing the image of events from a "fun thing to do", into an activity producing long term business benefits require a change of management mentality and a commitment to change and to succeed.

4. Implementing the Strategy

There are three key processes involved in implementing an event strategy to a concrete business situation. These are: planning, implementation and performance evaluation (and optimization).

4.1 The First Key Process: The Planning Process

There are two main levels within the events planning phase: A strategic level, where the business manager needs to evaluate event investment and industry performance and to understand where the company strengths and weaknesses are whilst searching for opportunities for gaining competitive advantage and bring business results through events.

Having completed this primal task and established the level of investment required and identified the type of activities offering the potential to gain competitive advantage; managers are ready to define the company's event portfolio.

An event portfolio is made of a combination of company-hosted activities offering the highest potential to support the achievement of identified business goals.

The second step in the planning process consists in understanding internal needs and the concrete value of event activities to fulfil these needs. This step encompasses the analysis of various factors such as:

- Need analysis: What market-segment has business/ brand issues to focus on, which can be addressed through business meetings or events?
- Business/Brand Goals Definition: Clearly define expected business outcome in a quantitative and qualitative terms and plan to communicate these to the relevant stakeholders
- Event Evaluation: What is the likelihood to positively influence a given business/brand goal through events (is an event likely to have any effect on driving and supporting sales, loyalty, etc vs. alternative marketing and sales levers (likely effectiveness)
- Stakeholder Definition: Which audiences are relevant to each business/brand goals and what is the best way to attract them and influence them through event activities. What internal audiences are relevant to identifying target audiences and managing stakeholders?
- Budget Definition: What is the adequate budget allocation for each individual activity in relation to desired/expected results?
- Summarizing: The planning process requires business managers to evaluate the value of events as co-adjuvant in the achievement of their business goals

Once it has been established that hosting an activity is the best tactic to support the achievement of a business goal (or part of it), individual activities need to be analyzed and evaluated for their potential value in supporting business goals.

The following chart depicts the thinking process behind the evaluation of individual activities at the planning tactical level in choosing the right activities (event portfolio evaluation):

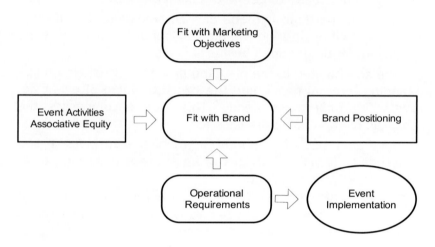

Figure 10: Fit with brand

Finally, when a group of activities to be hosted has been identified, it is recommended to plot these on a brand/business goals grid to ensure that the mixed of planned activities accurately represent the marketing and business priorities of the group and that the level of overall investment is adequate to the expected return on investment.

4.2   The Second Key Process: The Event Implementation

Once it has been establish that an event is the best marketing tool to support the achievement of a given business goal, the event activities go to the implementation phase.

Key stages in events implementation

- Project Management
  - Decide early who should be part of the project team
  - Communicate concrete business goals and get buy in
  - Allocate clear roles and responsibilities.
- Timing/Venue and Catering
  - Check and assert most convenient dates
  - Check for opportunities to leverage other company hosted activities
  - Select venue and catering reflecting your brand positioning
- Program
  - Make program relevant to both target audience and goal of the event
  - Take the chance to highlight brand values and embed brand promise
  - Evaluate opportunities to sale, cross sale, show case brand, products and capabilities in an effective manner
- Invitations
  - Align them to brand aesthetic and messaging strategies
  - Plan ahead of time and establish processes to identify key target audience involving the business
  - Proof the potential ROI of event
- Business Briefing
  - Create brief profile for participants and business script
  - Engage management in giving a business briefing, goals of the event and role of each company executive at the event.
  - Set up clear expectations
- Onsite Communications
  - Brand communication (align to brand campaign and brand values)
  - Company communication : i.e. company at a glance, or embedding related information into onsite decoration
  - Product segment communications: as relevant

- Identify "Take out message" What should your guest "take with him" from this event and use it consistently as a driver
- Onsite Hosting
  - The event project manager is responsible for the logistic results at the site and should be more than ever actively manage the event during the realization of the activity. The choice of production and catering partners is important but the ultimate responsibility is with the project/event manager. Their role during the event is to check, control and actively manage the events partners; put attention to detail and support the creation of a positive, lasting experience.
  - Executives attending the event are responsible for the business results of the investment and should behave according to the communicated goals for the event and agreed upon outcome
- Follow Up
  - As important as or more important than the event itself is the follow up. A thank you note, be from management or the relevant account manager, a follow up call and the careful recording of any new leads, prospects, quotes arising as a result of the event will help realize the potential value of an event.

4.3 The Third Key Process: The Event Evaluation

To measure is to know. Whilst the steps mentioned above provide us with a solid basis for success, we can only know the real value of hosted activities and the rate of success in achieving both return on investment but also return on objectives by carefully evaluating results versus identified goals. However, a measurement system does not guarantee success unless it is focused on optimization and recognition for work well done.

Why do we need performance evaluation and optimization processes?

- To identify and benchmark event performance in quantitative and qualitative terms
- To recognize people for their contribution to the realization of outstanding events and to the building of the Brand
- To become more and more effective in reaching our goal of aligning all hosted activities to brand values and business goals.
- To identify missed opportunities for market and industry leadership
- To support change of mindset from events focused on processes to events focused on business results
- To promote consistency of implementation, transparency of investment, knowledge sharing and high quality of events

What are the areas of evaluation?

- Event planning and budgeting
- Target audience definition and process
- Branding and communications (identification of key messages)
- Information management
- Event experience
- Follow-up
- Emotional value (motivation, inspiration, wow effect).

The authors have developed measurement systems and worked and measured many events themselves. For their own events they both work with experts outside their own companies in order to guarantee independency.

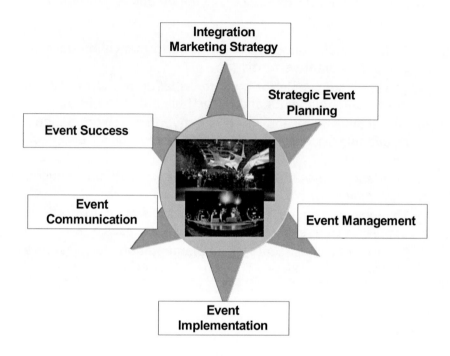

Figure 11: Eventflector, measurement method of MCI

The Event*flector* is applied in all major industries and is an approach by external experts. In a first step the goals are defined together. Then the experts elaborate a check-profile, which is composed by approximately 200 check criteria. In a third step the experts execute the check onsite. Step number four is the most labour-intensive part, where the experts write the evaluation profile and create a presentation. Step number five is the presentation to the stakeholders of the event, which includes benchmarks and proposals for improvement.

Putting it all together:

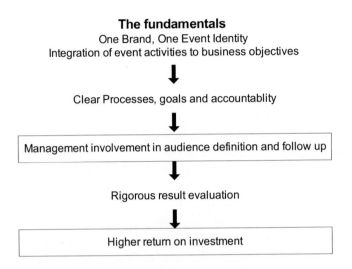

The fundamentals
One Brand, One Event Identity
Integration of event activities to business objectives

↓

Clear Processes, goals and accountablity

↓

Management involvement in audience definition and follow up

↓

Rigorous result evaluation

↓

Higher return on investment

Figure 12: The fundamentals

5.   Case Examples

5.1   No Limits – A Public Happening as Part of a Communication Campaign

Strategic business goal

To bring a brand (LG Electronics) alive and increase awareness for a specific target group in public space. Hardly any
other product family is as intensively advertised, hardly any
other target group receives the same interest and hardly any
other brand is as fiercely competitive. With so many extremes, the solution has to be nearby and a solution coming
from and inspired by extremes!

The task

How can young people aged between 16 and 29 and the forever young be motivated to buy the company's high-tech products?

The solution

Out of the ordinary advertising during the world-wide "Company's Action Sports World Tour" in a spectacular synthesis of extreme performance (skateboard, BMX, inline-skating competitions in the half-pipe and street course) and hip brandscapes (old overseas containers with stylish interior design and high-tech applications).

The Sports World Tour made 14 stops as it travelled around Europe, Asia, USA and South America visiting symbolic and world-famous venues including Barcelona's Moll de Marina, the Paris Eiffel Tower, the Berlin Brandenburg Gate and Olympiapark in Munich. Its visitors were given copious opportunities to see and experience fascinating in-sports and cool products.

The implementation

The agency designed a custom-built brand and product world for the company in line with the style of the Sports World Tour's action sports. An average of 40,000 visitors attended each of the venues lured by the 50 extreme athletes LG had on contract for the event. The audacious stunts of the world's best were there to be seen in the three half-pipe and street course competitions. The products were adapted for each locality, the interior of the five containers were filled with amazing product landscapes of the latest generation in the mobile and gaming market.

For days on end, the mobile games, ring tones and Xbox innovations were tested and found acceptance with the target group. Interactive competitions were staged in the containers creating a bond between the pros, the action in the half-pipe and street course and LG Mobile's brand world.

The result

Pure action and "extreme" interest! The sport and technophile community was mesmerized by the squad of superstars from the extreme sport scene on the half-pipes and trials amid the centrally located venues. The various brand worlds designed for target groups and showcasing LG Electronics' latest high-tech products in a contemporary atmosphere

5.2 Straight on Course – A Very Special Sales Conference

Strategic goal

To grow the business and to set sail for a successful future. This was the key vision delivered by the Insurance Company as it pulled anchor on its quest to discover new horizons together with its employees. Advised and supported by the agency, a highly motivated team broached the waves and landed at their planned destination without deviating from the course. The result was a rallying muster call for the future: full sail ahead, no matter how rough the winds!

What turns a sales conference into an experience to remember? On the one hand, the power of the messages being proffered. On the other hand, recognition that if you want to be part of a successful services community, you have to understand how to turn changing market forces into your own advantage.

But how can I get this across to my audience? The management and the agency designed the occasion side by side, and set about its realization with a highly motivated crew. The lead-in time was a sportsmanlike eight weeks.

Clever story lines rather than PowerPoint boredom, motivated, well-trained speakers in place of a platoon of statistics, empathy and authentic emotions instead of learning by rote – thus the sales conference was transformed into a conspicuous success for the 1,700 co-workers from the three language regions of Switzerland. Analogies with the Alinghi team produced vivid parallels and translated the core objectives of the company's strategy into the world of the professional yachting. Whereas in yachting there is talk of mooring, anchoring, "coiling up" and audacious manoeuvres, the subject here was expanding market leadership and the new five-year plan. The skippers themselves delivered the visionary messages. Authentic speeches by the directors emphasized key statements without the addition of sailor's yarn. Creativity and excellent performance ensured the success of the event. High performance both motivated and delighted the delegates just as much as it would in the yachting world. A standing ovation at the end of the three-hour session was the manifest proof that everyone was "on board" …

The opening of the sales conference showed it had listened to the pulse of changeable markets and natural law (sailing). The impressive percussion band "Power!" gave the event the right beat and rhythm to the themes that followed.

Patrick Magyar, former General Manager of the successful Alinghi team and multiple winner of the America's Cup, spoke about how a professional team makes the difference. Thorough preparation, well-rehearsed procedures, high commitment and professional teamwork – even in rough seas, shallows or adverse winds. Facilitated by multimedia staging, the visionary messages sailed right in the hearts and minds of the audience.

The ensuing strategy speeches by the management continued seamlessly from the brilliant opening and provided additional impetus and incentive for the delegates and were supplemented by compelling media recordings and a live transmission by the company from its "Centre of Excellence" in Barcelona.

After three hours, it was clear the company had reaffirmed its position as Switzerland's unchallenged number one – and secured it for the future, too.

5.3 Mission to the Moon – Change Management Example

Strategic business goal:

Performance improvement and increased sales.

The European Management of the world leading company in the medical device industry decided to change their approach to clients in the near future and to increase sales in a single division to more than a billion dollars within three years.

Opportunity: In many countries people die because they do not have access to the new medical devices. There is an opportunity to create a world where people, suffering from a specific disease which could benefit from new therapies, will get them.

Two senior managers from the agency were invited to participate in the strategic development of a plan, as communication with the stakeholders was crucial. During the development of the strategy, the clear need for an 18 month performance improvement program with different events emerged from the managers. That is where the knowledge and experience of the two people of the agency started contributing to the strategic plan.

The challenge

– The 500 sales oriented people in Europe were in different organizations and now needed to form one single organization
– The optimization into one simple sales organization resulted in a change management process
– The new target group was partly unknown

- This requires an innovation in the structural and cultural approach towards clients and involved decision makers
- Strong Emotional bonding of all stakeholders at a cost-effective venue
- Return of Investment of more than 30 % within 18 months

The solution for this change management challenge:

The events are embedded in a performance improvement program. During 18 months there is steady communication with the target audiences through different channels. All the aspects of the challenge are addressed within a focused and themed communication campaign.

The basic cost for a sales force of 500 people is considerate. Focusing a whole sales organization towards a common goal as well as raising the awareness results in a performance improvement.

Pre-kick-off

During the three months phase, the goal was to create awareness and interest amongst all the stakeholders. The annual European business meeting was transformed into a kick-off meeting for the "mission to the moon" and as the most important point for a good ROI the expectations are clearly managed by the communication as well as by the country managers.

Kick-off

The first time in history all the business units had their meeting together and came from all over Europe to Brussels. A strong bonding to the theme and to the brand with their corporate values was created during the event. 500 people got involved in interactive break-out sessions and strongly motivated in a plenary session where speakers, like the first astronaut on the moon, created a strong link between their own adventure and the challenges the 500 people are facing during the next 18 months. Social events were important for letting the people experience the changes emotionally, for example within a specially constructed rocket during the gala dinner, accompanied by an alien-musical specially created for them.

The campaign reinforced the strong emotional bonding, which took place during the kick-off. Creativity is crucial to keep the attention of the audience when daily life returns. Astronaut food doesn't smell so nice, but everybody talked about the meal they have tried. At the end of the year, the best performers are evaluated. Additionally to their internal incentive program, they received the invitation for the VIP Event from their president.

VIP Event

The exclusive astronaut training in the USA was such a success that all winners decided upon their return to share their experiences with their colleagues in their countries. This extended the awareness of the campaign and when the winners shared their photos and personal experiences with their peers, they brought alive not only the theme, but also the many experiences of everybody during the kick-off with the astronaut and other aliens.

It has become a lifelong experience for all people involved.

Conclusion:

The intensive workshop of the eight managers and the two external specialists on business goals, change management (changing the organization) and the measurement criteria was crucial for the planning and the success of this performance improvement program. For the implementation it was necessary to have dedicated specialists from more than 15 different professional fields available in order to execute the different parts of this program.

TransRockies Inc.: The Effective Use of Stakeholder Management in Event Projects

Donald Getz, Aaron McConnell

1. Introduction

It was a Sunday in August, 2005 and mountain bike race promoter Heinrich Albrecht stood at the start structure of the fourth annual TransRockies Challenge mountain bike stage race in the small mountain community of Fernie, British Columbia as over 300 mountain bikers prepared to ride the first 50 km of a 600 km race. The sun was shining and there was excitement in the air. The stage is set and conditions are perfect for the start of this fourth year of "the world's toughest mountain bike race". Conditions were much tougher two years ago. Forest fires forced last minute re-routing of the racecourse in 2003. In 2002, the inaugural year of the race, participants suffered through cold, snowy conditions to finish the grueling marathon race from Fernie to Canmore.

If Heinrich had been able to see into the future, he would find that the 2005 event was not to be without challenges, as participants battled record heat on the first day, only to face near-freezing temperatures, rain and hail on and off throughout the week. Despite these conditions, in a post-event participant survey, riders would rate the overall experience very highly. And even further into the future, the event would sell out for the first time in 2006, with 350 signing up seven months in advance. Although success looked to be just around the corner, 2006 would also throw a major problem at the Challenge organizers, as a restriction on growth was to be imposed by Alberta Parks. This would necessitate a major change in route, and would require establishment of new stakeholder relationships.

This chapter is a case study of the TransRockies Challenge, an ultra-endurance mountain bike race staged in the Canadian Rocky Mountains, owned and managed by the Calgary-based firm, TransRockies Inc. The study examines the event's origins, its planning and operations, and in particular how the principals in TransRockies Inc. have used stakeholder management as a key competence in the development and sustaining of a new event property.

This study is not about the struggles of the athletes participating in the TransRockies Challenge, but those of the organizers, Heinrich Albrecht, his partners Chester Fabricius and Kevan MacNaughton and others who have become partners and friends of the organization, TransRockies Inc. Specifically, the case discusses how the organization has created project networks and partnerships to make the event more successful and sustainable, and how one major challenge emerged to threaten the event. It was developed through interviews with those most involved with the event, and direct observations.

2.   Origins of the Event

In the late 1970's, Chester Fabricius owned a bicycle store in Germany and was one of the first to import mountain bikes to Germany from the United States. He shipped 30 bikes to his store, and needed a way to sell this new style of bike that was unfamiliar in the marketplace. He started organizing some of the first mountain bike races in Europe to promote mountain biking. Soon, he joined forces with Heinrich Albrecht to organize the German Cup of mountain bike races. The two men went on to become the premier mountain bike race organizers in Europe, organizing the first Mountain Bike World Cup races for the sponsoring German electronics firm, Grundig. In 1989, Albrecht co-founded Michael Veith Marketing GmbH with Michael Veith, a former champion alpine skier. The company specialized in organizing sport events, including mountain bike races. In 2001, Michael Veith Marketing GmbH merged with Upsolut Sports and Marketing AG, becoming Upsolutmv, part of the larger Upsolut Sports AG. Fabricius moved to the United States, where he launched Upsolutmv Marketing USA, in addition to other sport marketing business interests.

Today, Upsolut Sports AG manages a diverse portfolio of sport and athletic properties, including professional road cycling races and tours throughout Germany, a professional triathlon, a professional hockey team and a football club in Germany. The Upsolutmv division of the company primarily focuses on mountain biking events. In 2005, through a restructuring of Upsolut Sports AG, the company no longer is the primary owner of TransRockies Inc., the Canadian subsidiary which is now owned by three individual partners. This paper will concentrate on TransRockies' flagship event: the TransRockies Challenge – an endurance mountain-bike race modeled after the TransAlps.

TransRockies Inc. was founded as a partnership between Upsolutmv (Munich), Upsolutmv Marketing USA (Scottsdale, Arizona), and Read & Co. Event Management Group (Calgary). Read & Co. was the event management firm owned by former Alpine Ski World Cup Champion Ken Read. Read was a friend of Michael Veith of Upsolutmv, as the two competed together on the Alpine World Cup circuit. Read & Co. was initially awarded the management contract for the event.

TransRockies Inc. was formed for the purpose of producing an event to be known as the TransRockies Challenge. The weeklong event would emulate the already established TransAlps event, featuring teams of two riders, mountain biking from Fernie, British Columbia to Canmore, Alberta. In 2004, TransRockies Inc. operated a second event: a round of the UCI Mountain Bike World Cup, hosted at Canada Olympic Park in Calgary, although this event was not repeated in 2005 or 2006.

3.   The Event Concept and Operations

The TransRockies Challenge is an endurance mountain biking competition consisting of teams of two riders. The seven-day race covers over 600 kilometers of trails and back roads and over 12,000 meters of elevation gain. The course, beginning in 2006, runs from Fernie to Panorama Mountain Resort, both in British Columbia. Each day competitors complete a stage, similar in format to the Tour de France. Although the riders start together each day, the overall results are calculated based on the combined time from each day's stage. The stage starts and finishes are in towns at around half of the stages and in wilderness camps provided by the event organizers at the other stages. There are seven categories: Open Men, Open Women, Open Mixed, 80+ Men, 80+ Women, 80+ Mixed, and 100+ (80+ and 100+ indicate the combined age of the team). The $20,000 cash purse is divided among the categories.

The TransRockies Challenge is based on the TransAlps event in Europe. Although the overall concept is the same, the TransAlps starts and finishes each day in a town, whereas the TransRockies is more of a wilderness experience. The TransAlps, which started in 1998, sells out at 550 teams every year, and is extremely popular, judging by its waiting list of over 1000 teams. The TransRockies was first conceived in the year 2000, in preparation for the first event, which took place in August of 2002. Early support and encouragement for the TransRockies event, including the process of securing land use permits, was provided by Travel Alberta, who saw the potential for the international media exposure that the event could generate.

One of the unique aspects of this sport event is the logistics associated with creating and transporting the base camps, which have to be moved forward each day in advance of the competitors (see the photo). When the Challenge enters the backcountry, away from major roads, many issues arise, from how to provide showers and toilets to where to find a suitable area of level ground. Alberta Parks became very concerned that as the event grew there could be damage to the environment.

Control and Decision Making Mechanism

Xi Events took over the management contract for the Trans-Rockies Challenge when Ken Read sold Read & Co. Event Management to become president of Alpine Canada Alpin. The principals of Xi had been employees of Read and Co. and so it was a seamless transition to the new company and the people involved in organizing the TransRockies Challenge remained the same. Xi was responsible for the majority of the pre-event logistics planning and administration for the TransRockies from 2002 through 2004. After the 2004 Trans-Rockies Challenge event, Xi resigned its management contract for TransRockies Inc., citing a lack of profitability from the project and a desire to pursue other work. Aaron McConnell, an author of this case study, subsequently took over these management responsibilities in 2004.

The organization of the TransRockies Challenge is generally centrally controlled by TransRockies Inc. TRI is the sole organizer and responsible party for the overall operation and execution of the TransRockies Challenge, under the direction of Albrecht, Fabricius, MacNaughton, and McConnell. This senior management team is based in three different countries, but meets as a group several times a year, with more frequent meetings between some members of the team. The group typically works together to come to an agreement on the more complex decisions, while daily operational decisions are left to the Calgary based management team of McConnell and MacNaughton.

The event is staffed by a mixed crew of Canadian and German staff as well as volunteers, some of whom come from outside of Canada. Host communities are asked to provide key services to the event, and are also invited to organize their own festivals around the event. TransRockies Inc. uses a pool of contractors to provide certain equipment and services to the event.

Planning and preparation for the TransRockies Challenge takes place year-round. For the two months following the event, the primary activities are review and analysis of the past years event, as well as establishing overall directions for the next year. Registration for the next year opens on November 1st, approximately 2.5 months after the event finishes. Route planning typically commences in the fall, but is not usually complete until 1 month prior to the start of the event. Production of merchandise, awards, signage, and other race materials commences in April for completion in July.

Event Operations

Aaron McConnell manages the TransRockies Inc. offices and handles a large amount of the site logistics for the Trans-Rockies Challenge. This includes managing the relationships with host communities, land use permits, arranging for equipment rentals such as tents and generators, arranging catering and shelter for all the athletes, and many other specific details of the event.

When the event passes through towns, host communities are asked to provide amenities for the race, such as simple athlete accommodations and meals. The towns are also invited to organize a festival to welcome the race, which provides pageantry and allows TRI to focus on race operations. The start and finish towns for TransRockies organize festivals around the event featuring entertainment and attractions, with the goal of bringing the community out to welcome the race. The benefit for the community is the value of the international television exposure they receive. The support from towns started out not being very strong, but has increased every year. The town festivals are run with virtually no input from the race organization, which focuses on the operation of the race.

The TransRockies event has traditionally passed through a great deal of leased land, with a variety of landowners and land managers. The event requires a large number of permits to pass through the various lands. The primary government agencies that the event has dealt with are Alberta Forestry, outside of the Kananaskis Country area, and Alberta Parks, within Kananaskis Country. The primary concerns of these agencies have been environmental impacts of the event and safety of the event. The race has not been permitted to use certain trails that are popular for mountain biking due to the management plans in place for wild land park areas.

TransRockies Inc. has been sensitive to the possible environmental impacts of the event and has enforced strict policies on itself and its participants in terms of environmental impact. The organization uses the philosophy that trails and staging areas must be left cleaner than they are found. Travel Alberta provided support early on in the securing of land-use permits for the event. The organization's ties to the provincial government facilitated this process greatly.

A group of about 10 staff travels from Germany to work the events. The group forms the lead crew, which is responsible for moving the start and finish setups from stage to stage each day. There are two sets of all of the required equipment, so that the crew can leapfrog the setup from one day's start location to the next day's finish location. The German staff work alongside Canadian staff and volunteers. It is most efficient for TransRockies to use the German staff since they are already well trained in the race format from TransAlps and can run the event very efficiently. Some concern has been expressed by the principals of TransRockies Inc. about the amount of German spoken at the Trans-Rockies Inc. events, and they feel that Canadians may be unhappy to have Germans running the events. However, over time, Canadian staff make up a larger proportion of the staff, and the German and Canadian groups have become more integrated, working together as a cohesive team.

The TransRockies Challenge relies heavily on a volunteer workforce of approximately 30 volunteers. Volunteers are asked to volunteer for 7 days due to the logistical difficulty in re-training volunteers mid-event.

Budgeting and Event Finances

For the TransRockies Challenge, the primary revenue source for the event is registration fees. In the first two years, there was a single price of $3,200 Canadian dollars per team ($1,600 per person). In 2004 TRI offered three options providing different levels of amenity: Economy ($1,350 per person), Classic ($1,550 per person), and Deluxe ($3,350 per person). In 2002 and 2003 approximately 75 teams signed up each year, providing revenue of $100,000 to $200,000 (some of the teams received free entry in consideration of media coverage). For 2004, there were 115 teams registered, and in 2005, 157 teams signed up. Of these teams 5% deluxe, 19% economy, and 76% classic, providing revenue of over $400,000. The event was always planned to sell-out at approximately 300 teams due to space constraints.

In December of 2005, Alberta Parks imposed a new policy that would cap the TransRockies Challenge at 175 teams, and by March of 2006 the organizers decided it was necessary to change the event route to allow them to grow to a maximum size of 300 teams. They worked quickly to secure support for a route that would stay primarily in the province of British Columbia. Routing for the first half of the event remained similar to previous events, with a new route created for the second half, moving the finish of the event from Canmore, Alberta to Panorama Mountain Village, British Columbia. Due to this change, the event is expected to reach a size of 250 teams in 2006.

A secondary revenue source for the TransRockies Challenge, although still important, is sponsorship. The event has yet to attain the sponsorship revenues achieved by the TransAlps, but it has grown its list of sponsors, searching for a title or presenting sponsor.

The majority of expenses for the TransRockies Challenge (see Table 1) are directly related to event operations, including staff and contractor expenses, permits, medical support equipment purchase and rentals, and participant meals. Another significant expense is television production, as event coverage is broadcast throughout Europe as well as in Canada. The event relies on a relatively small marketing budget, with the support of media sponsors, as well as word-of-mouth reputation. Overall, the operating budget for the TransRockies is between $500,000 and $700,000 per year. It is not expected that the event will pay back the initial investment until year 6 or later, although it was making a small profit in year 4.

Items	Approximate cost in Canadian Dollars
Cost of Goods	13,000
Marketing & Public Relations	63,000
Materials and Equipment	56,000
Administration and Staff	136,000
Equipment Rental	45,000
Contracted Services	117,000
Logistics and Venues	71,000
Prize Money	20,000
Total Expenses	521,000

Table 1: TransRockies Challenge, Expenses

Marketing

The TransRockies Challenge is not primarily a spectator event. Significant crowds do attend the starts and finishes of some stages, when they are hosted in towns. The towns try to encourage a festival atmosphere around the race to capitalize on the international television coverage the event provides. However, a large part of the race does take place in a wilderness setting, where large crowds are neither feasible nor required for the success of the event. Marketing of the TransRockies Challenge, therefore, is primarily focused on the participants and on the event's reputation, as the world's most challenging mountain bike race. Additionally, the event offers a powerful tool for building the reputation of the region where it is hosted. This was exploited by Travel Alberta during the first four years of the events operation. With the new route in British Columbia, the Kootenay Rockies Tourism organization has pledged support, with Tourism British Columbia also considering becoming involved.

Initially, the TransRockies marketing plan focused largely on capitalizing on the popularity of the TransAlps event, and attracting participants from that event's large waiting list to register for the TransRockies. However, serious response from the European teams did not materialize at first, and the event has been largely populated by North American competitors, with a small but growing number of European teams. For the first time in 2006, over 50% of the participants are expected to come from outside of Canada.

The event's reputation as an incredible experience and a highly unique race became established early on and has been strengthened with each successive running. The event regularly receives mentions and coverage from a wide array of cycling publications, as well as endorsements from high-profile figures within the cycling community. This word of mouth advertising within the cycling community is of key importance to organizers, since most participants must plan and prepare to compete in the event for a year or longer. For the 2006, although registration was initially limited by Alberta Parks, a long waiting list formed, with the organizers estimating that demand for participation spots had nearly doubled over the 2005 event.

TransRockies Challenge participants make a high personal, financial, and emotional commitment to the event. Financial commitment includes travel to the event (from all over the world), additional equipment costs due to wear and tear from the event (often over $500 per person), additional accommodation costs (hotels at start and finish, some teams use RVs during the race), and race entry fees ($1300 – $3000 per person). Personal commitment includes time invested in training for the event (most are not professional athletes), time spent traveling to and participating in the event, and enlisting the help of at least one support person during the event, usually a close friend or family member.

Living up to its reputation as the toughest mountain bike race in the world, the TransRockies Challenge is a grueling and exhausting experience for most participants. The early days of the race sometimes create feelings of regret and fear in participants. As the race progresses however, moods elevate and most are elated by the end of the race, exhilarated with the thrill of finishing such an incredible event. Overall, there are very high barriers to participation in this event. It is accessible only to those with significant disposable income, time, and interest in the sport. However, completing the event brings a high sense of accomplishment and personal prestige.

The participant experience is a key priority for organizers, as participant fees are the most important revenue source. Although financial constraints limit the amenities that can be provided, the organizers strive to provide good food, showers, bike service facilities, and a high degree of safety and medical support. At the end of each stage, there is a well-presented awards ceremony where the stage winners are presented with medals and the race leaders in each category receive leaders' jerseys. This is followed by a motivational video presentation with footage from the day's race. This lifts the spirits of the athletes and motivates them for the next day. The organizers spend a great deal of time communicating with athletes prior to the event, and strive to create a brand community around the TransRockies Challenge.

A formal study of economic impacts has not been undertaken for TransRockies Challenge, although it is believed that the regional impacts of the event are very significant. Participants typically spend several days in hotels at the start and finish, and some rent motorhomes, buy additional food and souvenirs along the way, and cover the cost of ground transportation. This are also the direct expenditures by the organization, the majority of which are made locally. Total direct expenditures for the event are likely to exceed $1 million annually. The fact that over half the participants come from outside the country makes the Challenge a significant international tourism event in the context of the Canadian Rockies.

4. Media Management and Destination Promotion

An important product of the TransRockies Challenge is the transmission of contextual information about the locations in which they are hosted to audiences around the world. Through media coverage, television broadcasts, and information on the internet, people can learn about the hosting region in the context of the bike race. The TransRockies accesses significant distribution through its existing European contacts, as well as Canadian broadcast partners, and it received over 160 hours of international broadcast time for the 2005 production.

This international television coverage was an important reason for the involvement of Travel Alberta in the Trans-Rockies Challenge. The agency is charged with destination promotion for Alberta internationally, and understands the media value that events such as the TransRockies can offer. When competing for international tourism business, unique events offer a point of differentiation.

Travel Alberta was introduced to the organizers through Ken Read's early involvement with the event. Ken Read had been contacted through a former competitor on the Alpine Ski World Cup circuit, Michael Veith. Klaus Roth, a senior executive at Travel Alberta who has strong European connections, was able to investigate the background of Upsolutmv and TransAlps through trusted sources. The organization decided to invest in the TransRockies Challenge for the tourism promotion value it was expected to provide. Travel Alberta became an important champion for TransRockies, lending significant legitimacy as well as a financial commitment in the key first years. Travel Alberta supported both the TransRockies and the UCI World Cup due to the ability of each to showcase southern Alberta to international audiences through powerful visual images and contextual marketing.

Travel Alberta's role in the TransRockies Challenge is expected to end with the event moving away from an Alberta finish. Given that the event had become successful in Alberta, organizers were able to approach British Columbia with established value.

5. Grants and Sponsorships

TransRockies Challenge has yet to secure a title or presenting sponsor. The event offers a very unique opportunity for companies wishing to be associated with a property that is much different from other events. Sponsorship levels for the TransRockies have increased modestly each year, but it still remains a secondary revenue stream. A unique challenge for the Challenge is that a significant proportion of the measurable media value delivered by the event is widely dispersed, lacking focused strength in key markets. The events are ideally suited to sponsors who do business worldwide. There is growing interest from bike manufacturers in fielding teams that can possibly win the race, in order to gain prestige. This may have a secondary effect of driving participation revenue in the event.

TransRockies Challenge is a difficult platform on which to build sponsorship due to the lack of spectator opportunity at the mostly remote stages. However, the event does provide significant media value: over $18 million dollars worth of worldwide media exposure annually, using the advertising equivalence valuation method. At present the event has a number of medium-sized sponsors. The organization hopes to find a large title sponsor for the event.

6. Stakeholder Relationships

The Political Market Square Metaphor

Due to the large number of actors involved in these events, and the complex interactions between them, the political market

125

square model (Larson and Wikstrom, 2001) was chosen as a metaphor for studying the activities of TransRockies Inc.

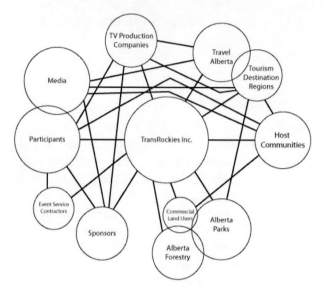

Figure 13: Political Market Square for the TransRockies Challenge, 2005

In Figure 13 each circle represents an actor, while the lines between actors are indicative of interactions between the two. The size of the circles roughly indicates relative importance, and overlapping circles represent actors effectively working together.

Stakeholder Conflict and Consensus

A key aspect of the political market square metaphor is the degree to which parties act in conflict or consensus with other parties in event planning and execution. A high level of conflict is typical when relationships are new or short-term, when there is a lack of goal alignment between parties, and when there is a lack of perceived legitimacy for one or both parties. Consensus is more typical when there has been a long-term relationship based on trust and defined roles, a high degree of goal congruence, and high levels of perceived legitimacy for both parties (Larson and Wikstrom, 2001).

TransRockies Inc. and Alberta Parks

Alberta Parks is the agency responsible for administration of various protected areas within the province of Alberta. Kananaskis Country is a vast tract of land to the west and south of the City of Calgary, through which the majority of the TransRockies route traveled from 2002-2005. Trans-Rockies Inc. obtained a permit from Alberta Parks for the event each year. The relationship between the two organizations tended towards conflict, as many of the best mountain biking trails were off-limits to the race due to group size limitations in place for areas within areas designated as Wildland Park. Although the TransRockies organization constantly made efforts to meet all the requirements of Alberta Parks, Parks would typically focus on problems occurring in the past year's race, while event organizers stressed the significant improvements made from year to year.

The conflict between Alberta Parks and TransRockies Inc. could be primarily attributed to a lack of goal alignment between the organizations. While Alberta Parks is charged with administering the lands of Kananaskis Country, its mandate does not include promotion of sustainable tourism or economic development. Faced with increasing pressure from recreational, agricultural, and industrial activity within the region, Alberta Parks' singular focus is on the protection of park areas. The organization's approach to events is not a customer service approach, but one of regulation and supervision. TransRockies Inc., even though it was supported and encouraged by many other groups and agencies including municipal governments and other branches of the provincial government, found itself at odds with Alberta Parks more often than not.

The conflict came to a head in the winter of 2006, when Alberta Parks introduced a new field limit policy for the region that would prevent the TransRockies Challenge from achieving the growth that it had always planned for. Despite strong support and lobbying efforts from other parties within Alberta, Parks held to their new policy. TransRockies Inc. made the difficult and risky decision to move most of the event to British Columbia. While permits will also be necessary in British Columbia, management agencies there appear to be very welcoming, with an emphasis on facilitation of the event. TransRockies Inc. hopes to obtain multi-year permission to use specific areas for the race.

TransRockies Inc. and the Bike Shop

The Bike Shop was a part of the TransRockies Challenge from the beginning, as a sponsor. In 2003, the owner and president of the Bike Shop, Kevan McNaughton, took on a volunteer management role with TransRockies Inc. and has since become a partner in the organization. McNaughton sees cycling events as an important way to drive the growth of cycling, which has a direct impact on his business as a bicycle retailer. McNaughton also has a personal motive in being involved with the event, being the new challenge of working with a number of international partners. The idea of being involved with events for profit is a long-term hope, not an immediate reality. While McNaughton and the Bike Shop are generally in complete consensus with TransRockies Inc., he sometimes struggles with conflicting priorities of the two businesses.

TransRockies Inc. and Travel Alberta

Although TransRockies Inc. and Travel Alberta had different goals and objectives, within the scope of the project there was agreement from both parties about what needed to be done together in order to achieve individual goals. There is recognition from the organizers that it may not have been possible to launch the TransRockies Challenge without the support of Travel Alberta. Travel Alberta was very pleased with the exposure that it received from the event. Initially Travel Alberta made a three year financial commitment to the event, but extended its partnership in light of the high return on investment that it received through international television value.

There were some minor tensions in the relationship, arising primarily from the fact that neither party had the resources to fully leverage the opportunity for media exposure. Travel Alberta wanted to see a satellite television truck travel with the event, but the $2,000 per day cost of this was out of reach for the organizers and Travel Alberta.

With the move of the event to British Columbia, TransRockies Inc. hopes to achieve a similar consensus-based relationship with Kootenay Rockies Tourism and Tourism BC.

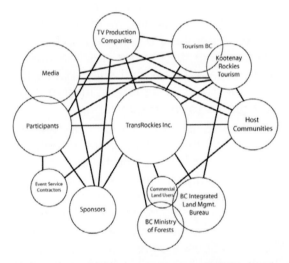

Figure 14: New partners in the stakeholder network – political market square for the TransRockies Challenge, 2006

Although TransRockies committed to the move before securing any commitment from either agency, there should be a good basis for a relationship. TransRockies has been operating nearby for four years and has established a good reputation in Canada; it is a highly legitimate operation that leaves

Alberta with a strong reference from Travel Alberta. In addition, the organizations have a high degree of goal alignment, with the tourism agencies and TransRockies both striving for a "best in the world" reputation, and building a brand that is "rugged, adventurous and real."

TransRockies Inc. and the Host Communities

A goal of TransRockies Inc. has been to provide value to the communities that host the event. This includes both the international media value and direct economic impact provided by the event. In exchange for these benefits, organizers requested financial support from the communities. In the first year, there was conceptual support from the communities for hosting the event, but a lack of interest in providing funding. Communities either did not understand the value provided by the event, or simply did not have the funding mechanisms in place to support it. Community interest and support has increased since it started, but it is still generally in-kind support as opposed to direct grants to the organizers.

The organizers would like to use their option of running the race through other communities as a bargaining tool, although changing the route is a complex undertaking and the alternatives are in fact always limited. The lack of community funding makes the event more financially challenging for organizers in North America than in Europe. The relationship between the organizers and host communities has always been positioned as one of consensus based on mutual benefit. In reality, it was been somewhat conflict-based early on, evolving into more of a consensus. Consensus is growing due to the organizer's increasing understanding of the capabilities of the host communities, and the communities' increasing understanding of the benefits from hosting the event. With the recent re-routing of the event in 2006, there is growing recognition that the event is established enough to survive without fixed host communities.

7.   Key Stakeholder Management Themes

Building Legitimacy and Trust

On the surface, the idea of German organizers coming into the Canadian Rockies to create a new event may have seemed unrealistic, but several factors made it possible. First, proper introductions through high-profile individuals in the local community provided early legitimacy to the organizers. The establishment and success of the TransAlps event was a major factor in securing the support of Travel Alberta, which became a major champion of the event. The European connections at Travel Alberta also provided it with the ability to carry out due diligence in the decision to support the event. Travel Alberta, through its connections to the government, lent its reputation to the organization in securing permission to use the public land required for the race. Travel Alberta also helped to influence the host communities to support the event.

The organizers have built trust with other stakeholder groups through successfully implementing their plans, and delivering on their commitments. This has engendered a greater degree of cooperation and support for the Challenge. TransRockies Inc. had already established local legitimacy and credibility when they moved the majority of the event to British Columbia, facilitating cooperation from Kootenay-Rockies Tourism. As the new route in B.C. evolves, TransRockies will need to focus on building relationships with a new group of stakeholders.

According to Larson and Wikstrom (2001), a high degree of legitimacy tends to lead toward processes based on consensus rather than conflict in the political market square. It appears that TransRockies Inc. has been able to achieve a high degree of legitimacy in its operations, and through legitimacy-building practices, has continued to build consensus within its network. Further, as the event recurs annually, there is a tendency to develop trust in the relationships over time, which further improves cooperation. Working within a framework of consensus is believed to be the most effective way for all parties to achieve individual and mutual goals.

Adapting to Cultural and National Differences

The organizers experienced several key differences in bringing the TransAlps concept to North America. First, the tourism interests of host communities are funded much differently in North America. In Europe, communities compete to host stages of the event and support it with large marketing budgets. In North America, far fewer resources have been made available to support the event.

The TransRockies takes place largely in wilderness, whereas the TransAlps is much more of a "front-country" event. Amenities, services, and support are more readily available for the TransAlps. This means that the TransRockies is much more logistically challenging and operationally expensive, as well as being a much different experience for participants.

The preferences of North American participants differ from those in Europe. For example, North Americans prefer tent camping to sleeping in a gymnasium, which Europeans are quite happy to do. Cycling in general is not as popular in North America, which means there was less interest in the event from the general population than for TransAlps.

Event Sustainability

This case study illustrates a number of harsh business realities within the event industry. It might take years for new events to become financially sustainable. According to the organizers, TransRockies Challenge became operationally profitable in its fourth year, but the owners' very substantial capital investment is not expected to be paid back for several more years. A payback period of 6 or more years is not typical of most industries, and puts for-profit event management in an unattractive light from a business perspective.

The major change in routing in 2006, in response to the new capacity rules put in place by Alberta Parks, was a move intended to secure the growth and financial sustainability of the event. A field size of 250-300 teams is required to pay back the initial investment at an acceptable rate. The organizers took significant risks in making this move quickly in response to the changing environment. Uncertainty about the new host communities and potential tourism funding all contributed to the risk. In the end, the senior management team of TransRockies felt that it was crucial for the event to maintain its momentum, and to find a more favorable climate for the ongoing success of the event.

Clearly, the principals of TransRockies Inc. have taken a long term perspective on this business venture, and with the event business in general. The promise held by the Trans-Rockies Challenge is of eventually building it to a size where it can create a consistent and significant return on investment.

Those looking at entering the event management field must be aware of the financial realities of organizing events, and the commitment involved in making such a venture profitable. It may be difficult to find financing for a new event due to the long payback period and high risks involved. Those without strong financial backing would be advised to start small and work on establishing a number of smaller events that can eventually support larger ones. Developing legitimacy, trust and strong stakeholder relationships is a must. In the case of TransRockies Inc., the firm's principals started when mountain biking was a new sport, and are still building the events two decades later.

8. Conclusions

This case study has examined the management and operations of the TransRockies Challenge, a high profile cycling event that requires a large degree of organization and support from a highly varied range of stakeholders. The organizers worked with regional tourism interests, land managers, contractors and participants to build a unique event that is in keeping with their core business, as well as providing value to the host communities. TransRockies Inc. was able to capitalize on the reputation and legitimacy of Travel Alberta to help open other doors in Alberta, which has, in-turn created a degree of legitimacy that is transferable to other locations.

Management Implications

The case of the TransRockies Challenge provides some valuable insight into an essential aspect of organizing events, the development of functional project networks. The establishment of the Challenge would not have been possible without the ability of organizers to create and develop a network of event partners and supporters half a world away from their core operations. The organizers always attempt to work in a consensus mode with event partners, although sometimes conflict is inevitable.

This analysis suggests that event managers should look for opportunities to build partnerships with key stakeholders that are based on trust and common goals. This may sometimes take time and the effort of not only delivering value to partners, but demonstrating value and shared benefits. Stakeholders may be reluctant to play the role of "partner" in the political market square, especially early on, as it may be much easier to be a vendor, contractor, regulator, or host.

Finally, prospective event managers must be prepared for the financial realities of event management as an entrepreneurial venture. Risks are great, and even well-capitalized, professionally managed events can require years to break even, and several more to pay back the initial investment. Many lessons derived from the TansRockies Challenge can be applied to other events, and in particular it has to be stressed that owners and organizers must always focus on being effective stakeholder relationship managers.

Literature

Larson, Mia, and Ewa Wikstrom (2001). Organizing events: Managing conflict and consensus in a political market square. Event Management, 7(1): 51-65.

Some Ideas on Specifics of Event Evaluation

Ulrich Wünsch

"The food was great, the singer wasn't bad, the dance routine was even better, especially that act – whatever it was – in the air, this old factory building just fantastic, great interesting stage here at the marketplace, lots of visitors here really perfect for business, terrific opportunities, ideal networking at the conference, helpful meeting, entertaining leisure program, sure – lovely colleagues," this one might here at or after an event of whatever kind. In short: enthusiasm everywhere. Enthusiasm that something had taken place, that one was looked after, that one was noticed, that one was entertained, that the cash register was and still is full. However: what product was it about, which service was presented, did the city expect something from the citizens or the visitors, what knowledge was conveyed?[15] The impact and success of events have many mothers and fathers. It would be wise to know what works, what helps, what enriches and what only costs money. In the following, possibilities of criteria are considered and a model for the assessment of event communication is contemplated. The perspective is one of a general approach to reflecting all kinds of events looking for the intangible aspects of effects and its constructions.

1.   Problem Area

With the beginning of the 1990s "events" became a widely recognized phenomenon in Germany. Gerhard Schulze, a

---

15 *Similar to the area of advertising where the consumer is, in the meantime, only touched very little and the so-called recall dwindles or even disappears, it could be stated that an overkill of events might cause the much desired experience to disappear: result of an experiential-overflow.*

German sociologist, conducted a groundbreaking study titled "Die Erlebnisgesellschaft" (experience society), published in 1992. He researched the trend towards entertainment in form of enhanced experiences that seemed to emerge in society, especially recognizable in the way that leisure time and products or services were being marketed. He stated and proved a change of attitude and context. In 1999 B. Joseph Pine and James H. Gilmore followed with their management handbook on experiential product and service marketing: "The Experience Economy – Work is Theatre & Every Business a Stage". The focus was and is on experiences and emotions, those constructs as old as mankind, of which no one – to put it very bluntly and simply – really knows what they are and how they work with human beings. The gates of epistemology, philosophy, neurosciences, psychology, ethnology and many other fields stand wide open, inviting scholars to further research. Yet: all of a sudden those happenings that happened anyway – i.e. cultural productions and life cycle events in their context of an enveloping year – became strategic factors and marketing or communication tools. All this, now in an economic context, needed and needs to be managed, organized, controlled, benchmarked and put to best practice.

A problem though arose and continues: definitions, agreed standards, classifications that are accepted everywhere and accepted within intercultural contexts are lacking. Especially the strong cultural subtext of events makes it difficult to standardize. This applies to any public event as well as to any event organized by a corporation. Yet standardization and best practice are prerequisites of modern management. They stand for success in a mass market. Thus: how to evaluate events?

Many questions remain open: what should be evaluated, with what intent should be evaluated, which already established methods should be used, which model of event experiences should be created? Are we looking for the hard facts, the tangibles – such as visitor numbers, turnover, sales figures and more? Or do events stand for intangibles, the soft facts – like image, reputation, recognition, inclusion and more? Or are both advisable? Approaches from many neighbouring disciplines or practice areas have an effect on today's event assessment. For example advertising impact research, media resonance count, given social science methodology as well as communication theory related approaches are available in their whole width and depth. In addition, there are data collections of every kind, mystery shopping and participatory observation as a method of the ethnology, project management related approaches, broad studies of economic effects, reports on the sustainability and long term effects of events – all combined with individual heuristics of any practitioner of the event genre. Since there still has not been a consensus on what "works" at an event, how can the desired experiences actually be conveyed and finalized, how can a situation be totally comprehended and described? In a substantive speech, Donald Getz outlined the future tasks and indicated deserving ways for the next steps in a topic description, subsequently followed by Glenn A J Bowden with his comprehensive description of the research in the area of events in England.[16]

In the context of corporate controlling practices, evaluation is understood as a basic measurement instrument that provides guidance for the controlling of fundamental data. Controlling thus serves as a steering tool. Putting outside and inside perspectives in a row, the Balanced Scorecard provides a special steering tool that might be applied in all its complexity to events. It will have to be developed for events though. Evaluation often is wrongly associated with the term "control" and all its often-negative connotations. The term "control" alarms and often hinders the carrying out of evaluation. Instead, placing an emphasis on reflective evaluation in

---

16 Donald Getz, presentation at the Annual Conference of the "Association of Irish Festival & Events" in Tralee on November 7, 2003: "Establishing a Research Agenda for Event Management" and Glenn A J Bowdin et al. "Identifying and Analysing Existing Research Undertaken in the Events Industry: A Literature Review for People 1st", AEMA, Leeds 2006.

the area of testing of hypothesis, comprehension of what is happening, conclusion drawing, creating a 360°-view, coordination of process and above all improvement and learning should be an appropriate approach. Evaluation serves as a means within the ideal postulated as the learning organization: to turn information into knowledge in order to create new heuristics that then again need to be evaluated over and over. One might also call this professional project management.

In general evaluation is about hard factors (numbers / tangibles) and soft factors (opinions / intangibles) and their assessment, compilation and interpretation. For the area of public events as well as exhibitions, the determination and analysis of the money spent in regard to the money taken in – as direct or indirect return – as well as a visitor count remains the first choice for tangibles. This holds true even if a public celebration is a catalyst to generate pride, affiliation and other intangibles. The difficulty here lies in classifying and separating the returns. What can really be attributed to the event as the trigger for specific revenues and returns? How can the indirect routes of indirect returns be described and what would the categories be? Could that be: hotel accommodation, restaurant visit, use of transportation and gas stations, private shopping in general and all what is leased and bought for professional use? Yet how to draw the magic geographic circle within which the data needs to be collected? But what about all the picnic-boxes bought somewhere outside this circle to be taken to an outdoor event? And do we count all the people on site at time x, or does one only count those who come from out of town? What about the long range and sustainable effects like a second visit, triggered by the positive experiences of the location or business? How to know about that? What can be calculated as an offset – orders that are given to another location; use and wear and tear; damages; deployment of law enforcement forces? How will the residents judge the impact of any given event? This is to name but a few. Apart from standard procedures like counting visitors or asking for simple feedback ("how did you like the speaker, the food,"), an individual mix according to the specific event objectives will have to be created for each event.

For corporate events it is necessary to designate a goal that is more concrete than "create emotions". Who would want to anger the consumer or cause fits of rage with their product, those being emotions as well? Often this general goal does not mean anything more than "create excitement – hopefully in connection with a product". A connection to sales and the goal to "increase revenue" is not being constructed here and cannot be. In this multi-factorial situation called event the relationship corporation-product-consumer is hard to identify. Especially what really triggers the act of purchase. Unless there is a concrete sale closing taking place directly at an exhibition we do not exactly know what happens. The often quoted AIDA-formula does promise solid ground, however daily experience has taught that justification is an instrumental rationalization first applied after the act (of purchase) – "I was so hungry, that is why I bought the chocolate". Purchasing takes place imbedded in situational complexes, which are not easy to fathom.

The magic word ROI (Return On Investment) is up front for management as a guiding factor and as a goal to evaluation today. In this case too, as mentioned, the classification of effects on single measures as well as the actual and explicit determination of returns and surplus proves to be rather difficult for events. The term ROO (Return On Objectives), which is conventionally used in management processes and in project management, is more to the point here. The determination of quantifiable goals at the beginning of the project, the pursuit and adjustment of these during the project, the measurement of dependent costs and finally the examination of the results in relation to the set goals will produce clarity and reliability. As success necessarily is defined as reaching set goals or objectives of any kind and can be measured with a simple target-performance comparison (via quantifiable goals), ROO is surely appropriate as a test of an event's success. The crux here is located in the determination of goals, especially quantifiable goals. Those intangibles prove to be difficult beyond the tangible goals of 100,000 visitors at a festival, a million of contacts via the media or 500 contacts or leads at an exhibition.

How can a sustainable communication success be determined and assigned to a definite measure? At the beginning of a project it often seems to be hard to determine goals past the very general. Besides, it is well known from project work that goals can change during the process of a project. Many, sometimes too many, stakeholders are involved and influence what is happening. Relevant goals are not defined due to lack of time or overview or experience. Goals are formulated too vaguely out of fear that a failure could be measured. Here it is important to establish a matrix of goals and objectives that is accepted and utilized by all. Goals, purposes and intents according to their degree of conceivability, their evaluation related conceivableness and the depth of the conjunction with the measure are to be differentiated. Goals might be defined as the actual significance of an event, as its not precisely measurable centre that can still be indirectly ascertained. Intentions would not be directly measurable wishes and visions that follow certain aims and exceed the individual activity. These are the fundaments of an event and can be described. Objectives eventually would be the measurable parameters of an event. They are chances that are comprehended und result from the intents and goals. More to this later.

The evaluation itself then can actually fall back on all methods and theories being used in the above-mentioned neighbouring disciplines. At the moment the hope for insight from neurobiology is determining the method discussion in the area of advertising research: will those purchase provoking impulses be traced, identified and localized in the brain and could it be determined how to activate them? This "open sesame" would then solve all problems of recall and purchase stimulation. Unfortunately human behaviour is embedded in situations and processes that go beyond a simple stimulus-response interaction that is being researched at the moment. Furthermore, one could fall back on the audits that are popular in quality-management and change these to special topic oriented and moderated focus groups. Additionally, it seems advisable to point out the difference between feedback and evaluation. Here, feedback only means the collection of data, gathered by asking whoever non-tested questions without having a hypothesis of any kind or knowing the usual bias of questionnaires. Evaluation means a strategic und coordinated interest in recognition that exceeds the specific event. The evaluation concept is based on models, hypotheses and test validating results. Various methods in the quantitative or qualitative realm could be applied and the event is placed in a larger context or whole. This can be done.[17] Feedback in the colloquial sense as a survey on site is part of an evaluation.

2. "Experience" and "Emotion" in the Context of Events

It is widely agreed on that an event revolves around experiences and emotions. That is what "works" and what is better and different from other communication instruments in creating certain, often intangible, results. In contrast, it could be simply argued that those human beings who don't feel or experience anything are dead. It simply is part of being human, part of our make-up as humans, to continually and spontaneously feel and experience. Those terms might function in a marketing context as promises of success, yet what it really takes to stage and produce planned, desired and focused experiences and emotions is not easy to determine. Even Hollywood does employ script-doctors, and still a lot of movies fail to attract a large audience.

---

17 *The consumer goods industry, trade and tourism are leading in the compilation of specific experience dimensions in the product area.*

A pragmatic and concrete definition would be: experience is the processed sensory perception; emotion is the feedback machinery between those. And "event" (as a staged and produced experience) is a group communication phenomenon achieved by relating situational components through the direction of staged and condensed specifically emotional moments focused on a certain target group. To state the process idea very generally: something within somebody is moved by the participation in the event by whichever motive, and linked with whichever emotion, in his/her individual and our shared day-to-day reality. This moves the event past the barrier of perception landing within a specific situation that then receives special attention. This then moves the event across a second barrier and creates a specific experience. This is then processed and condensed into a story connected to the specific emotion and experience is stored as a recollection. What then exists as an experience is retrievable as a specific story[18] about an experience – which will be retold differently every time it is being remembered and shared.

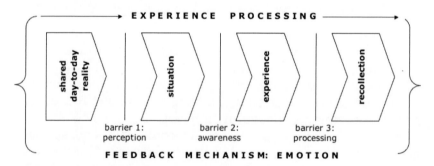

Figure 15: Experience processing model

The problem of relevance would need to be clarified and researched here: what causes something to become relevant in

---

18 Here, story means a "narration" following a typical and topical structure.

daily life for the subject and thus crosses over those barriers of perception and attention?[19]

In order to be able to explain and further clarify the phenomena of event communication in its practical exercise as well as its communicative and social funding, further steps are necessary. It would be effective to find a fitting language with which the acting body and visitor-spectator-audience can communicate with each other. This partially means an appropriate and precise terminology as well as partially a discourse on art. Furthermore, the motives that move the audience to the event and at the event should be researched. Therein an examination of the uses and gains or gratifications that the audience receives and retrieves from the event needs to be conducted. In addition, the phenomenology of the situation and situations that usually can be found at an event would have to be contemplated. And finally, one would deal with finding a way to describe more precisely how the individual reaches an agreement with the group about how the collective reality in the event is created and experienced.

3. A Communication Science Oriented Approach to the Evaluation of Event Communication

First steps towards a communication specific approach for typology, model and procedures of event communication will be introduced here within this limited space. Individual justification contexts have been shortened or have the status of assertions.[20] However, in the presentation of the general context a first exemplary approach can appear and already be generative for further research now.

An event, as an experience that is driven by certain goals and is professionally organized, that takes place in the three dimen-

---

19 The deliberations of Alfred Schütz on this complex should be pointed out here.
20 In order to clarify the background of the considerations, among other things, the systems theory of Niklas Luhmann, the theories of frame analysis from Erving Goffman, the thoughts towards a social construction of reality by Peter L. Berger and Thomas Luckmann, the constructivist theories of Heinz von Foerster and Humberto Maturana and the evidence to the indissoluble procedural connection of reason and emotion that was put forth by Antonio R. Damasio, should be referred to.

sions in real time and that a certain initiator allows to be carried out or a certain organization implements, is understood here as a means of communication. It is defined as a communication form at the intersection of mass communication (TV, radio,) and inter-personal or face-to-face (meeting of two) communication as a special form of group and large group communication – not to be mistaken as, for example, telephone communication otherwise labelled as group communication. At the same time it should be pointed out that mass communication mainly serves the purpose of announcing something or creating a layer of general awareness but that the acceptance of something (opinion, fact) is reached and solidified through interpersonal communication. Not until a meeting, a personal exchange, the communication characterized by feedback beyond the one-sided mass media, has taken place will a further step be taken past the mere physical reception of messages. Thus the event can be seen as a social network that is made up of close and less close relationships that are constantly oscillating in a sphere of associations. The characteristic of a so-cial network consists of establishing congruence (apart from drawing distinctions and creating boundaries), i.e. agreement, safety and well being. Here it would be worthwhile to examine uses and gratifications (adapted from an approach to TV impact research), as well as moments of the image transfer from other contexts and relationships. What also should be taken into con-sideration are the models of conviction through low-involvement models that are constructed in the persuasion research. Events should also be understood as a hybrid form, where both low-involvement and high-involvement can be found.

Give and take

A model that focuses on the determinant of return will be presented here, acknowledging that companies – like human beings – want something in return. Return in this context means the general construct of the overall success.

The superior determinate used to assess an event's suc-cess and return is defined as ROC (Return On Communica-tion). This value contains the specific ROO (Return On Objectives) meaning the level of achievement of specific goals; the individual ROE (Return On Event) meaning the specific level of mediation of individual attitudes; as well as the specific ROI (Return On Investment) meaning the specifically recognized value of the means employed. A formula for reckoning with this special case of communication would look like this:

$$ROC = (ROO \times z1) + (ROE \times z2) + (ROI \times z3)$$

$z1$, $z2$, and $z3$ represent the respective values attached by various stakeholders (government, public, guests, management, employees, citizens,) to this specific event, thus providing a multi-perspective approach. For each event and object of investigation the plus sign could be replaced by a multiplier (division is also possible), to specifically value the dependency of the individual factors among themselves. Return On Communication is understood as a result beyond the classic controlling only by means of numerical factors, because the soft facts that really determine the reality of live communication cannot be translated one to one in the world of hard facts. Therefore the formula represents an approximation to reality and does not express a numerical ascertainable solution, rather proportionality and perspectives in the framework of a special case. The central question of companies, organizations and public bodies of "how expensive is affection" allows for many different answers. Nevertheless, the numerical financial compilation and assessment of an event communication measure should naturally be part of every evaluation. Effectiveness and efficiency, perspectives that together depict the success (i.e. often economic, artistic, social elegance plus customer satisfaction), are cornerstones of the interpretive compilation of a Return On Communication. The following perspectives determine the examination of the ROC: total, stakeholder, participants and organization. Whereby the commitment for something, the satisfaction with something, the relationship to someone or to something, the positive image of something, construct the central achievement of event communication.

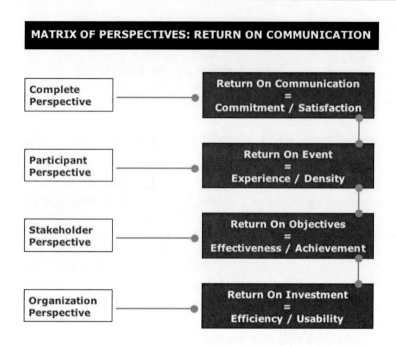

Figure 16: Model of return on communication-perspectives

The participant perspective is determined by the character and density of his/her individual experience. The stakeholder perspective is determined by effectiveness or the best possible achievement of objectives. The organizers or organizations perspective is determined by efficiency or the appropriate and best use of means. These perspectives determine and influence one another.

Determining these perspectives in the form of objectives should be done at the beginning of every event planning. At the same time goals, intents and objectives need to be differentiated. This helps to assess the application of appropriate evaluation methods (not too much effort, not too much cost) and an adequate differentiation of the ROO for the given event. A goal is defined as the inner core; the central meaning that stakeholders attribute knowingly or unknowingly to an event. Goals cannot be assessed via quantitative methods[21], only interpreted within individual worlds. Intent is defined as the coordinated directions, wishes, visions based on the goal(s). These could be qualitatively described and ascertained using refined quantitative assessment methods as well. Objectives are defined as decisive parameters formulated by the planning and arranging bodies (i.e. the ones paying for the event) on the basis and as a reaction to the intents and goals. These are open for qualitative evaluation methods and their computerized evaluation in all their facets.

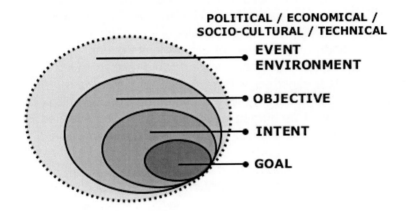

Figure 17: Event parameters

A uses and gratifications approach for events

Since the sixties, the handling and use of mass media (mainly TV) has become a relevant topic for social debate. General research on a theory about motives of use as well of expectation clusters of the user were innovatively formulated by Blumler and Katz[22] within the theoretical framework of a reception orientated approach.

---

21 Goals might be approachable via the method of "thick description" as developed by anthropologist Clifford Geertz within the framework of symbolic interactionism and symbolic anthropology.
22 Blumler J.G. & Katz, E. (1974). The uses of mass communications: Current perspectives on gratifications research. Beverly Hills, CA: Sage.

Uses and gratifications served as the main terms of the research with the following question: which gratifications were sought for, which ones were satisfied by media consumption; how are the sought and obtained gratifications connected; and which media behaviour was inferred from this. It became clear that the perceived gratification depended on social and psychological parameters (sex, age, social position, education, authority, identity). The construct of expectation captures a central position: users (or guests) must have a rudimental knowledge of the alternatives that could serve to the satisfaction of their needs, in order to choose and to behave appropriately. For this reason the expectations that are built up in the pre-phase of an event make up a considerable and formative part of the complete event. If the expectations are fulfilled then satisfaction should take to effect. Satisfaction itself is a construct with multifaceted dimensions inside and outside of the event and its attaining individual. A matrix of the motives as well as human needs that are to be satisfied is fundamental for the uses and gratifications approach. The assumption that a person actively decides about the use is relevant for the theory. This process then can be described as a multi-step selection process, where interpretation and feedback in the acceptance of contents come in to play.

In 1962 the psychologist Abraham Maslow tried to comprehend human needs in his known hierarchy of needs (in ascending order: physiological needs, safety needs, social needs, the need for esteem and finally self-actualization). Bert Brecht formulated this a little differently in the nineteen twenties: "First the grub. Then the morality"![23] This theory was further developed, for instance by Clayton Alerter who defined the ERG (existence, relatedness, growth) pyramid. Further research from didactics and learning motivation then lead to the following presumptions about the motive construction, the uses, and sustainable effect of events.

For the complex of event communication, represented by events of all kinds as a means of group communication, following

---

23 The character Mack the Knife sings this in a ballad from "The Threepenny Opera" about the question "finally what keeps a human being alive".

need factors and their uses and gratifications are designated.[24] These considerably influence the Return On Communication of every event and provide information about its success.

Factor: SOCIAL
acceptance, being part of something, integration, involvement, love & being loved, commitment, group formation

Factor: COMPETENCE
experience of own ability, realization of own ideas, accomplishment, experiencing of own capability

Factor: AUTONOMY
self-awareness, self-esteem, self-assurance, individuality, power, recognition, pride, choice

Factor: INFORMATION
knowledge, content, understanding, eloquence, presentation, density, exchange, novelty, relatedness

Factor: DRAMATURGY
rhythm, theme, packaging, story, suspense, meaning, sense, sensibility, timing, congruence

Factor: UTILIZATION
applicability, private & professional usefulness, instant & long-term practicality, social & group standing

Factor: BALANCE
not too much, just right for recollection, appropriateness, experience, adjustment, making sense

Factor: FUN/JOY
pleasure, style, entertainment, diversion, site, location, design, luxury, context, sharing, thrill, adventure

Factor: QUALITY
catering, accommodation, organization, material, transport, sustainability, social responsibility

Table 2: Matrix of event related need factors and their domains

This matrix can be seen too as an independent control instrument forming the individual programming, planning and creation of an event, likewise pointing to basics of the specific implementation. For the phases of an event (pre-beforehand, beforehand, creation, planning, during, directly after and after) this matrix serves as a guideline for process and controlling. The factors make a structured and reasonable observation possible like the evaluation of the various happenings for the determination of success.

Finally, a first model of the event field with its parameters and influences that constitute the event as such will be very briefly attempted here. The single items serve a) as domains for further research and the foundation of a specific theory and b) as practical fields for creation, controlling and evaluation of events. Terms to be

---

24 My thanks go out to Hermann Will, PhD, and the Wup-Summer Academy 2005 for inspiration in every point, as well as Professor Andreas Krapp, PhD, for valuable indications.

further researched and defined are: the event environment = the general setting in which the objectives of the event are embedded – also the macro environmental domain / the event situation = the specific setting in which the people are embedded with their specific needs, wants, uses and gratifications – also the meso-environmental domain / the event scene = the relevant setting in which the actual process is taking place – also the micro environmental domain. These domains are embedded and ruled by the central parameters of the function and effects of events: experience and emotion. I propose that along those lines, taking into account the verification and utilization of the advanced research of the terms and concepts of "emotion" and "experience", further progress can be made.

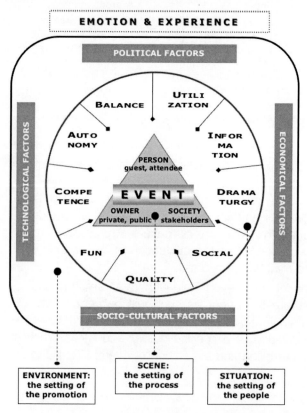

Figure 18: Model of the event field with its domains and parameters

The allocation of the particular approaches and a development of a typology of events that finally will be accepted globally remain for the future[25]. At the same time ways and standardized methods will be crystallized that could be considered secure in a multitude of cases after assignment and inspection. This focuses on the already successfully used methods from social research in the area of advertising research and communication science. Here it is necessary to follow the connections further and more precisely and to describe the division of events more precisely and smoothly. The big assignment beyond the compilation and classification of hard facts and data is the designation of soft facts for the evaluation in the above mentioned. At the same time it will be necessary to integrate the up-to-date findings from psychology and biology, as well as those from systematic and reflected research and explanatory approaches of event practitioners. Yet, what never should be lost sight of is the foundation on which the event as an effective communication medium is based on: theatre, ritual and street.

---

25 As of an initiative of the Canadian government and its Canadian Tourism Human Resource Council an attempt is being made in 2008 to develop an International Event Management Standard. This needs to comprise a description of what an event is.

Fira de Teatre al Carrer de Tàrrega – A Performing Arts Market

Mike Ribalta, Francisco Juárez Rubio

Since 1981 when it was founded, every year on the second weekend of September, the Fira de Teatre, the most important performing arts fair in southern Europe, is held in Tàrrega. It draws over 800 professionals and around 100,000 spectators who transform the town into magnificent showcase for the contemporary performing arts and an impressive popular festival during four days.

The Fira is a great fair for the different scenic arts disciplines and covers a wide range of shows both in closed venues and in the streets. There is an extensive, plural and carefully chosen programme of Spanish and international productions, which places its emphasis on contemporary and visual forms to guarantee innovation and artistic diffusion.

The basic aims of the Fira de Teatre are to promote artistic production, facilitate contracting and make the circulation of artists and companies possible for the most varied exhibition circuits. In other words, the objective is to make a decisive contribution to invigorating the performing arts industry.

1. The Show of Spectacles

The core of the Fira is the more than 200 performances from around 80 companies (in 2005: 47 companies from Catalonia, 31 from the rest of Spain, ten international) who cover the full range of current theatrical tendencies. From street spectacles to those in closed venues, text, visual, dance, circus, cabaret, etc, for children or adults. All the performing arts have their place in Tàrrega. Most of the shows pro-

153

grammed are new, first performances or previews and are held in closed venues or in the street (up to 21 venues), and are watched by a loyal audience.

Some of the leading theatrical companies, such as Comediants, El Tricicle, La Fura dels Baus, Teatre de Guerrilla, Cirque Eloize and Teatro de la Arena, have found a springboard to national and international recognition in the Fira. For young companies, the Fira represents an open forum for their creations and the platform for reaching the distribution circuits.

The Fira de Teatre al Carrer began in 1981 as an activity in the local summer festival. A few years later, it had become a small festival that programmed prestigious companies from all over Spain and small emerging groups from European street arts. From 1991 on, with the 11th edition, the transformation took place from a Street Theatre Festival into a Performing Arts Market. Nowadays, the Fira is an essential meeting point for contacts and purchase spectacles in the Catalan and Spanish calendar and a reference point for the European street arts circuit.

2. Quality and Artistic Renewal

One of the aims of the Fira is to promote the creation and distribution of new spectacles by Catalan companies. Until 2005, the organization reserved a budget of 12,000 EUR destined to helping, through co-production, those proposals that the artistic director considered most attractive.

In 2005, through the Fira, the Generalitat de Catalunya (the Catalan Administration) set up a new campaign of assistance for the street arts financed by a total of 150,000 EUR, in which the companies that benefit from it have to return as their show generates profit through the performances contracted. Thanks to the good results of this first experience, the Generalitat will finance four new street theatre productions by Catalan companies per year.

3.   Organization

The Fira is run by a Board of Directors, The Municipal Board of the Fira de Teatre al Carrer de Tàrrega, which is made up of:

Tàrrega Town Council
  Department of Culture – Generalitat de Catalunya
  Institut d'Estudis Ilerdencs – Lleida Provincial Council
  INAEM – Ministry of Education, Culture and Sports

The event is organized through a permanent office with a team made up of a Chief Executive Officer (CEO) who puts the lines set by the Board of Directors into practice and coordinates all the areas involved in the organization.

3.1 Artistic Area

In charge of following up the street art scene, selecting the proposals that reach the Fira, searching for innovative products on the international market and finally, the configuration of the programme for each edition. The Artistic Area is also in charge of analyzing the proposals that are candidates for financial help from the Generalitat de Catalunya

From November to February, those companies interested in taking part present their proposals (proposals were received from 500 companies for the 2005 edition). Simultaneously, the artistic director looks for outstanding high quality companies who are programmed to complete the selection and are guaranteed to attract both the public and professionals. The programme is decided in May with the 80 chosen companies.

3.2 Technical and City Services Area

Besides the Artistic Area, the Technical Area is responsible for coordinating the montage of the 80 companies in 22 venues while the City Services is the direct link between the organization and the other services in the town to facilitate the

155

many changes the town undergoes in the fortnight before and after the Fira.

3.3 Professionals Area

This is the contact between the Fira and the performing arts professionals. It is in charge of providing registration for the professionals at each edition. As those responsible for the Market, they coordinate the contracting of stands and the setting up and organization of the Fair Pavilion and all the activities arranged for professionals.

3.4 Communication Area

The Communication Area coordinates the Press Service, the Public Information Service, the Box Offices and entrances to the spectacles and is in charge of the public image, documentation and management of the information, publications and graphic supports, publicity and diffusion through both traditional channels and the Internet.

The main aim of the Press Service is to provide journalists and the media with access to the textual and graphic information that is generated throughout the year. Thus it manages interviews with members of the organization; the Board and the companies programmed and organises press conferences.

The Public Information Service offers various channels of access to the programme and information about the services offered by the Fira de Teatre for the spectators who attend or wish to attend the event. Attention is offered by telephone, e-mail or in person through the public attention office.

The Box Offices and the entrances are organized to facilitate access to the spectacles, by both the audience and the registered professionals. The ticket sales are managed through a multiple distribution channel (telephone + internet + office) and facilitated by an electronic banking service (http://www.telentrada.com).

The documentation and information management is done through a database system linked to Internet. The different areas of the Fira can handle a large part of their administrative procedures and through the Web.

3.5 External Resources Area

This area centres its activity on finding economic resources to complement public resources and the ordinary budget of the Fira de Teatre, essentially through sponsors, patrons and private collaborators. Similarly, it manages those parts of the Fira that represent complimentary sources of income.

The responsibility of the External Resources Area is to incorporate sponsors; the management of the San Miguel Awards by popular vote (prize financed by a brand of beer); the Club dels Mecenes (Patrons' Club) (local companies who help the Fira with the purchase of tickets at a special price, which they then give to their clients or suppliers); the production and sale of merchandising; the artisan market (a market of hand-made products that is organized simultaneously with the days of the Fira); Public Way occupation (process of public offer by which the bars, handcraft stalls with foodstuffs and other businesses that are set up on the days of the Fira are allotted); La Llotja Virtual (catalogue of performing arts companies that can be consulted on www.firatarrega.com); Publicity on our own supports (publicity in the catalogue of the Fira and in the magazine for the public and all the publicity on the Web)

The organization has permanent departments for administration, protocol and secretariat that work full time to guarantee the agility and efficiency of the team, one of the fundamental aspects for a good external image of the event.

4. The Performing Arts Market

Although the work of the Fira goes on all year long, the market revolves around the holding of the festival on the second weekend of September, with two main targets:

1. Put the buyers (programmers) in contact with the sellers (theatre companies). That is why there is a catalogue published for every edition with full information about the companies and a manual with full details about the accredited professionals. These two books are given to all the registered professionals as basic tools for their work.
2. Promote the diffusion through an intensive communication campaign, to attract public and give the event a high profile.

The Fira de Teatre has an annual cycle that begins in November with the call for artistic proposals and ends the February of the following year with the sending of survey on contracting to the professionals, through which we ask the promoters to inform us about the contacts and purchases of spectacles made at the Fira.

5.   The Fair Pavilion (La Llotja)

La Llotja is the area where professional activity is concentrated at the Fira de Teatre.

It is a meeting point for exchanges between the accredited professionals, and the nerve centre for activities (talks, debates, presentations, etc.). However, the main space at La Llotja is the Fair Pavilion, a 1,000-square meter thematic area with over 80 exhibition stands, which allow the institutions, businesses, networks and companies to promote their work and projects.

Over the years, La Llotja of the Fira de Teatre has become an essential reference point for the international theatre management community. La Llotja is the meeting point where theatrical and cultural agents from all over the world buy and sell shows; and a place for free and spontaneous contacts between artists, managers, producers, distributors, companies and public and private institutions linked to the world of the performing arts.

La Llotja is of growing economic importance in the workings of the theatre industry as, directly or indirectly, it generates an important volume of business deals. This is the reason for the enormous interest that companies show in participating in the Fira, which gives them a unique opportunity to open up new markets for their shows.

The public offer of stands begins in April each year and ends in August. In the last edition, La Llotja housed 80 exhibitors who took up 84 stands, 100% of the space available. The exhibitors were mainly agencies, institutions and companies.

6. Evolution of the Fair Pavilion

Unlike other countries, where the performing arts markets are common events (one of the clearest examples is the Kulturbörse Freiburg, which will soon celebrate its 20th anniversary) in Spain, the first performing arts fair pavilion opened in Tàrrega in 1991. Following the model of Tàrrega, there are nowadays four other theatre fairs in Spain that have places for exhibitors in their events (Alcoi, Palma del Rio, Galicia, Huesca). Similarly, there was a similar initial experience with the Performing Arts Market in Seville in 2004.

These markets are especially orientated towards Spanish professionals, who are still not very used to this model and respond coldly to these initiatives.

Implanting this model of contact in Spain is slow and difficult, but, despite everything, the response of the Fira de Tàrrega is positive. In the last three years, since the area of stands was implanted in a marquee, its capacity has grown every year: from 63 in 2003 to 75 in 2004 and to 84 in 2005.

The type of client who contracted stands in the Llotja at the Fira de Tàrrega: in the 2005 edition were: 50% agencies from Catalonia, 31 exhibitors (39%) from the rest of Spain and eight stands (10%) were for foreign entities, mainly companies who were offered a stand as a meeting point with the buyers of their spectacle programmed in that edition.

7.   Diffusion of the Fira de Teatre

The Fira has no specific budget for publicity. It is worth mentioning that after 25 years the existence of the event has a great inertia and a loyal audience. The publicity is generally a vehicle a through collaboration agreements with the national, regional and local media. Thus publicity is obtained in exchange for the presence of the media on the publicity supports of the Fira (catalogue, web page, poster, events diary and the newssheet *L'Èxit*) or in public acts (press conferences, presentations). Indirect publicity is also obtained through agreements with institutions, such as the ticket sales service, managed by a banking entity or discounts through student cards or others.

The diffusion of the Fira, apart from the traditional graphic supports, is done through Internet, either directly on the portal http://www.firatarrega.com (12,000,000 hits in 2005) or through newsletters.

7.1 Graphic Supports

- Poster. Diffusion all over Catalonia
- Catalogue. Includes all the companies on the Official Programme, general information in four languages and generally orientated towards professionals.
- The newssheet of the Fira (L'Èxit). Support for the programming for the public that includes information about all the participating companies and the performance times together with a plan of the town. Newspaper format. Diffusion around all the tourist and youth information points in Catalonia, as well as other registered entities. Publication in various newspapers (Segre, La Veu de l'Anoia), RENFE stations in Catalonia, pre-booking points (all branches of Caixa Catalunya), Tourist Offices and public attending the Fira.
- Caixa Catalunya leaflets. With the application of the image and the dates of the Fira. Diffusion via Caixa Catalunya by mailing to its clients and in the branches.

7.2 Publicity in the Press

- Insertions in the newspapers, Segre, El País, El Mundo, El Periódico, La Vanguardia and the magazines Artez, Escena

7.3 Publicity on the Radio

- Catalunya Ràdio, Catalunya Cultura, Catalunya Informació, Segre Ràdio and Ràdio Tàrrega (230 broadcasts)

7.4 Publicity on TV

- TV spot. Insertions on TV3, Canal 33 and TV Lleida (100 showings)

7.5 Presence on the Internet

The Fira de Teatre's presence on the Internet goes back to 1996. At that time, when many people in Spain did not yet have e-mail, the Fira made a firm commitment to the use of these new technologies and a presence on the Internet. Specifically, it committed itself to designing a first informative website, in three languages with general details about the 16th Fira: Catalan, Spanish and English.

By 1997, the Fira had already acquired its own domain, www.firatarrega.com, and it began to use e-mail as a communication system with professionals and the public. With that address, a second, more elaborate, Web site came into operation, and the Fira Virtual was promoted – an initiative intended to offer Web services to the companies linked to the Fira's programme.

At the end of 1999, the services of a specialized company were contracted to redesign the Web site and to make it possible for a database service to be set up so the Fira could organise a system for compiling information using on-line forms. In 2002, the sending of information via electronic distribution lists began, and the idea of the Fira Virtual returned. With La Llotja Virtual (www.lallotjavirtual.com), what is nowadays one of the best-known specialized virtual dramatic arts catalogues took shape.

In 2003, a step was taken towards converting the Fira's Web site into a thematic portal which, beyond being a simple support for publicizing news and information organized into areas, has become a very useful tool for organizing the Fira. Using this, requests by artists to take part and applications for professional accreditation, among other things, could be managed and useful downloads could be provided for the communications media or for students of cultural events.

With the years, the number of visitors to the Fira's Web site has grown spectacularly. From the first records from the end of 1997 to today, the number of visits per year, from all over the planet, has increased tenfold. The figures for 2004 can be used for reference: 89,000 recorded visits, involving a total of 9,800,000 hits on the portal's pages.

8.   Audience

One of the characteristics that the Fira has tried to promote is its double character as a Theatre Market and Festival. Tàrrega is not a showcase in the strictest sense as the companies do not do present from their spectacles aimed at a specialized professional public but rather show their complete spectacle to a heterogeneous audience of spectators and programmers, which puts less pressure on the performers.

8.1 Professional Public

The professional public who come to Tàrrega are from the artistic field (directors and performers), the professional management field (programmers, promoters and managers) and from the media.

The accreditation of the performing arts professionals who come to the Fira to acquire spectacles and contact professionals begins in June. The inscription is open to all professionals linked to the performing arts (agents, festivals, institutions or companies)

The Fira, as well as the representation from around Spain, includes an important choice of theatre companies from around the world. The management professionals are mainly from Spain and Europe. Most the main Spanish media come to Tàrrega, together with the news agencies and the most prestigious European media.

Since 1995, the number of programmers interested in coming has increased steadily until a peak of 900, which was reached in 2003. Given the high number of professionals registered in 2004, it was decided to charge a registration fee, with the aim of eliminating the inscription of non-professional programmers and raise the quality of those inscribed and improve their working conditions. Table II shows the drop in accreditations because of the new measure and the normalization in 2005

	2005	2004	2003	2002	2001	2000
Catalonia	431	339	480	409	427	374
Rest of Spain	209	189	257	245	225	177
Abroad	167	116	164	220	178	181
TOTAL	**807**	**644**	**901**	**874**	**830**	**732**

Table 3: Evolution in the number of professionals registered

8.2 Spectators

The audience that attends the Fira can be divided into three types:

Young people, who spend over 48 hours and get involved in the festive atmosphere of the Fira.

Public over 30, with a medium to high cultural level, professionals, who are interested in theatre as such and who attend the paying performances.

Family audience, with children, mainly interested in the programme aimed at children and street theatre.

9. Culture and Economy

The Fira de Teatre al Carrer de Tàrrega is a cultural event with many economic dimensions, some of them difficult to quantify but no less valuable for that. For example, it has turned the city into a place that is internationally known. Although this does not have great immediate economic effects, it is an investment for the future, as any new project enjoys the advantage of not having to start by putting the town on the map. It has also consolidated a framework in the world of theatre fairs, with a market that appreciates its work and which, year after year, renews its interest in the cultural product offered and in the contracting space. This opens the doors to expanding what has been achieved up to now.

Together with these assets, there are others that can be quantified. These include the public and private funds attracted by the event and, at the end of the chain, the spending by those who attend. The first of these items is shown in the Fira's budget, which gives the town the option of a greater than proportional part of the national budget for culture because of its contribution to cultural production through the creation of a professional infrastructure that maintains and expands the acquired specialty. Tàrrega does not just organize the shows offered in its streets and venues. In La Llotja, it also hosts groups offering their productions and those who contract this kind of show. A considerable proportion of the shows that will be seen throughout the year in many cities have their origins in La Llotja in Tàrrega, with an important economic component for the participants. It is a service offered by the town thanks to the infrastructure deployed, which requires the dedication of many people throughout the year.

10. Economic Impact of the Fira on the Town

The section covering spending by those attending is very important and has been measured by the 2000 and 2004 surveys directed by Francisco Juárez Rubio, director of the Department of Business Administration and Financial Management at the University of Lleida (UdL).

Given that the Fira is organized around the public holiday of 11 September, the way the days fall is different every year and consequently, the numbers of spectators varies. The surveys make it possible to put the number of those attending at 85,000 (year 2004) and 110,000 (year 2000). They spent EUR 20.34 per person per day on refreshments in 2004, mostly in Tàrrega. This figure does not differ much from that obtained as an average in the 2000 survey (EUR 22.33 per person per day), taking into account the variability of the measurement. Total spending on refreshments ranges between EUR 1,730,000 and EUR 2,400,000. In other establishments (petrol stations, pharmacies, souvenirs and others), spending in 2004 was estimated at EUR 572,020 (EUR 684,718 in 2000). A considerable proportion of those attending the Fira stay in and around Tàrrega, with total spending on accommodation ranging between EUR 120,000 and EUR 150,000 each year.

At the 2004 Fira de Teatre al Carrer de Tàrrega, estimates of total spending per person per day are approximately EUR 30.13 (±0.48), and total spending was EUR 2,561,050 (in 2000 estimated average spending per person, per day was EUR 31.23 and total direct spending was EUR 3,357,438).

The origin of people attending the Fira is very varied, although an important percentage (88%) come from Catalonia and, more specifically, from two large geographical centres: Barcelona and its surroundings on one hand and Tàrrega and the neighbouring districts on the other. Tàrrega provides 8.6% of the total and Lleida without Tàrrega 23.6%, Barcelona 42.5%, Tarragona 9.6% and Girona 3.7%. Finally, 9.4% of the audience comes from the rest of Spain and 2.6% from the rest of the world.

The audience attending the Fira shows a high degree of loyalty. 27.5% of those attending were going to the Fira for the first time in 2004. 25.4% attended for the first time less than four years ago, 25.5% between 1990 and 1999, and the remaining 21.6% before 1990. Those attending the Fira know about it being held largely through friends and family (51.71%) or have it scheduled as a cultural/leisure event year after year (25.27%).

All the data indicate the consolidation of this cultural event, which makes it a very valuable economic asset. Because of its specialization, Tàrrega has been capable of making a significant contribution to the production of cultural assets with services of great value, obtaining, in exchange, the economic remuneration we have mentioned.

11. Economic Impact of the Fira among the Performing Arts Professionals

Six months after each edition of the Fira all the programmers who attended are sent a questionnaire about contracting to evaluate the volume of contracted business that each edition generates among the performing arts professionals. This survey is awaited by all the agents involved and is a key tool for valuing the importance of the Fira as one of the most vigorous performing arts markets in Spain.

Valuation of the data obtained from the survey of the 24th edition

On the basis of the survey carried out by the external consultant directed by Ms. Maria Vidal, a graduate in Sociology from the University Autonoma de Barcelona 1995-1999, the university carried out the postgraduate degree on Participation and Sustainable Development 1999-2000.

The most outstanding data from the study is that some 90% of the programmers accredited in Tàrrega bought something. This shows that Tàrrega is consolidated as a meeting point and the most important place for buying and selling in

Spain. It is not only the place where most performing arts agents gather, but also where these professionals make more business deals.

Among the entities accredited, 27.5% acquired one or two spectacles; 25.7% bought three or four; 24.8% bought more than seven and 17.4%, five or six.

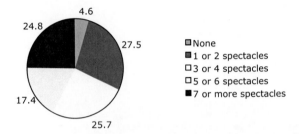

Figure 19: Volume of contracting of spectacles at the Fira during the 2004-2005 season

The basic conclusion from the figures in the study is that, if any doubts remained about the effect that the professionalization of the system of accreditation at the Fira de Tàrrega, it is clear that, despite there attendance being lower, their purchasing power has increased rather than decreased.

From the analysis of the registered professionals it can be seen that 50% of the Catalan entities inscribed in 2004 were local councils. From the rest of Spain, half of those inscribed were from local councils and the other half from festivals. More than 50% of the foreign entities were festivals.

This profile is very positively rated by the Fira, as with this typology of professional buyer the twin mission of the Fira is guaranteed for the companies: direct sale of the spectacle to the promoters who attend and promotion of their proposals, which ensures sales in the middle and long term.

With regard to the market, the professionals from Catalonia are still the ones who buy most at the Fira, although they are not the ones with the largest programming. The foreigners and those from the rest of Spain increased their purchases compared with the previous study. The purchases by programmers from the rest of Spain now are almost as high as that by the Catalans.

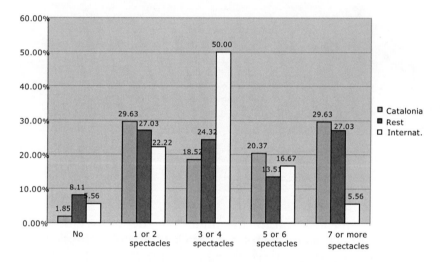

Figure 20: Volume of contracting of spectacles at the Fira by origin

The typology of the spectacles acquired at the Fira ratifies Tàrrega as a good market for street theatre as well as for text theatre, although it has also managed to obtain the loyalty of professionals who buy other genres, mainly children's theatre, circus and puppets.

The study was carried out on a sample of the questionnaires sent to entities registered at the 24th edition who purchased spectacles (214), eliminating from the same those professionals who do not buy (such as companies and distributors, who come for promotion and sales). The high number of questionnaires returned (111) gave the study a margin of error of only 6.6%, thus the results of the study are completely representative.

12. Budget

The first budget of the Fira de Tàrrega in 1981 was 11,287 EUR; the one for the latest event amounted to 1,551,842 EUR.

In this latest budget, the income section breaks down as follows: 66% from subsidies; 22% from the organization itself (ticket sales, "La Llotja" space, permission to occupy the public highway and refreshments, sale of programmes, etc.) and the remaining 12% from sponsors and advertising.

In the costs section, 66% of the budget corresponds to organizational costs, 26% to the costs and contracting of groups and 8% to communication.

If we analyze the subsidies, 42.84% is from the Catalan Government; 10.71% from Tàrrega Town Council, 7.28 % from the INAEM of the Ministry of Culture; 6.08% from Lleida Provincial Council and, finally, 0.09% from Urgell County Council.

If we analyze the budgets overall, we will see that the Fira pays for itself to a level of 33% and that the costs section is conditioned by those of organization (staff and infrastructure), with the remainder for communication and marketing.

1981	11,287	1982	23,113	1983	52,198	1984	68,125
1985	149,754	1986	278,269	1987	285,649	1988	257,233
1989	210,965	1990	330,557	1991	389,213	1992	450,991
1993	308,686	1994	432,053	1995	461,316	1996	539,786
1997	763,070	1998	728,933	1999	899,813	2000	883,725
2001	893,149	2002	970,793	2003	1,098,129	2004	1,161,077
2005	1,551,842						

Table 4: Budgets for the past 25 years (in EUR)

The Meetings Industry Yesterday, Today and Tomorrow

Tony Carey

Human beings are a tribal species, so the story of meetings goes back into the mists of pre-history. Whether it's the Bible, the Odyssey or Norse sagas, every culture, legend and folklore tell of people coming together to achieve a particular purpose – much as we do today.

And the components of a meeting have remained unchanged for millennia. Apart from the participants themselves, there is always an identified need for people to congregate (even if it is to fight), there is a meeting place or venue, which usually entails them leaving home, and there is an organizer or leader – whom, today, we call 'a planner'.

Only the means and methods change.

So, however attractive the technological alternatives, people will always have a compulsion to gather together. The need is ingrained in the human soul.

1. Evolution

But it has only been in the last 50 years that this natural human activity has been analyzed, dissected, systemized and made into a specialist procedure. For this we have to thank the Americans and a handful of (mainly) European pioneers who sowed the seeds of the global, professional, multi-billion dollar industry we know today. They were visionary.

The conference or meetings industry (I use the terms interchangeably) has evolved remarkably quickly since the 1950s. In those days it was not recognized as a specialized field. In the corporate sector, any spare manager and his secretary could be given the task of 'organizing the annual sales conference'. Associations would often co-opt their members to stage the annual convention. There were no training courses, no manuals, little guidance and scant respect for the hapless organizer.

Of course, governments and large corporations, political parties, academic institutions and others, organized very professional conventions, but their success was often due more to the leadership and experience of one person in the organization than to generally accepted procedures or standardized systems.

It was probably in the 1960s that the realization dawned on people in the developed world that huge sums of money were being spent on meetings and the scramble to get a share of this lucrative business really started.

Many different specialists became aware that they contributed to the success of business meetings so sought to become involved in this new industry: caterers, audio-visual providers, interpreters, entertainers, transport companies, presenters, printers, photographers and many others, joined hotels, convention centres and convention bureaux in promoting themselves to event organizers.

2. Destinations

Some cities had long seen the benefits of attracting conferences (in fact, the first Convention and Visitor Bureau (CVB) was established in Detroit in the early years of the 20th century). By the 1960s, cities all over the world were centralizing their marketing efforts to gain a bigger share of this expanding business. And the services they provide have evolved and been growing ever since.

Today, bureaux are often public-private partnerships with contributing members drawn from the commercial community. The most successful, such as Vienna and Copenhagen, have created a strong brand and instantly recognizable image.

In the future, we can expect to see CVBs offering even greater support to visiting events, including accommodation booking services, transport management and the provision of local staff.

It can confidently be predicted that the ex-communist countries will attract an increasing share of the European market as infrastructures improve and hotel chains expand. But the destination of choice for long haul and international events in the next 20 years is likely to be China.

3.   Venues

In the 1970s and 80s, congress centres, like cathedrals in the Middle Ages, were built to add prestige to cities and towns throughout Europe, and although they attracted business to their regions, few in the early days, were self-supporting. Perhaps because, as venues proliferated organizers were spoilt for choice so competition kept prices artificially low.

The design of convention centres continues to evolve – usually a step behind client requirements – but with one common trend: they get larger. Hotels too are increasing their conference suite capacities. All are aware that the current trend is for fewer plenary sessions and lots of variable size, concurrent, breakout sessions.

Rooms with natural light are – thankfully – replacing many of the subterranean meeting spaces favoured by the architects of the 60s.

Perhaps the most significant development in recent years is the emphasis that attendees, and therefore organisers and venue managers, now place on standards of service and food quality. They have become important differentiating factors.

In the future, we can expect a proliferation of health suites and wellness centres in hotels, as the public's obsession with health continues. In this connection, venues will need to pay greater attention to water and air quality. They will also have to cater for a public that is getting taller and wider and older.

In the final analysis, meeting planners will continue to select their venues on the basis of the attractiveness of the location, accessibility and standards.

4. Industry Associations

If humans have a tendency to congregate they also have a tendency to regulate and both of these became apparent in the 1950s when conference practitioners in the USA started to form their own associations, with the aim of protecting and promoting their interests.

In fact, the Convention Industry Council (CIC), an umbrella body comprising a handful of American industry associations was formed in 1949. Today all the major international associations are in membership.

The International Congress and Convention Association (ICCA) was established in 1963 to develop this 'new' industry, and the International Association of Professional Conference Organisers (IAPCO) was created in 1968.

1972 saw the foundation, in the USA, of Meeting Planners International, (MPI) – now Meeting Professionals International, with the aim of bringing together conference organisers with their supply-side counterparts and raising the bar of professionalism. Today it is a global association providing professional education and networking opportunities for its 22,000 members in 68 Chapters. (There are 2,000 members in Europe). <www.mpiweb.org>

Conference venues, too, have always identified themselves as specialist properties and have had their own associations to further their interests for many years. Global marketing consortia are, however, a relatively recent phenomenon.

5. Industry Media and Exhibitions

It is possible to judge the health of an industry by its media and one of the first magazines in Europe aimed exclusively at meeting professionals was 'Conferences and Exhibitions' published in the UK in the late 60s.

But within a few years, specialist publications were springing up everywhere and by the turn of the century there were probably more than 60 titles in Europe – reflecting the strength of advertising. Today, these publications are augmented by scores of magazine-style Web sites and portals.

Another major platform for promotion by suppliers has always been trade shows. London's CONFEX was first staged in the late 70s and EIBTM (now in Barcelona) opened in Geneva in the early 80s. One of the largest international shows is IMEX held annually, in Frankfurt, in the spring.

Almost every European country now has its own national trade show for the industry and many attract buyers from across the world. But the trend is for the distinctions between conferences and exhibitions to blur. They are becoming multi-media experiences.

6. Organisers

Who were the organisers in the early days of the industry? In the corporate sector, the stereotypical conference planner was a middle-aged male with project management experience and an interest in food and wine. He might be a Sales Director, Administrative Officer or Personnel Manager. Typically, he would be assisted by younger, female, staff.

Many associations, in the early days, had not realised that a conference, far from being an annual overhead, could in fact become a profit centre. Their events were often organised by committees of volunteers – with all that that implies.

As organisations began to appreciate the importance of their human capital, so more and more meetings were taking place, with groups travelling further from home and seeking more exotic or unusual destinations and venues. The days of the amateur planner were numbered.

Most major corporations now employ specialist departments to manage their meetings. Sometimes these include staff from agencies that are 'embedded' for a limited time.

7. Intermediaries

It was in the 1970s that a new breed of organiser emerged: the independent professional. Some were freelance, some set up agencies, some specialised in specific industries such as medical or pharmaceutical, according to their background. They became known as 'Professional Conference Organisers' (PCOs) – but not in North America where the term is still relatively unknown.

Another type of intermediary which appeared on the scene early on was the Destination Management Company (DMC). In the tour operating field, they used to be termed 'ground handlers'; they are specialists in a particular geographic locality and – having the local language and contacts – organise all the arrangements for a client, at the destination.

It is a role that has become increasingly important with the march of globalisation. Simpler and cheaper air travel has enticed events further and further from home, where a local, on site, facilitator is a necessity.

The dramatic increase in the number of venues in the 70s meant that organisers could rarely spare the time to research them all personally, so third parties appeared to undertake that task – in return for an agent's commission. These venue-finding agencies are now established in every European country.

The industry was becoming more structured and by the 1980s 'professionalism' was on everyone's lips.

8. Professional Development

But professionalism implies accepted standards and, originally, there were few training courses and – outside North America – no manuals or guides. The accepted mantra was: 'You can't teach meeting planning; you have to learn on the job."

When I established an annual, five day, residential training course for conference organisers in 1983, it was only the second such programme in Europe (IAPCO was the first) and attracted attendees from across the continent.

But there were, by this time, many experts who had spent decades successfully managing meetings and conventions. Their contributions to the seminars, workshops and trade shows, which were now servicing the industry, were invaluable in raising professional standards.

It was the industry associations such as MPI, ICCA, IAPCO, IACVB, (now MMAI) and others who really raised the professional bar in the 80s and 90s. They saw their role as primarily educational and still provide some of the best programmes and materials for the industry. Today there are national associations for conference professionals in almost every European state, making a useful contribution through educational activities.

The past 30 years has seen parallel development taking place around the world. North America is usually a step or two ahead of Europe and Asia Pacific in recognising trends, establishing standards and encouraging professional development.

In the 1980s, in an attempt to establish uniform standards and best practice, the CIC instituted the Certified Meeting Professional (CMP) designation, for which an exam is set. As at 2008, over 10,000 people have been awarded the CMP.

Few other certifications have achieved the same international credibility, although a recent phenomenon has been the emergence of university degree courses that include event planning. Their popularity is growing year on year.

A challenge to the academic teaching of meeting management is the fact that social attitudes, economic circumstances, the global situation, technology and delegate expectations are constantly changing. We work in a very dynamic industry which is influenced by scores of external factors whose impact varies from sector to sector. Keeping up to date is a constant challenge.

9. The Role of the Planner

The past decade has also seen a fundamental change in the way meeting professionals perceive their role. In the past they were administrators and logisticians, today they see themselves as communicators who create the optimum environment for successful communication.

Globalisation is having a profound impact on the manner in which events are organised. Planners are required to be more culturally aware than hitherto. And ideas are being shared, globally.

It used to be considered almost impossible to quantify the success of a conference, unless its objectives were financial (such as a sales meeting) but, in the late 1980s, MPI rolled out a guide for measuring the return on investment (ROI) of a business event. Today this tool and modern variants have been universally adopted to evaluate and refine procedures and outcomes.

And possibly as a result of this, the larger corporations now require their event departments to work closely with (or under) their procurement executives in order to achieve best value for money.

Another fundamental development in recent years has been a new emphasis on creativity and ideas. Conference attendees increasingly expect to be entertained while they are informed and educated. This requires imagination and innovation. The traditional formats no longer appeal. The terms 'infotainment' and 'edutainment' and 'imagineer' have entered industry parlance. The future is likely to see a more holistic approach to meetings as planners adopt multi-sensory techniques to communicate. This may result in a further blurring of the work-leisure divide.

The collapse of the Soviet Union and the demise of communism in the late 1980s gave a fresh impetus to people's expectations of democracy and therefore the freedom to choose. Today's conference attendees no longer accept the diktats of an authoritarian organiser, they demand choice. Planners now have to consult the delegates as to their wishes. Meetings are becoming attendee driven.

Fortunately, technology now permits a more personalised approach, so individualised marketing and personalised programmes are becoming commonplace.

In future, demographic changes will require the meeting planner to prepare special programmes for accompanying senior citizens and children, while abbreviated attention spans will lead to shorter business sessions.

Conference catering has become a key component of planning in the last few years. The days of set menus with a dull vegetarian option are past. Attendees now expect planners and venues to offer wide selections of menu to allow for allergies, intolerances, diets and preferences. This has led to fewer formal, set meals and more buffet-style functions. Many planners now adopt the 'grazing' principle of snacks and light meals being available continuously from food stations; a solution that also facilitates networking.

A comparatively recent development is an awareness of the need for organisations, and their events, to display 'Corporate Social Responsibility' (CSR). It is now expected of companies that they will concern themselves with their impact on the environment and on the localities in which they operate.

Conventions and congresses can have a major, albeit short term, impact on their chosen destinations and planners must now ensure that this impact is benign. Recycling of food is just one example. At the same time, consideration for minorities such as the disabled or those of different faiths is now much higher on an organiser's list of priorities.

Other recent developments in the way meetings are organised reflect the new professionalism. Planners are researching needs in advance and creating more relevant programmes. Lead times continue to get shorter. Meetings are becoming more intense to save time. Sessions are more participatory – because we now have a better understanding of how adults retain information. Networking is higher on the list of desired outcomes. These may be passing trends – but I doubt it.

10. Security

Today's professional meeting planners have to concern them-selves with a far greater range of responsibilities than hitherto, and security is one of them. Obviously the welfare and safety of delegates is paramount, but security of information and measures to protect against identity theft are also important.

It is unlikely that the global terrorist threat will disappear in the near future and large gatherings of people will always present a vulnerable target. Meeting planners will be taking this seriously for some years.

11. Travel

In the 1970s and 80s research showed that 70% of corporate meetings took place within two hours travel of a company base. Today it is a different story. The growth and relative cheapness of air travel is enticing groups to previously unknown destinations. Even the low cost carriers are targeting the business travel mar-ket.

As European roads become more congested and petrol more expensive, conference attendees are shifting to rail travel as a cheaper, less stressful and more environment-friendly option. This trend is likely to continue as European rail systems improve.

Certainly, the accessibility of a destination remains a crucial factor in site selection.

12. Standardisation

Attempts to establish national, let alone global, standards for the industry are fraught with difficulty, but are still a long term goal. The CIC is leading the field in this regard with its work on APEX (Accepted Practices Exchange). This is a project to collect and col-late best practice and methodology from around the world with a view to distilling these into systems and procedures for interna-tional use. The APEX Glossary gives some indication of the extent and complexity of the task. <www.conventionindustry.org>

The industry has always had a problem with measurement. Every country and each association has evolved a different definition for a conference, congress, meeting or seminar. So the collection of statistics has tended to be a.) local and b.) open to interpretation. APEX is helping in this standardisation but until there is international agreement on what constitutes a conference, meaningful measurement is impossible. So, at present, the global value of the industry can only be guessed at.

13. Technology

More than anything else, the new technology has impacted the meetings industry and will continue to do so. The internet has changed the way we promote and manage events, how we communicate with participants and how we measure outcomes.

Certainly, the planner needs to be au fait with the latest developments as meeting attendees are bound to expect a modern, technological environment on site. The trend will be for venues to provide the means for fast, efficient communication – free.

Time will tell if the cell phone or the smart card will become the 'key' of choice for conferences, but both will be capable of facilitating the management of registrations, on site payments, access control, data collection, etc.

The latest cell phones are proving both a distraction and a useful tool for event organisers who will have to learn to both exploit and control them. Technology is even coming to the aid of networkers.

It is dangerous to forecast where technology will take us next, but virtual-reality Web sites dedicated to meetings is an area to watch.

14. Specialisation

As the industry becomes more sophisticated, so it inevitably splinters into specialisations. Incentive Travel has, for over 40 years, been a distinct sector with its own association (SITE) and methodology. Now we are seeing the emergence of 'Team Building' as a separate business travel activity, distinct from meetings.

Venues are starting to specialise and focus on specific markets in the business sector. An example is the advent of 'conference centres' which target the corporate meeting and education market.

On the agency side, we are entering a period of consolidation where small agencies are linking with, or being absorbed, by the larger multinationals to create networks with a strong brand and global reach.

15. Conclusion

The meetings and events industry, which two third of the world refer to with the acronym MICE (Meetings, Incentives, Congresses, Exhibitions), has come a long way since the 1950s and is now universally accepted as an important generator of local income and a valuable communicator of ideas. It is an industry destined to grow in size, value and importance.

Meetings play a key part in the communications spectrum and I fully expect that the role of meeting professional to gain even more (well-deserved) kudos in the future.

German Protestant Kirchentag – Sustainability Strategy for a Large-scale Event

Gabriele Nottelmann, Tilman Henke

1. The German Protestant Kirchentag

The German Protestant Kirchentag ("Church Day") is the same age as the German Federal Republic. It was founded in 1949 in Hannover by Reinhold von Thadden-Trieglaff together with a number of his friends – as a movement by Protestant lay people, for whom two things above all were dear to their hearts: their freedom as Protestants in relation to the official Church, and a Christian faith which combines piety with a responsibility for society and the world. The objectives of the Kirchentag are set out in the preamble to its rules:

The German Protestant Kirchentag aims to draw together people asking questions about the Protestant faith. It aims to bring together Protestant Christians and strengthen them in their faith. It encourages a sense of responsibility in the Church, to equip people for witness and service in the world and to contribute to the fellowship of world-wide Christianity.

The Kirchentag takes place every two years during a week in May or June. It lasts for five days, from Wednesday to Sunday and is hosted by a different city each time.

The participants come from all over Germany and indeed from all over the world. Of those people who travel to the Kirchentag, around 100,000 come for the whole time, and another 50,000 buy daily tickets; altogether a Kirchentag has on average around 1.1 million visitors. The age profile is a good mixture, 41% of participants are under 30 years old, 29% between 30 and 50 years and 30% over 50. Each time about half are there for the first time, for the rest it is already their second, third or fourth Kirchentag.

The Kirchentag is spread over approximately 1 million square metres of performance areas on Exhibition Centres and in the town centres, indoors and in the open air. The framework for the programme is provided by the central Opening Services of Worship on the Wednesday, followed by the "Evening of Encounters" in the town centre of the host city, with over 400,000 visitors. This is followed by three days of around 2000 events: platform discussions, workshops, exhibitions, concerts, worship services, theatre performances etc. The Kirchentag ends with a communal Closing Service on Sunday morning.

Preparations for a Kirchentag begin several years earlier with the choice of the city. A good eighteen months before the event happens a local office is established, where the staff are responsible for handling the practical organisation of this huge event. There is also a permanent office based in Fulda: the staff there is essentially responsible for the planning and carrying out of the content of the main event. The budget for a Kirchentag amounts to around 13 million Euros on average: the budget costs are borne in approximately equal shares of one-third each by the fees paid by the participants, by the host Protestant Regional Church (Landeskirche) and the contributions received from public funds from the federal state, the region and the city. The biggest item on the expenditure side, amounting to around 4 million Euros of the budget, is the hire of rooms (above all the Exhibition Centre) and the provision of technical equipment in all the locations. Altogether the cost of the presentations and events (preparatory meetings, organisation, bookings administration, publications and publicity) amounting to 9 million Euros represents more than two-thirds of the budget. The rest of the 4 million Euros covers the costs of offices, management and personnel.

Tens of thousands of people, up to half of the participants, are actively involved in the planning and formation of a Kirchentag. Their commitment is voluntary and unpaid. Thus the Kirchentag is not something organised from above but it grows from below.

The Kirchentag is a place where the grass roots and the establishment from both Church and Society meet each other. Working alongside high-profile personalities from the worlds of politics, science, business and church, or popular artists, you will find unknown singer/songwriters, amateur cabaret artistes or people sharing personal experiences from their everyday life. This diversity is what gives the Kirchentag its attraction and its liveliness.

2. Kirchentag and Sustainability

With any large event there are inevitably environmental effects – participants' travel, the construction of platforms, the adaptation of exhibition halls, presentations which are held on grassed areas – all of these and much more use up environmental resources. The interests of the environment play a role in almost every aspect of the preparation and carrying out of such an event. For many years now the Kirchentag has made great efforts to minimise its environmental impact. This is a natural consequence of the Kirchentag movement's commitment to making a contribution to sustaining the integrity of creation. But there are also some concrete organisational motives which come into play: so, for example, the movement of streams of people between the various locations for events is dealt with by using public transport only. And good, solid crowd control of visitors is not only necessary in the interests of the environment – in order to avoid unnecessary time wasted on travel or on waiting around – but is also essential for the sake of ensuring the smooth running of single large events such as for example the Closing Service with up to 200,000 visitors.

Particular features and challenges

An event of this magnitude would normally be organised and carried out by a team of permanent staff, sometimes with the support of a handful of enthusiastic volunteers. With the Kirchentag it is different: alongside the employed staff, of whom there are as many as 80 at the peak period, there are just under 50,000 volunteer comrades-in-arms who feel themselves to be part of the

185

Kirchentag movement. They commit themselves to involvement in the running of the event at many levels – and that includes having to undertake some advocacy work with many different groups and interests. An example: on the "Market of Opportunities", a kind of Trade Fair held during the Kirchentag, there are around 800 organisations, initiatives, associations and interest-groups which set up stalls with presentations of themselves and their work. Almost every organisation produces – for understandable reasons – a leaflet about the relevance of what they are doing. Not to mention the free-riders – attracted by the huge mass of visitors – who hand out their own printed messages and advertisements outside the main venues for the events. All in all, this amounts to several tons of printed paper which is handed out to Kirchentag visitors – and for the most part ends up in the rubbish bin. In this area the Kirchentag has been working for many years on a major propaganda exercise to persuade groups on the one hand to produce as few brochures as possible, in a realistic quantity, and on the other to use recycled paper. All the groups in the "Market of Opportunities" have to agree to the Market regulations, in which attention is drawn precisely to these issues, amongst other things. A further challenge is faced in the local organising office: a good two thirds of the staff is only employed by the organisation for a few months. So at the beginning of the period of employment they have to familiarise themselves with their highly complex sphere of duty in the shortest possible time, and at the same time be persuaded of the relevance of the environmental task, which is sometimes very demanding and even irritating. This also requires the use of a considerable amount of advocacy, which is done by the environmental team based in the office. For example, the environmental team regularly invites in advisers and trainers with expertise on waste disposal, paper recycling and fuel-saving, who run training workshops in the office. In addition, every new arrival has to be involved in a small workshop in the so-called "environmental pig-sty office": one of the offices is set up with a whole range of environmental "sins" (heating left on, windows open, all the lights left on, coffee left in the machine instead of being put into thermos flasks, mistakes made in the separation of rubbish etc) and the new recruits have to set out on the search for these – with the motto "hunt the mistake".

Environmental control

In order to combine all the many individual activities, which traditionally make up the Kirchentag movement, into a single strategic and systematic policy for environmental protection, the organisation introduced during 2002 to 2003 an environmental control system as promoted by the Federal Environment Agency and the Federal Government Environment Ministry. Environmental control fulfils in essence three functions: firstly, it provides information about the flow of materials and energy usage of the enterprise (information function). Through this, the environmental effects can be foreseen and assessed. On the basis of this information the establishment of environmental aims and the planning of environmental actions can be put into place (planning function). Furthermore, the continuous collection and recording of data makes it possible to assess the success of the measures which have been carried out and how well the environmental aims have been fulfilled (control function). The German Protestant Kirchentag is the first large-scale event to have its own environmental control system at its disposal and since 2001 it has had a comprehensive overview of its environmental effects.

The environmental effects have been and are being measured in the following areas: energy use (water, electricity), volume of waste material, travel to and fro, provision of food, use of paper, office materials, accommodation (during the event) and articles for sale. An environmental controller is employed for 3 – 5 months to collect the data during and after the event. Much of the data can be provided from the in-house database. Sometimes it is simple figures that are requested: on the aforementioned "Market of Opportunities" volunteers specifically look for leaflets and publications. They ask those responsible about the number of copies printed and thus make an assessment of the total use of paper in this segment which the Kirchentag has christened "uncontrolled paper".

3.   The Kirchentag Offices

In both offices – both in Fulda and in the relevant Kirchentag location – there is an Environment Team. Great importance is attached above all to the Environment Team in the local office: for
their concern covers not just the environmental effects within the
office itself, but also for the whole event. Staff from the widest
range of areas of work within the office is represented on this Environment Team: purchasing, administration, domestic management, IT-services etc. That means that not only is there the possibility of considering a particular question from a lot of different
points of view, but it also helps towards making changes. It is no
secret that changes, however small they might be, are a lot easier for staff members who are themselves (or one of their direct
colleagues) involved in the decision.

A couple of examples of how the Kirchentag office acts in an
environmentally-friendly way by very simple means: in every office an electric socket strip with an on/off switch has been installed and thus every individual staff member can avoid wasted
use of electricity by the stand-by function of the various office
machines. Also, an initiative of the Environment Team has led to
the exclusive use at meetings of organically produced and fair-
traded coffee. Fruit juice is sourced from the local region and bis-
cuits from eco-fair trade. Energy is bought 100% from renewable
sources. Glues containing solvents are not to be found anywhere
in the offices, the proportion of recycled paper used throughout
the local office is just under 85% and overall the proportion of office equipment (files, containers, folders) which is re-used makes
a contribution to a good eco-balance.

In the Fulda office similar efforts are made: here too the whole
of the paper supply (letter-quality and photo-copier) was recently
replaced with recycled paper. In addition to buying electricity
from green sources, solar panels have been installed on the roof
in Fulda to produce our own green energy; and furthermore, the
Kirchentag holds shares in a wind-farm in Thuringia run by church
supporters. These actions mean that around 17 times the amount
of electricity used by the Fulda office is produced to some degree
from "clean" sources.

For its office in Fulda the Kirchentag has been granted an EMAS certificate (EMAS stands for Ecological Management and Audit Scheme). A prerequisite of this European environment certificate is that the office has committed itself to the observance of the nationally applied environmental regulations and to the appropriate level of continued improvement of environmental protection within its internal systems. It has set its own selected goals in relation to the environment, instituted an environment management system, undertaken self-examination in relation to the environment and has drawn up a so-called environmental declaration for public release. The observance of all the more precise requirements as prescribed has been examined by a registered external environmental expert.

4.   The Event: 1.5 years of Preparation End in Five Days of Kirchentag

The Kirchentag is well justified in giving itself the title of one of the most environmentally friendly large-scale events. A lot of effort is put in to achieving this aim, which needs to be done afresh every two years. In doing this the Kirchentag receives support from a circle of expert volunteers who are members of the "Standing Committee on Environment". This small circle of people is made up of representatives from various environmental institutions, from the Kirchentag Praesidium, from the environmental work of the Church, and from the business world; it meets twice a year and offers the Kirchentag advice and stimulus for action.

Since the 1999 Kirchentag in Stuttgart there has been an organic food market at the main Exhibition Centre site. Here visitors are offered a wide choice of ecological and fair-trade foodstuffs, ranging from fried rice or crepes through to traditional German Bratwurst. From its origins as a niche offering, the Organics Market has blossomed over the years into a veritable pivot for the provision of food, serving almost 15,000 portions per day.

A further ecologically-friendly offering for visitors is given by the "Glass Restaurant": this is where the Protestant Academies (conference centres) in Germany come together to demonstrate what a huge variety of tasty regional and ecological dishes can be cooked and offered. As the name suggests, you can actually watch the chefs at work. Altogether, the quantity of food provided from organically certified production at the Hannover Kirchentag in 1995 was over 20% of the total consumed. Even the official commercial food outlets at the Exhibition Centre were drawn into the environmental concept of the Kirchentag and obliged to co-operate: in Hannover all the cafés situated at the venues for events were only allowed to offer exclusively "eco-fair" coffee. All in all, this led to a proportion of over 90% out of the total con-sumption during the Kirchentag.

Another pillar in the concept of ecological food provision is the "eco-fair" breakfast. Around 40,000 participants sleep in school premises in the Kirchentag city (communal accommodation). They are looked after by volunteers, mostly from the local par-ishes, who also provide breakfast – organised by themselves, but supported by the Kirchentag. Staff at the Kirchentag office train the teams and offer the availability of help with the shopping. The care teams get a budget from the Kirchentag for the costs of the breakfasts. In order to provide a financial incentive for providing ecological food, there are three aspects of the procedure: the ac-commodation teams receive a lower payment if they only buy conventional products. They get slightly more if they buy a mix-ture of conventional and ecological products and the highest sub-sidy is paid for purely ecological products. Proof of what has been bought must be backed up by receipts from the respective shops and/or products. Thus the choice is handed over to those respon-sible for the accommodation and not to the participants. There is therefore no correspondingly higher charge made to participants who are receiving an ecological breakfast. This means that it is the Kirchentag that bears the recognised higher cost of providing ecological and fair-traded foodstuffs in the communal accommo-dation. This is all the more the case, the more schools participate in these measures. Nevertheless, the Kirchentag advertises the eco-fair option and tries to convince as many as possible of the accommodation teams of the quality and lasting value of these products. A good third of the breakfast food provided at the Hannover Kirchentag came from controlled organic production – a record which is expected to be broken at the coming event (in Cologne). As has been the case at previous Kirchentags, the training of the accommodation teams, well-designed brochures and not least the financial advantage offered, all help to draw attention to the expectation of the Kirchentag.

With regard to the numerous suppliers of goods, the Kirchentag takes care to ensure that these are locally sourced from the region. On the one hand, this makes economic sense, for in the end the region ought to get something back from its own Kirchentag – and on the other it means the avoidance of unnecessary transport. Ecological criteria have hitherto only been prescribed for the suppliers in exceptional circumstances: the 80,000 scarves for the climate campaign, for example, were bought on condition that the fabric has the international "ökotex" label.

A good ecological balance for many conventional products is also achieved at the Kirchentag through a high rate of re-usage and of re-sales. The classic example of this is the cardboard-box seat ("Papphocker") – a practical seating item, which is folded like a cardboard box and functions in the Exhibition halls in its umpteen thousands as an ersatz stool. At the end of the Kirchentag many of the visitors buy a Papphocker for one Euro and take it home with them. There are lots of smaller events in the areas of youth work or church activities which are glad to make use of the practical and lightweight boxes. Thanks to the storage facilities of the Kirchentag the remaining stock are available for use all year round from the local office.

5. The Main Environmental Focus of the Kirchentag

With the 2005 Kirchentag the idea was conceived of having a main environmental focus: at each Kirchentag a special stress would be laid upon one particular environmental topic, which would be presented both as part of the content and through campaigning action. In this way the organisers wish to give stronger expression to their efforts on behalf of the integrity of creation and at the same time to use the opportunity of reaching 100,000 people with the message.

The climate campaign was the environmental focus of the 2005 Kirchentag in Hannover. The goals were defined as: a minimum of 50% of the participants should come into contact with the topic of climate protection and at least 5% should be motivated to make a concrete change to their behaviour. In order to achieve these goals, a range of different instruments of communication were chosen:

The Climate Market

On the open area in the middle of the Exhibition Grounds in Hannover a "Climate Market" took place over three days. Weatherproof tents were set up where 18 organisations presented their commitment to climate protection and demonstrated the possibilities available for individuals to contribute towards reduction in emissions in their own everyday lives. A particular highlight of this was the exhibition Energy@home, which was presented in one of the Exhibition halls adjacent to the Climate Market. In the Market itself a café offering fairly-traded products offered an opportunity to sit and rest for a while. While you drank your coffee, you could gather information about the Kirchentag's commitment to the environment from one of the advertising columns. In a neighbouring hall, the theme of sustainability was also to be found in a culinary context: the Glass Restaurant offered an invitation every lunchtime to enjoy a regionally seasonal and eco-fair menu, which proved to be very popular. A cookery book passed on a variety of information on ecological dietary change and on the topic of cookery and climate. The people involved in the Climate Market were amongst others the General German Cycling Club, the Federal Association for car-sharing and wind energy, the German Railway Company with its own environmental centre, the Climate Association and the energy advisors of the consumer office of Lower Saxony.

"Have you changed over yet?" – Changes on offer.

In order to attract as many Kirchentag visitors as possible to the Climate Market and in order to provide an incentive for concrete action, a "climate card" was designed, with 110,000 copies being printed and included in every programme booklet. This card could be exchanged for one of six different "changes on offer" available on and around the Climate Market, for example an initial credit balance when establishing an account with an ecological energy company, a low-energy light bulb at a special price or a free expert's report on heating costs.

The blue climate-protection scarf.

The main instrument used for confronting the mass of visitors with the relevance of the topic was the 80,000 blue scarves printed with the slogan "Kirchentag for climate protection" which were distributed in exchange for a donation. Here the organisers were able to use a certain tradition when suggesting this campaign, as there have already been scarves printed with slogans at different Kirchentags in the past. Kirchentag guests like to wear these scarves as a sign of belonging and in doing so maybe incidentally learn that the Kirchentag attaches great significance to this topic.

6.   Events

Climate protection needs to feature also in the Kirchentag events themselves. Thus there was a half-day platform discussion with the title "Change Now", in which representatives from politics, business and environmental associations held a debate about the energy-mix of the future, the creation of work-places through renewable energy and about sustainability as a model for global politics. Every day between 11.00 and 13.00, short "climate talks" with music were held on a stage set up near the Climate Market. Protagonists of climate protection gave a full justification for their position on topics such as the renaissance of nuclear energy, compensating for flight emissions, innovative forms of mobility among other things. People living in the Alps reported on the melting of glaciers and guests from Pacific islands reported on the effects of climate change on their homelands.

The Glacier wager

As part of its regional network, the Kirchentag worked with the climate-protection agency of the Hannover region. They organised a "Glacier wager" from the beginning of April up to the beginning of the Kirchentag. A $2m^3$ ice cube was set up inside an insulated cover in the city centre of Hannover. The wager was opened by the Lord Mayor of the city and the General Secretary of the Kirchentag. Estimates could be made as to the percentage of the ice which would not have melted at the end of six weeks. Attractive prizes awaited the winners. In this way the campaign was also carried into the city and communicated in advance of the Kirchentag.

Good examples at the forefront......

The wide range of measures which are described in this article demonstrate that the Kirchentag itself does not just talk about climate protection, but actually takes action:

- green electricity used in its offices
- green electricity used at the Exhibition Centre during the event
- photovoltaic solar panel equipment used in Fulda
- investment in two wind farms
- building work to ensure energy-saving in Fulda
- compensating for flight emissions

In total, through these measures 21.4% of the CO2-emissions of a Kirchentag have already been avoided or offset.

Partners in the climate campaign

The Kirchentag used its own personnel to take on the overall concept, organisation and implementation of the campaign, including the planning of the Climate Market by its own architects and also the graphic design of the materials used. In addition, however, it sought out different partners to provide financial and conceptual support. Thus the individual topics and possible ideas for action in relation to climate protection were presented by the actual organisers of the Climate Market themselves, who registered an application to participate and paid a modest exhibitor's fee. Volunteer Kirchentag staff supervised the Climate Market during the setting up and the running of it.

The Federal Environment Agency and the Federal Environment Ministry supported the campaign with a financial contribution which made it possible to establish an additional project post for two months. Alongside this, an invitation was sent out to all the certified eco-energy companies operating nationwide to tender for becoming partnership sponsors, which would include, amongst other things, the right to bid for contracts for energy supply on the Climate Market. The tender from Greenpeace energy was the one that was accepted. Together with those responsible for the enterprise the idea was born, that for every contract that was agreed support would be given to a development-aided climate project. This project – the construction of clay ovens in Tanzania – was chosen in co-operation with Bread for the World.

What has been learnt during the Climate Campaign

The various elements of the campaign were successful in different ways. The response to the blue scarf ensured that the 50% target was well exceeded. Similarly, the Climate Market was very successful. Its central position and the good weather ensured that it was continuously bustling with visitors. The exhibitors expressed themselves as very satisfied with the organisation and the location and were positively surprised by the great interest and the responsiveness of the Kirchentag participants. It was obvious that for the public the most attractive stands were those with interactive features – for example a quiz, a solar café, the opportunity to send an e-mail with a photo or the calculation of a personal emissions balance.

As a criticism it could be noted that the climate talks turned out to be not controversial enough and the stages used were too big. For the small-scale format of this event a more intimate setting for a discussion closer to the public would have been better.

The card offering an exchange for change was only used by about 1000 visitors, which corresponds to an approximate return of 1%. So the statistically measurable transactions fell short of the expected 5%. What can't be measured, however, is how many of those who made enquiries at the Climate Market concerning climate-protecting behaviour, may have done something about this in their own daily lives or in the workplace (e.g. in local church congregations). In considering this we should not underestimate the function of staff in local churches and schools in spreading the word and disseminating information.

7. Communication

In the period before the Kirchentag there was a press conference for the introduction of the scarf and also an opening of the whole climate campaign involving well-known people. A number of press releases were issued during the preparatory period by the Kirchentag, by Greenpeace energy, by the German Environment Foundation and the German Energy Agency. A Web page was devised to go with the Kirchentag focus on the environment, appearing on the Internet under www.kirchentag.de/umwelt.

However, the organisers were not really happy with the media response to this commitment to the environment – neither in the run-up to the Kirchentag nor during the event itself. Here too – as with the take-up of the theme by the participants – it was clear that with all the multitude of topics covered at a Kirchentag, the media representatives still look for their own main focus of interest for their reports. Since it was evident that the main focus is most noticeable when an event features prominent people, the climate campaign has learnt the lesson that next time they need to acquire a prominent patron.

Internally, too, it was not always easy to get those involved to be interested in this commitment and to motivate them. Since the Kirchentag is, as already explained, a movement of the laity, it has a whole range of committees which are involved in various

ways. In general, these are positive in their views on environmental projects – who can be against it these days? Yet, they
clearly allow it to suffer from a lack of interest. The highest rank-
ing committee of volunteers in the Kirchentag, the Praesidium,
consisting of around 30 people, showed hardly any willingness to
support the climate campaign. Externally, this was visible for example with its appearance on the Web site, which is not so easy
to find – needing to navigate three pages to get there. No-one
out of those with leadership responsibility was willing to make a
strong effort to get this topic more into the foreground.

8. Acquiring partners and sponsors

These days, work on the environment is a topic which every business really needs to ask itself about. Firms whose actual production doesn't lie in the environment branch of industry – for sim-
plicity's sake let's call them "conventional" firms – will of course
find it difficult to find a place for themselves in sponsoring something like this. A lesser role is played by a fear of being put into an
"eco-niche" by potential customers, but a much greater one is the
fact that there is a yawning gap between desirability and reality.
Conventional firms and concerns mostly have their own environmental programme and give themselves an environmental value,
but in terms of practical implementation there is a clear failure to
anchor it in what is actually done. For this reason the main sponsor of the climate campaign is someone who offers an eco-
product. Here once again, the Kirchentag had the luxury of being
able to choose from three candidates, of whom the two who were
turned down were clearly disappointed by the rejection. The conclusion of the organisers: it is certainly possible to get sponsors
for work on the environment, for this area is an attractive part of
the Kirchentag happening.

9. Environmental Focus on Transport – a Look into the Future

90% of the carbon emissions of a Kirchentag are caused by traffic. Personal travel by participants to and from the Kirchentag alone accounts for 53 million kilometres – without taking into account the air kilometres as well! Almost 13 million kilometres are then covered by Kirchentag visitors within the locality during the event. A further 4.2 million personal kilometres are travelled by staff and volunteers during the months of preparation.

It is therefore worth looking more closely at this area. In relation to transport too, the Kirchentag has led the way in terms of environmental friendliness. From an ecological point of view the range of distribution amongst various different means of transport is well above the German average.

For comparison: The Fifa World Cup in Germany in 2006, with its 'Green Goal' programme, set itself a target of 50% for the proportion of spectators travelling to matches by public transport – for the Kirchentag this has already been over 90% for a long time. But because there is always room for improvement, the Organisation has committed itself to tackling this as a focal issue for the 31st Kirchentag in Hannover.

From as long ago as 1981, the full admission ticket for the whole Kirchentag has also included at the same time a travel pass valid on local public transport. Since 2001 this has been done with the day tickets as well. As a rule, the combined ticket covers a larger transport area, and therefore many participants and visitors from the whole region come to the Kirchentag by train and by bus – the cost is, after all, already included in the price of the ticket.

In addition, the Kirchentag organises special ticket offers with German Railways (Deutsche Bahn) as well as special chartered trains from both the local region and across the country.

The Kirchentag motor pool

During the preparatory setting-up period and throughout the event itself, the Kirchentag runs its own motor pool of around 100 vehicles, with about 180 volunteer drivers, providing transport of all kinds for moving people and goods from place to place. During those few days these vehicles alone cover around 390,000 kilometres and in Hannover they used over 10,000 litres of fuel. For this reason the drivers for previous Kirchentags have been required to complete a special fuel-saving course. By knowing some simple tricks, fuel use can be cut by more than 20% – as our volunteers notice for themselves in their own purses when driving their own cars after the Kirchentag is over.

In the last few years the transport fleet for the motor pool has been sponsored and put at our disposal by one of the large German motor manufacturers – the last one by Volkswagen. As a result of this the Kirchentag has little influence over what type of vehicles are provided and so far has not had any vehicles available in the pool with low consumption or using alternative fuels. On the other hand, the big involvement of a formal sponsor has enabled an increase in expenditure in other areas.

Since the 1999 Kirchentag in Stuttgart there has also been a bicycle courier service for short distances and small items. This spares the environment from lots of short car-trips which have a particular high fuel-usage rate.

And Kirchentag visitors can also use pedal-power: as long ago as 1997, a bicycle shuttle service was firmly established. A bicycle hire-station is provided in the city centre area and a corresponding one at the main location for events, the Exhibition Centre, where individual visitors can borrow a bike in exchange for a returnable deposit, in order to cover short distances by using their own muscle power. This puts several hundred cyclists into circulation, making their own contribution towards an improvement in the transport eco-balance.

Guidance for visitors

As already mentioned the Kirchentag already invests a lot of time and energy on giving guidance to visitors and ensuring crowd control, for purely organisational reasons. Every visitor receives a programme folder sent to them in advance, containing amongst other things, a town plan with precise transport information. General information offering guidance and directions are also included in the programme booklet. With just this information alone, a lot of unnecessary journeys can be avoided. Furthermore, the planners can forecast the traffic flows that will ensue from their choice of the locations for events – and therefore take these into account when making their choices. Short routes between locations are often a crucial factor in making the decision for a particular place.

At the "Evening of Encounters"', the opening celebration of the Kirchentag, over 350,000 people are moving around the city centre. To cope with this mass of visitors, the organisers have established a sort of traffic roundabout system, which functions rather like a one-way system. Potential trouble spots and streets can only be used in one direction during the evening, to avoid traffic jams.

For groups travelling together, there is a special service: all the groups which have registered in advance receive a letter from the Kirchentag giving precise information about parking places and travel directions for the bus driver. Detailed instructions are given in writing about the best route for the bus driver to take on the day of arrival in order to reach the place where accommodation is being provided. Parking tips are given for the main period of events from Thursday to Saturday, especially for the Exhibition Centre. Sunday, with its Closing Service, presents a very special challenge for the organisers. On that morning there are many thousands of participants all wanting to get to the same place. Most of the groups who have come by coach get their bus drivers to drive them to the Closing Service, so that they can set out on their homeward journey straight afterwards. This means around 500 coaches, all of which receive in advance a description of the route to take from their place of accommodation to the coach parking areas near to the place where the Closing Service is being held. 250 stewards are there to direct the coaches and every coach passenger is given a diagram of the exact location before they get off the bus so that they can find their bus again after the Service. About 100 coaches drive directly to the Closing Service, in order to collect their groups from there and chauffeur them back home. These are allocated a specific parking place in advance and the group is informed in good time of the place where their bus will be. A special left-luggage facility is designated for these groups nearby, so that cases, bags and rucksacks don't have to be carried around the area unnecessarily.

At least 40,000 participants are provided with overnight accommodation in local schools, where detailed information about transport options is made available. For each school location the Kirchentag prepares a recommended travel plan for getting to the Exhibition Centre or into the city centre by bus and train. And of course the host region also needs to be given information about what to expect in terms of traffic during the five special days that make up the Kirchentag: the Kirchentag calls a major press conference in advance in order to give detailed information about all the street closures and delays that are to be expected during the period of the event.

CO2 offset for air travel

Air travel is well known to be particularly relevant for its impact on climate through high fuel consumption and the production of emissions at sensitive altitudes. The Kirchentag has therefore made a decision to compensate for any flights which are undertaken in relation to the event, by making payments to climate projects, corresponding to the amount of carbon dioxide which is released. The payments have gone to atmosfair; an organisation which specialises in carbon offset compensation for air flights, and also to help finance climate projects in developing countries. Of course, carbon dioxide that has been released into the atmosphere can't be taken back through these payments, but at least a contribution is being made towards the world-wide reduction of emissions. Through these payments a total of about 981 tons of carbon dioxide is saved in other places by atmosfair.

Looking ahead to the 2007 Kirchentag

At the time of writing this report the plans for the 31st German Protestant Kirchentag in Cologne in 2007 are well under way. Concrete projects and events relating to the environmental focus for 2007 are not yet clearly decided. What is clear, however, is that all the previous efforts made in relation to transport and the avoidance of emissions will be undertaken once again at this Kirchentag – they are now regarded as "standard" in forming the basis for further minimisation of the ecological consequences of a large-scale event.

Now that the office in Fulda has received the much-desired EMAS certificate, the Kirchentag has set itself the next challenge: the event itself is working towards being the first event of its kind in general to achieve the EMAS certification. The process for this is beginning a good year in advance, in early summer 2006.

So the organisers are once again reaffirming their aim of being the most environmentally-friendly event – and of remaining so. In concrete terms the aim of be a "zero-emission-Kirchentag" has moved to being within reach. The use of energy from renewable sources ("green electricity" and our own solar and wind-power sources) is a great step in this direction.

Translation: Sheila Brain

IMEX – A Case Study in Launching a Trade Show

Carina Bauer, Simon Naudi, Brian Wiseman

IMEX is the worldwide exhibition for incentive travel, meetings and events and takes place annually at Messe Frankfurt, Germany. Launched in September 2001, IMEX has become the pre-eminent trade exhibition for its sector and was awarded the 'Best Trade Show' award in 2006 and the 'Best Visitor Experience at a Tradeshow' award in 2005 – both by the Association of Exhibition Organisers.

IMEX 2006 brought together over 14,000 industry professionals from 150 countries, including 3,300 exhibiting companies; 3,400 hosted buyers (who travel and stay free as guests of the organisers) plus over 4,000 additional trade visitors.

IMEX is organised by Regent Exhibitions Ltd and the founder is Ray Bloom. (www.imex-frankfurt.com)

1. Pre-Launch – Research

The most challenging requirement before launching a tradeshow is to identify a need. Whilst in some cases this can be a matter of personal hunch or preference, the most crucial element is to research the market carefully. The research phase for IMEX was extremely important, although due to the organiser and founder's existing knowledge and links with the industry this phase was less intensive than might be undertaken during a traditional trade show pre-launch phase.

In researching the market some of the following tips are useful to consider.

- Identify lists of potential exhibitors in trade directories, professional associations, the catalogues of existing shows in that

sector and by examining advertisements in the trade media for that industry.
- Question whether your target companies will pay to exhibit at your proposed trade fair, especially if it is not the first in the sector.
- Identify prospective visitors – their attendance in sufficient numbers, and at the right level of decision-making, is the basis of the whole viability of the event.
- Identify industry professionals through the readership of trade publications and contact the appropriate trade associations.
- Estimate your hypothetical worldwide total of prospect attendees and then be ruthlessly realistic in trying to predict the probable percentage that might attend the exhibition.
- Analyse the strengths of competitor exhibitions and why some of these do well and why others may have failed.
- Consider the ideal time of year for the exhibition and the most sensible duration for the event, as well as its desirable frequency that fits in with the supply and demand cycles in the market concerned.

During the pre-launch phase it is also extremely important to consider the most appropriate location – country and city – of the exhibition, as well as the selection of the exhibition venue itself. For IMEX, Frankfurt in Germany was an ideal location for a number of reasons. For a highly international event Frankfurt provides unrivalled transport links with the largest airport and train station in continental Europe, an excellent rail and road network and enormous hotel capacity with over 35,000 hotel rooms. Germany itself has one of the largest buyer markets in the world for the meetings and incentive travel market and with no competing events in the country it was an ideal location. In addition, Messe Frankfurt – as the third largest exhibition halls in the world and an extremely modern venue – provided unrivalled facilities for the exhibition, plus the numerous seminar sessions and meetings which take place around the show. At IMEX we put much time and effort into developing our relationship with the management of Messe Frankfurt and we see them as an integral component to the success of the exhibition.

At the pre-launch phase it is also very important to consider your investment and financial needs. This is the case irrespective of whether you are a professional organiser of exhibitions, a specialist publisher planning a spin-off event, an exhibitions venue organising your own trade fair, or, as in the case of IMEX, an individual entrepreneur with an enthusiasm for a particular sector. In each of these situations the achievement of a return on the capital invested will matter, although possibly the required timescale for recovering such a profit may vary. The preferred approach at IMEX has been to consider profitability only in the long-term and therefore to invest heavily, and sometimes disproportionately, from the launch of the show in order to attract visitors. Whilst it is possible that exhibitions can be profitable from the first year; many shows which have the greatest long-term success take a three to five year view of profitability.

2. Developing and Cultivating Industry Support

It is crucial to win the support of the wider industry, usually in the form of trade associations, at an early stage in the development of the exhibition concept. The benefits can be their endorsement – creating the sense that the show has 'official' blessing – together with the access they can provide to reaching their members – would-be visitors and/or exhibitors. IMEX has sought such support – and developed the resulting sense of partnership – using two strategies. The first is to work hand-in-hand and as true partners with the professional bodies that represent the industry worldwide. IMEX is endorsed by SITE[26], ICCA[27] and DMAI[28]; is a European Partner and sponsor of MPI[29] and is a corporate partner of AIPC[30]. Supporting trade associations include JMIC[31], ASAE[32], ESAE[33], IAPCO[34], IAEM[35], ISES[36], CIC[37] and

---

26 *SITE: Society of Incentive and Travel Executives*
27 *ICCA: International Congress and Convention Association*
28 *DMAI: Destination Management Association International*
29 *MPI: Meeting Professionals International*
30 *AIPC: International Association of Congress Centres*
31 *JMIC: Joint Meetings Industry Council*
32 *ASAE: American Society of Association Executives*

EFCT[38] to name just a few. IMEX's engagement with such organisations helps us to talk to their members, and attract their attention, but equally it enables us to know what the industry is thinking and wants from IMEX and what we can further do to help in their work. We value such relationships as the basis for seminars or research, award schemes and joint projects; but above all, their support means that their members are far more likely to participate in our show.

The second strategy is to seek the support of the local industry and trade bodies. For example, the German Convention Bureau is a strategic partner of IMEX. Their support and influence has helped us to create close relationships with key German partners including Lufthansa Airlines and Deutsche Bahn; as well as local organisations such as the DGVM[39], VDR[40] and Frankfurt marketing club. Their involvement in our visitor marketing campaign has also been a key factor to its success.

This process of gathering enthusiasm and backing for the exhibition also includes the targeting of relevant media, whether published magazines or e-magazines and whether domestic or international. At IMEX we work with over 70 trade publications across the world and employ press relations agencies in both the local German market and for our global audience. A key factor in developing such media support was the formal launch which IMEX organised early in the planning stage inviting a cross section of media, trade associations, industry leaders and potential exhibitors. We explained the concept behind IMEX and demonstrated the difference between IMEX and previous industry events – i.e. the unique combination of a large international hosted buyers programme together with access to the huge German buyer mar-

---

33 ESAE: European Society of Association Executives
34 IAPCO: International Association of Professional Congress Organisers
35 IAEM: International Association of Exhibition Managers
36 ISES: International Special Events Society
37 CIC: Convention Industry Council
38 EFCT: European Federation of Conference Towns
39 DGVM: Deutsche Gesellschaft für Verbandsmanagement e. V.
40 VDR: German Business Travel Association (Verband Deutsches Reisemanagement)

ket. During this launch we also emphasised the importance of the visitors and outlined both our visitor projections and plans for attracting them.

3. The IMEX Team

Of great importance in the development of IMEX has been the creation of a strong and focussed team; the majority of whom came from the industry and therefore had a prior knowledge and understanding of our sector. An essential component of the team is the sales department which makes the effort to meet as many exhibitors as possible – both pre-launch and between each annual exhibition. This approach at salesmanship places an emphasis on the creation of long-term goodwill – achieved through constant contact, getting to know people well, meeting them at the show, helping them to be successful and becoming their friends. The IMEX team has a philosophy of never forgetting to say thank you for our exhibitors' support.

A special emphasis is also placed on the organising team who must not only understand the logistics of organising an exhibition, but also understand fully the levels of service expected for our exhibitors and visitors. As much as any part of the team, the organisers help to create a culture of goodwill which touches every participant. Therefore, it is important that they should pay special attention from the start to the quality of the infrastructure that is offered during the exhibition and the IMEX organising team has developed a close relationship with each one of the suppliers within Messe Frankfurt ranging from cleaning services, shuttle buses, catering, security, cloakrooms, signage and more. Taking an interest and active involvement in such detailed work is crucial for the smooth running and ultimate success of the show.

4. Visitor Marketing and PR Campaign

The visitor promotion, visitor attendance and visitor experience ultimately determines the success or failure of any exhibition and as a result we take the visitor promotional campaign extremely seriously at IMEX.

The IMEX hosted buyer programme

A hosted buyer programme is an extreme form of visitor promotion whereby key industry buyers are literally hosted to the exhibition – with the flights, accommodation and transfers being paid for by the organiser. The buyers are invited through intermediaries – key businesses around the world (for the meetings industry they include airlines, hotel groups, media, convention bureaux and agencies) who select, invite and manage the visit of their top customers to IMEX. Naturally the cost of running and, therefore, the cost of exhibiting at exhibitions which run such programmes are significantly higher than average. At IMEX, we run the largest such programme in the world and in 2006 hosted over 3,400 buyers from 57 countries to the exhibition. However, whilst such programmes eliminate the degree of uncertainty you may have about attracting visitors; they should be looked at in context and it should be noted that a 'hosting' approach is virtually nonexistent in other exhibition markets, and where it does exist, it is arranged on a modest scale – say, for two to 300 buyers maximum. On the other hand, it is highly possible for every exhibition to target some key buyers to host, even if limited to, say the top 50 executives in their relevant industry sector.

Direct Marketing Campaigns

Direct marketing campaigns are the traditional way for exhibitions to attract visitors. At IMEX we used a number of avenues to develop and build a strong database for our campaign – trade media, trade associations, local business and marketing associations, local media, etc. The exhibitors also play a key part in our direct marketing campaign and we supply them, for free, with professionally produced leaflets and encourage them to send them to their key clients inviting them to register for and attend the exhibition.

Our visitor promotional campaign includes a mixture of direct marketing by post, email campaigns, telephone marketing, advertising, magazine inserts and, of course, PR work which we will touch upon below.

Travel discounts are also an important part of attracting visitors to attend an exhibition. At IMEX we developed a close relationship with Lufthansa as our official airline and they offer 50% discounts to all pre-registered visitors and exhibitors. In addition, Deutsche Bahn also offer discounted rail travel and we have negotiated with hotels in Frankfurt to offer special rates. Other incentives might include free or heavily discounted public transport, restaurant and cultural offers and weekend packages through the local tourist office.

IMEX year-round PR

Whilst the exhibition has 'news value' when it is first announced, at the official launch, during the inaugural event and also afterwards when attendance figures are announced it is also essential to secure coverage on a year-round basis. In the case of IMEX we work to secure year-round coverage from around 100 meetings, incentive travel and other business tourism titles and we achieve this by working on a continuing campaign of industry-friendly initiatives that rely on innovation, and thereby create news interest. We call this our New Vision programme. This project is not intended to be money-making – on the contrary, the exercise costs a great deal to organise, together with the time of several IMEX executives. On the other hand, the value of supporting the wider industry, continuously working on projects hand-in-hand with the major trade bodies, as well as being constantly newsworthy is a priceless investment. The IMEX 'New Vision' programme encompasses 12 individual projects including a Wild Card promotion which gives four unknown destinations the opportunity to exhibit free of charge; our environment project that encourages buyers and suppliers to minimise their environmental and social impacts; the Future Leaders Forum which encourages dynamic young students to enter the industry and is now held in three countries through-out the year; as well as our Politicians' Forum that brings together politicians and industry leaders in an effort to explain and promote the potential of the meetings industry.

5. Managing Successful Exhibition Attendance

Having taken a strategic and hopefully long-term view about retaining the support of exhibitors, and attracting the interest of buyers, it is important to try to manage the exhibition attendance of those who attend.

At IMEX this means helping to ensure that both exhibitors and visitors leave the event with deals having been done. This is a business approach that can be adopted by any exhibition, albeit in varying ways according to the markets concerned. It is literally a process of social engineering. At IMEX, we use the website in order to promote the use of an online appointment system by giving online diaries to all exhibitors and pre-registered buyers and we continually encourage buyers to make online appointments with exhibitors in the weeks prior to the show. At IMEX 2006 over 18,000 individual appointments were scheduled prior to the opening of the exhibition. This system also encourages buyers to research the exhibitors who are attending before entering the halls. Through the website they are able to read about the exhibitors on dedicated web pages, ask for brochures before the event and even request proposals. Such systems not only promote a business focussed approach, but also make it possible for buyers to do their work more effectively and efficiently. Ensuring that educational seminars are held during out-of-show hours also ensures that buyers are on the show floor during business hours. In addition, we encourage exhibitors to arrange out-of-exhibition social and educational events where further networking and prospecting can effortlessly take place; as well as encouraging the construction of professionally designed booths which enhance networking and meeting possibilities. It is also important to ensure that exhibitors are sending senior staff to the event – this will inevitably attract a higher quality of buyer and vice versa.

The IMEX website is also used as a year-round tool for the industry. This has the effect of continuously promoting our exhibitors in a year-round live environment, as well as serving as a constant source of promotion. The IMEX website includes a virtual exhibition where each exhibitor has their own page for one year; provides useful information on industry associations, events and publications; as well as providing research pages highlighting industry sources and IMEX surveys and research. As the world becomes increasingly used to working online it is important to keep up with current trends and allow visitors and exhibitors to manage as much of their participation online as possible – for example offering online registration for visitors, press and exhibition staff; displaying the exhibitor manual and other key elements of the exhibition information online in a secure password-protected area of the website and offering online appointment systems as explained above.

The weeks following an exhibition are also a crucial time and one which many often forget. At IMEX we encourage our exhibitors to do their exhibition follow-up quickly, taking advantage of a two-to-three week exhibition 'after-glow' when buyers are still excited and still remember their meetings and the new products that they have seen. IMEX also takes advantage of this period by releasing results quickly, contacting the industry press, sending out a list of attendees to exhibitors and saying thank you to our industry partners.

6. Conclusion

The IMEX story is one of positive momentum and growth. It proves that in a market place where a genuine need has been identified, a professionally run and forward thinking exhibition can grow and achieve success in a relatively short time-period. A successful launch is crucial, but just as important is the need for the exhibition to stay ahead of trends, to become a central meeting place for the industry and to continually work with industry organisations to drive the marketplace forward.

7. In General: on Launching New Shows

The 'Art of Launching New Shows' is not so much a science as a journey that is beset with potential obstacles and set-backs. This chapter is designed as cautionary advice developed over forty years through many successful and also many unsuccessful ideas rather than a prescriptive methodology. It will help pre-empt and in many cases eradicate potential obstacles and help an idea reach fruition in the most painless way possible. Whilst it is true that no two launches are the same it is also a truism that there are certain fundamentals that if ignored can account for the majority of launch failures we see today. One of the most common is that someone develops an idea and envisions a multi-billion EUR launch with multiple spin-offs and globalisation like there is no tomorrow. The passion that often grips one when faced with such a situation can be overwhelming and so the need to house your event at the right venue becomes paramount. Venue owners (and I hope I am not doing them a disservice) are wildly enthusiastic also – to get you a signed tenancy contract and a deposit banked equally quickly. Once the reality begins to dawn that maybe the idea is not quite so large the enthusiastic entrepreneur is now facing a situation where a deposit has been paid and so they 'might as well' launch because they are going to lose their deposit money. This is not a good omen for launching a new event! Work with the venue owner to engineer a situation where everyone benefits and you will avoid probably the most common pitfall in one easy step.

8. Why is a Launch so Different?

It is important to realise that with a launch, there is no track record or previous visitor or exhibitor statistics which to use as ammunition in the sales process. You need to become the central office or channel for information about the event and the industry. We talk on our courses about the need to become the industry 'guru' and the ability to replace statistics from previous events with statistics about the industry itself. In selling your concept all you have here is a 'media picture' and you will have to describe who you hope to reach (by way of visitors), through which channels and what the irresistible proposition will be. If you are launching a show into a market that has never had any shows or events associated with it (a rare situation) then you will need to establish the traditional routes to market, the costs of those routes and where you fit in to this. This will help you justify your price per stand and per meter. As a general guideline, with a Business to Business event the cost of an average stand should equate to roughly the rate card price of a full page colour advertisement in the trade press. From a marketing point of view this will have implications for positioning but this seems to be an obvious entry point.

9. Where to Start

It is always imperative to remember that adopting best practice for a launch is still no guarantee or indeed a way of making a bad idea into a good one. We recommend dividing the launch process into three distinct phases which will avoid the pitfall of investing money on something that thorough research can later prove to be not such a great idea after all.

9.1 Stage One

The first phase is to spend time and not money, time that is research based. There are a whole host of ideas that are worthy of your time investment in phase one. Are your ideas competitive or compatible with another event? It may be that you have an opportunity for a flying start or the possibility of co-location and thereby 'trade' off the established visitor figures and demographics of that other event. Are the products of your potential exhibitors 'exhibitable', as this may determine floor space requirements? If your exhibitors are mainly service providers then their need to take larger stands will be doubtful and impact upon the meterage you need to sell, which in turn will affect your business plan and cash flow. It may also artificially determine the amount of sponsorship revenue you need to generate in order to reach break even. Are your exhibitors and visitors readily identifiable? We know that an idea is better received where the visitor and exhibitor population are tangible and specific. What is happening in trade or professional journals and magazines? Are there key advertisers who dominate the space or are there many smaller companies all competing for business? What is the international interest and can your idea be rolled out nation-wide or across borders? What might affect the timing, dura-tion and frequency of your event – are there traditional buy-ing cycles and peak periods you need to factor in to your de-cision? Are there any special services required that may im-pact on the venue or location? Who are the trade bodies and professional bodies involved and have you made contact with them? They may be a useful sounding board as well as a good source of information and business intelligence that will be useful to you in the future. Remember too that a re-spected industry body that is sponsoring or at least suppor-tive of your event means you gain instant credibility by de-fault. Specifically, this is the time to establish the value of in-dustry sales, imports and exports and the sheer numbers of manufacturers, importers and retailers that are active in the market, to name a few. It is also the time to build an accu-rate profile of the typical visitor and exhibitor as well as writ-ing down the rationale behind the event. By the end of phase one you should have a credible clean database with decision maker names, e-mail addresses and ideally direct dial tele-phone numbers. In modern times it is all too easy for your key prospects and influencers to hide behind voice mail and automated e-mail replies. As we will discuss later, it is impor-tant to have direct access to these people. This therefore as stage one, is the time to ensure that your idea is sound and viable. Do not sign any financial commitments until you have completed this phase. A basic business plan should also be drawn up covering at a minimum:

- Rationale
- Timing
- Profiles (visitor, delegate and exhibitor)
- Size of the Customer Universe
- Support groups and other trade / professional bodies
- Political / environmental considerations
- Legal issues
- Competitor analysis
- Industry overview
- Management plans
- Staff support structure
- Growth and profitability potential

It is also worth involving outsiders – people who have not given birth to the idea, who may view the 'evidence' more impartially than an avid enthusiast! These referees are a useful tool in the quest for impartiality and for playing devil's advocate.

9.2 Stage Two

Assuming you have completed the first phase, you are now in a position to allocate a sum of money and a period of time to this phase. This should take the form of a mini-budget – an extract from your event budget of what you need to invest. It is very hard to establish what this should be and will vary from company to company and from one individual to another. Typically as a guideline, it is commonplace to assign a GBP£30,000 budget for again typically a three month period, although it is only a guide. If you have good in-house facilities and technological expertise, web sites and desk research may be carried out more cost effectively and at minimal cost, therefore reducing the need for such a large budget. Phase two is where you need to get out into the market place and talk and more importantly listen. You need to have face to face discussions with potential media partners, trade, association and government bodies. You should also aim for at least ten wish list sponsors and fifty wish list exhibitors. It is important that you are open about your concept but you need to be flexible and listen. It is not unusual for an enthusiastic entrepreneur to listen to negative feedback about their 'baby' and rather than listen and assimilate the feedback, resort to hostility! It is important that you collect all the news – good, bad and indifferent. Recognise the fact that not everyone will share your vision nor indeed actively support your ideas but you need a clear understanding of what their reaction may be, their perceived objections and benefits that they would like to realise. Also recognise that many people will from politeness often say it is a good idea but when asked to dip into their pockets will hide behind some other reason not stated at your meeting. It is important therefore to set the scene so that they can be frank with you and in this way the information will be of maximum use. It is also important for you to set expectations and educate your potential exhibitors that a successful event is not just about visitor numbers. You can work out the maths yourself, but at a typical three day event, if you see a visitor for five minutes every five minutes, without so much as a break, typically you will get to see no more than 360 visitors. So drive home the message that success or failure is not overwhelmingly dependant upon visitor footfall. Some products or services likewise will need a lot longer than five minutes to explain so get them to shift their focus on the quality of the visitor rather than sheer numbers. The detailed research you carry out during this phase will help establish whether reality matches the anticipated plan. It is also worth building a spreadsheet when planning how to reach your visitors. You have two issues you will need answers to: firstly, how to reach them most effectively and how often and secondly, how to make them come. The spreadsheet should itemise which media you intend using and when, another column, for example may itemise the number of repetitions and the third column, say may have total number of exposures or 'hits'. In this way a potential exhibitor will be able to judge the awareness that you intend creating and use reasonable judgement about the likelihood of attracting potential clients to the event. Likewise a reputable PR agency involved with your industry will often be able to secure you better column-inch coverage and awareness than traditional paid for advertising. The second aspect should be a compelling reason why a visitor will consider your event to be a 'must-attend' rather than a possible or probable one. What will be your hooks, what can they gain from attending that they cannot achieve through traditional or alternative methods? Your budget will additionally be used on further initial tasks needed for launching an idea, which can include database building and cleaning, fax and e-mail campaigns, contacts with the key groups, getting letters of support from venues, ministries and trade bodies. Your business plan should now be re-visited, with promotion costs, sales forecasts, predicted costs and profit as well as cash flow forecasts becoming clearer. It is also worth incorporating some 'go-no go' milestones to ensure you are disciplined in your approach. (For example you will achieve x amount of contracts out there, y amount received back with deposits by z date etc). It is also the time when floor plans can be drawn up but do not enter into any financial commitments other than the business planned mini-budget as agreed for these three months. Good practice is to draw up a conservative floor plan and fill it so later on you can announce that due to demand you have to secure larger hall space. This will always make better press material than 'consolidating' the floor plan to be less ambitious than your initial forecast as you failed to achieve the take up you expected. At the end of the three months or when the mini-budget is spent it is time to consider whether to move on or abort. Consider the levels of support achieved for your event to date. Are they agreements in principle or have they indicated solid cash sums they might allocate? Again an outsider can see the wood from the trees more clearly perhaps. Also it is worth considering that in these fast moving times, global economies and world events can have a huge impact upon your plans – have things moved on since your embarkation on this journey?

9.3 Stage Three

Assuming you have passed phase two successfully, it is time to consider the next step. This is where you need to set a critical path and begin your sales campaign. If you are recruiting a sales team you will have identified possible candidates and costs in phase two, now you need to pay them. Opinion says that sometimes cash flow can be funded through pre-payment for stand sales and sponsorship money. This is no longer a credible approach in the market and becoming increasingly less likely. The risk is often too great for the bigger players to invest when they have no assurance of a successful launch. There are many examples of launches that have collapsed despite the solidity of their idea through poor or insufficient funding, sometimes only a matter of months away from the doors opening. If you need to raise finance be sure to consider what equity terms you will offer for the funding. Likewise check on any legal obligations in your home country, for in many instances gate money (at a business to consumer event say) cannot be released until after the event is completed and so deposits for contractors and venue owners will need to be met from elsewhere.

As indicated, launching a new event is not a rigid process, rather a series of pre-cursive measures that when added together amount to best practice and the least fraught route from inception to launch.

Exhibition Events – A Revolutionary Campaign

Tony Erpelding

Delphi Productions was approached by Wind River, a device software company, to help them create an "in your face" campaign to revitalize their company and the device software industry at large. Wind River was looking to create a new business category, Device Software Optimization, or DSO. With a new Chief Executive Officer and Chief Marketing Officer on board at Wind River, they were looking to create an impacting campaign that would redefine the software industry with the launch of this new business category.

Delphi partnered with them to create The Wind River DSO Revolution, a nine-month marketing campaign. The overarching goal of the campaign was to make the DSO category a reality by gaining industry acceptance of DSO. Tied into this goal was the aim to position Wind River as the DSO industry leader. DSO is a revolutionary way of approaching device software. Out of this, Delphi came up with the idea of creating a Revolution.

A revolution is not typically a single event, but rather a movement. The traditional trade show or event approach would not capture the essence of a revolutionary movement. Thus, Delphi looked beyond the traditional and instead approached the task as a campaign rather than an event or series of events. The idea was to create an integrated marketing campaign, manifested through web, print, media, event and trade show elements.

Delphi and Wind River wanted to start the campaign off with a viral, underground revolution feel – the beginning of a movement. Web and email efforts, supported by direct mail, were utilized to create this feel. These efforts were used to gain momentum leading into the first series of events. Conferences were staged regionally, continuing the viral feel of the campaign. The momentum gained through these efforts set the stage for the movement to come above ground, targeting the industry at large, accomplished through a presence at a major industry trade show. The revolution was completed with a global conference, which finally brought all the players together. The web and email efforts were continued throughout the manifestation of the campaign to maintain a consistency and constancy in messaging and to keep up momentum between the live events.

1. The Premise

The premise of the campaign began as "The Big Lie". It challenged the developers' roles as designers of software. In reality, the software developer was the unsung hero that could shape the future. DSO was the vehicle through which the developers' untapped potential could be released. The aim was to have a grassroot, viral feel to the campaign – an underground revolution. The campaign started by recruiting the developers then moving outward and upward through the embedded systems industry at large, revolutionizing the way people think about the industry.

The campaign utilized many mediums for its physical manifestation. Every element of the campaign supported the overriding goal of the campaign, to gain industry acceptance of DSO, and each element played into and supported the other elements. The revolution was played out through email and web campaigns, trade shows and events. Every element of the campaign was infused with the revolutionary theme – from language used to the color scheme of the graphic elements to the look and feel of the media and every other element. This was not just a series of events, but rather a fully integrated marketing campaign.

2. The Call to Arms

The implementation of the revolution began with an email campaign in August 2004. Delphi was responsible for all of the creative direction of the email campaign and the corresponding direct mail campaign. The look and feel was consistent with the schematic concept created by Delphi for the Revolution. A third party implemented these elements of the campaign.

The email campaign consisted of banner ads, links sent to developers where they could find out more about DSO and email blasts to a targeted developer audience. The goal of this element of the campaign was to start to garner interest in DSO by the developer community. The messages in the emails were provocative teasers promoting DSO and the upcoming Regional Developers Conferences, the first live event.

The email campaign was a call to arms, the beginning of the viral campaign. The intent was to begin by targeting the developer community to play into the viral feel of the underground revolution. It was a bottom up implementation. Wind River needed the developers to see the benefits of DSO and to see it as a viable alternative to embedded systems before they could target the industry at large. In order to accomplish this, the developers needed to know that DSO was out there and then become educated about it.

The imagery used in the email campaign played off the idea of the "inner superhero" of the developer. They were more than developers of software; they were the unsung heroes. The idea was conveyed that the developers were suppressed by the status quo, but that Wind River could offer them liberation from the status quo through DSO. The revolution was the means to liberation.

3. The Cell Meetings

The email campaign was used to encourage participation in the Regional Developers Conferences that took place from September through December 2004 around the world. Through the links provided, the developers were able to register online for the conferences. In keeping with the feel of an underground revolution, the campaign started with these local conferences – cell meetings.

Delphi provided the creativity for the Regional Developers Conferences, including media, graphics and logo wear. Two sets of graphics, which traversed the world, were produced by Delphi. Logo wear was designed for wearing by the Wind River staff at the conferences, maintaining the revolutionary feel throughout.

There were eight Regional Developers Conferences held in 2004. They were held in Chicago, San Jose, CA, Boston, Dallas, Paris, Munich, Oxford and Tel Aviv. Each conference had between 100 and 250 attendees. The budget for each conference was in the 25,000-50,000 USD range. Unusual venues with a warehouse look and feel that supported the feeling of an underground movement were used whenever possible.

The "recruits", or developer attendees of the conferences, were given a task designation during the registration for the Regional Developers Conference. The task designations were made based on the recruit's role in the developer industry. Color-coded tags based on the task designation were used at the conferences to visually alert the recruits to their fellow task members. The seating was also color-coded, arranged in a circle. The circle was bordered by floor mounted banners featuring provocative slogans and images that suggested an underground resistance movement.

The messaging included such slogans as:

"You are not a line of code. Freedom is in the code."

"You are not a cog in the machine. Nothing is what it pretends to be."

"You are not a title on a business card. Your business card is irrelevant."

"You are not a box on an org chart. Who do you really work for?"

This messaging encouraged the developers to rethink their role in the industry. It underscored the idea that they are the ones that can make the revolution happen, they are the unsung hero. It provoked them to rethink the status quo and look outside the embedded systems box.

The recruits were told that they were part of a growing world-wide movement, that they had a great mission before them and that Wind River could arm them as they charged ahead, ready to take on the future. The conferences were used as a motivational and educational platform. Wind River presented their products that were the foundation for the DSO platform. They showed the problems facing the device software developers and the solutions that each product provided. There were in-depth product tracks that the recruits participated in to learn more about how the DSO platform could directly affect them.

At the end of the conferences, the recruits were given access to a message board where they could keep in touch with their fellow recruits and get logistical support from Wind River. The continued web campaign was in keeping with the viral feel of the revolution. It continued the momentum of the campaign and kept the buzz going and growing.

The goal of the Regional Developers Conferences was to create a buzz about DSO. Wind River was looking to start this buzz locally and then expand it globally. The conferences were successful in this as the underground movement was taking off.

4.   The Massing of the Troops

The next step of the campaign was to bring the movement above ground. This was done at the Embedded Systems Conference (ESC) 2005 in San Francisco in March 2005. DSO was announced to the industry at large. The primary structural elements of the booth were huge D S O letters, proclaiming its arrival on the device software scene.

Delphi fabricated the trade show booth for Wind River, each booth element keeping with the creative schema of the campaign. Media was produced by Delphi as well, integrated into the architecture of the booth. The budget for the booth was in the range of 175,000-250,000 USD.

The Wind River booth at ESC was used as a platform to promote the next event in the campaign, the World Wide Users Conference. Posters and other marketing collateral with the revolutionary look and feel were handed out to publicize the upcoming event. The idea was to pique the interest of ESC attendee about DSO and in turn, the World Wide Users Conference. The architecture of the booth was designed to promote this goal.

In the side of the giant letters, there were peepholes into which attendees could look. Through the peepholes, media clips could be viewed. The media was intended to be visually stimulating and tease people with what exactly DSO was. It was a fast paced piece with the images rapidly changing. Phrases such as "Faster", "Better", and "Increased Productivity" were interspersed throughout the piece, along with "DSO", hinting at what DSO is.

Other media was used in the booth as well. A piece promoting the World Wide Users Conference was created. It began with an image of a giant fist with "Don't just think outside the box" overlaid on it. The fist then broke through the words and "Destroy the Box" appeared on the screen. Details about the conference then followed, along with registration information.

Each of these media pieces supported the two parts of the goal respectively of Wind River's presence at ESC. Together, they supported an integrated experience in the booth that wrapped the two parts of the goal together. The peephole piece piqued interest in DSO and the "Destroy the Box" piece provided the information as to how the attendee could become part of the revolution.

The web, email and direct mail aspects of the campaign continued throughout. Their focus now shifted to promote the next piece of the revolution, the World Wide Users Conference. A website was set up for online registration for the event. Email blasts and direct mail were used to keep up the momentum of the revolution and to point the recipients to the registration site.

5. The Overthrow

Delphi provided all of the creative treatment and production for the World Wide Users Conference, including the structural elements, graphics, media, logo wear and overall look and feel. Delphi partnered with a destination management company for the registration, bookings, food, etc. The overall budget for the event portion only was in the 500,000 – 1 million USD range.

The World Wide Users Conference was a way to bring the regional movements of the revolution together. At this point, the revolution shifted from local movements to a global force. The conference positioned DSO as something that had a growing world wide following and was something to be reckoned with. It was "The Overthrow" of the embedded systems standard.

The World Wide Users Conference was held at a resort in Orlando, Florida in June 2005. It was a three day event including group sessions and track sessions, with more in depth product focuses. Wind River broadened the scope of its target audience for the conference, moving toward a strong emphasis on recruiting c-level executives and partner companies along with the developer community. There was a higher level focus of the messaging at the conference than at the Regional Developers Conferences. The original aim was to recruit 1,000 attendees. There were about 450 attendees in actuality, with about 30 partner companies.

The recruitment of partner companies was critical to the success of the conference. The partners were paying sponsors for the event, funding it through the revenue generated. Three sponsorship levels were implemented – Platinum, Gold and Silver. There was a sliding cost scale for participation based on the sponsorship level chosen. The sponsorship level determined the placement and prominence of the partner company on the promotion material for the conference. A "Partner Pavilion" was set up at the conference with the sponsorship level of a partner company determining the size and placement of their booth space in the pavilion. The selling point for the partner companies was the access to the attendees to market their products and services that the Partner Pavilion afforded them.

Wind River intended to use the conference to promote its products and services, generate leads and drive revenue and build relationships with the developer community, especially on the executive level, and with partner companies. The conference was a platform for Wind River to position itself as the industry leader of Device Software Optimization.

At this point, the revolution shifted from a philosophical movement to a practical solution. The conference was a venue in which Wind River could promote the practical ways that DSO could alter the embedded systems landscape. The messaging reinforced the idea that traditional notions of device software development must be defied and the long-help assumptions about the role of the developers in their companies summarily rejected and revised – the box must be destroyed. This was symbolically accomplished at the kick-off of the conference when the Chief Marketing Officer of Wind River literally smashed through the box onto the stage. With sledge hammer in hand, he proceeded to destroy the box. Yet throughout the conference, there was also a transition to messaging that positioned DSO as the road to rebuilding the software design infrastructure in a radical, practical new way.

The World Wide Users Conference spurred the momentum of the revolution on an industry-wide basis. The revolutionary work had been done and there was growing acceptance of DSO in the embedded systems industry. The DSO Revolution had taken hold.

6. The Measurements of Success

From this point forward, the purpose of the continuation in the spirit of the campaign was to continue to concrete DSO's place in the industry and Wind River's place as the DSO leader. Wind River is continuing to use the tools utilized in the DSO Revolution campaign – events, trade shows and web efforts – to further DSO. Delphi has continued to provide direction and implementation resources for the ongoing efforts. The results of the ongoing efforts all point toward the success of the Revolution in achieving its goal of cementing DSO's place in the device software industry.

6.1 Increased Conference Attendance

Regional Developers Conferences were held locally again throughout 2005-2006. This series of conferences expanded from eight in the previous series to twelve. The conferences this time expanded into Asia, as well as maintaining a presence in the other regions where conferences had been held in 2004. The attendance of the conferences doubled to the 2004 series.

A second annual World Wide Users Conference was held in 2006, paving the way for it to become an annual event. The attendance of this conference doubled as well. The partner companies rose from 30 in number in 2005 to 40 partners in 2006. This was a complete sell-out of the sponsorship slots available.

These increases in attendance year to year exemplify that there was a learning process involved in recruitment methods for these events. But the lessons were learned and strategies adjusted. The increases also point to the growing acceptance of DSO in the industry.

6.2 DSO World

At the Embedded Systems Conference 2006, Wind River partnered with the show organizer to host a venue where companies with a vested interest in DSO could come together to educate the industry about DSO. This was called DSO World. Participating companies each had their own area in DSO World. There was a central theater that was used for scheduled presentations by the participants. A coffee bar was set up as a place where the presentations could be viewed and, while there were not presentations going on, the attendees could network and interact with other attendees. It created an environment where the DSO buzz could continue its "viral" expansion.

DSO World was set up to be a show within a show. The architecture of the booth was intended to give the attendee the feeling that they were stepping off the show floor and into another world when they entered the booth. Fabric structures enclosed the booth, sectioning it off from the rest of the show floor. It was a movement out of the embedded systems world of the rest of the show and into the world of DSO, in keeping with the goal of the DSO Revolution. It was a sort of turn away from the old standard of embedded systems toward the new solution of DSO.

DSO World at ESC 2006 indicated the beginning of the industry acceptance of DSO. Wind River is now working with the show management company for ESC to possibly change the show name to DSO for future shows. This is indicative of the level of acceptance DSO has attained in the industry.

6.3 Incorporation of DSO in the Industry Landscape

The Gartner Group, a technology industry analyst organization, has accepted DSO as an emerging business category and has predicted it, in their hype cycle, to continue its forward momentum and become a major industry player. DSO.com, a website dedicated to exploring trends in the device software industry, was launched by a publishing company. Competitors of Wind River are now using DSO language on their marketing materials and websites. DSO has become a device software industry reality.

7. Conclusion

Delphi looked outside the box to create an in your face, integrated marketing campaign. A series of events was utilized to create a movement. Each element of the campaign was a progression toward the overall goal of the campaign, while still maintaining a consistency in the look and feel and keeping with the schematic creative concept of the campaign. The various manifestations were not stand-alone elements but rather a part of an overarching campaign, aiming toward a higher level objective. All of these elements came together to create a marketing campaign that successfully accomplished its overall goal of launching a new business category.

How a Perfect Storm Created Spectacular Success

Joe Goldblatt

"That ceremony was the moment the world began to understand how modern and dynamic Greece had become and how extraordinary the Athens's Games were going to be. We aimed to show the world the new face of Greece this summer, thanks to you we did."[41]

A "perfect storm" was rapidly developing in the United States during the early part of 2001. Three years later, one organization was at the center of the perfect storm as it reached the apex of its 60plus year history by producing the opening and closing ceremonies of the Athens, Greece Summer Olympic Games.

The largest television audience in history, estimated to be 1.5 billion people around the world, viewed these magnificent ceremonies that, as their client stated, "showed the new face of Greece to the world."

How did this organization not only survive the perfect storm but also achieve what many journalists described as "the miracle in Greece"? The short answer is that they discovered and used a business secret far more powerful than the ancient oracle in Delphi. This article strives to reveal the secret of their success and shows how to sustain and grow similar success for an event organization and produce the deserved outcomes.

---

41 Gianna Angelopouos-Daskalaki, President Athens Committee for the Olympic Games (2004)

1.   Event = Outcome

The term event is derived from the Latin term, "E-venire". "E" means "out" and "venire" means "come". Therefore, the term event literally means outcome.

The championship organization and its successful and valuable products and services are the outcomes of hundreds of thousands of micro and macro events. Today's and tomorrow's leaders must precisely plan and flawlessly execute these events to produce sustainable outcomes for their organizations.

2.   A Producer is a Leader

The management-model used by the Athens Olympic Games Opening Ceremony event-production company Jack Morton Worldwide is called The Olympic Achievement. It demonstrates step by step how you can become a more effective producer/leader and how your organization can use the same tactics employed by the producers of the Olympic Games Opening and Closing Ceremonies to achieve unprecedented success for your very own organization. Both special events and all types of organizations require similar processes to achieve their full potential.

In fact, every championship organization is the ultimate result of many successfully produced individual events.

According to our research, the process of organizational self-actualization (similar to Maslow's Hierarchy of Needs: physiological, safety, love, esteem, and ultimately self-actualization) is a direct result of many individual events or outcomes that were achieved individually by utilizing a unique system comprised of six rings of influence. The Olympic Achievement is formed by eight distinct phases or rings and within each ring there is a specific process that may be used to achieve success. Figure 14 demonstrates how the Olympic Achievement applies to both spectacular events and organizations.

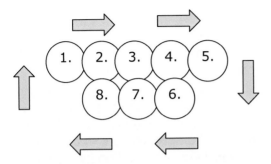

Figure 21: The Producer's Eight Rings of Olympic Achievement model
(Goldblatt/Morton)

Key:

1. Strategic Planning and Management
2. Human Resource Facilitation
3. Financial Control and Management
4. Risk Assessment and Management
5. Strategic Marketing
6. Create the Event
7. Orchestrate the Event
8. Continuous Professional Development

Special event producers as well as leaders of small and large businesses have discovered that the same system to produce major events such as the Olympic Games can also insure the success of every sized organization. Bill Morton, now chairman of the firm founded by his father 64 years ago, recalls how he discovered the secrets to Olympic Achievement and how it helped his business not just to survive, but to stabilize and ultimately thrive.

When Bill Morton was president and CEO of Jack Morton Worldwide, he experienced "the perfect storm" between January 1 and December 31, 2001. According to Morton, "the combination of an increasingly slow U.S. economy, the tragedies of September 11, 2001, and the impending acquisition of our largest competitor

(Caribener) combined to produce a strong undertow." Morton often uses the analogy of sailing to describe his role as captain of the firm that was created by his father in the 1920s. "My associates counted on me to get them through the storm", is how Bill Morton describes his approach to this perilous time.

So how did Morton and his leadership team get his firm through the perfect storm and go on to not only produce the Olympic Games Opening and Closing Ceremonies but also become the most successful organization of their kind in the world? The answer, according to Morton, and later verified by his team, and further validated by hundreds of interviews with successful leaders, is encapsulated in one phrase: "steady as she goes."

The phrase "steady as she goes" does not appear in most business school textbooks. However, a fundamental truth of all organizations is that without stable leadership, as exemplified by Morton, there is little incentive for anyone to show up for work and much less incentive to follow them.

Strategic vision is important for the leader to demonstrate; however steadiness of purpose is critical to long term success. This is especially important during challenging times such as the perfect storm experienced by Morton. These eight ovals are the critical phases for developing and producing special events. Our research and professional experiences further confirms that these same eight rings develop and produce successful organizations. So, how do you become a producer of individual, seeming separate events that when linked together, produce high achieving, championship organizations?

Whether you are planning a simple meeting or running the entire organization, the strategies and tactics for sustainable success are identical. For example, when producing the Athens, Greece Olympic Games Opening and Closing Ceremonies, Bill Morton's leaders faced what appeared to be insurmountable obstacles. Similar to starting, growing and sustaining a business enterprise, the producers of the ceremonies encountered the following six expectations:

1. The expectation of creating and delivering the brand promise of Greece before billions of people worldwide.
2. The expectation of assembling and training a diverse workforce in record time in record time.
3. The expectation of creating a process for managing this project on time and within budget.
4. The expectation of developing a project management system that was both efficient and flawless.
5. The expectation of producing a high quality, high value product.
6. The expectation of producing a profit for their organization.

Every organization faces similar expectations from their owners, employees, stockholders, stakeholders, and customers. The individual event must first define or align with the sponsor's mission and vision before the brand promise may be crafted and delivered. Indeed, every organization's success is the direct result of hundreds or perhaps thousands of daily events that must be researched, designed, planned, coordinated, and evaluated.

During the period when Jack Morton Worldwide was in the process of acquiring its largest competitor, Caribener, Bill Morton recognized that his firm would soon be faced with nearly 700 potential new employees. Morton and his father before him recognized that, first and foremost, their firm was in the people business. However, he needed greater expertise than he possessed to manage this critical transition. His colleague, Josh McCall, suggested retaining the Hay Group, a leading consulting firm with expertise in human resource planning. Morton, therefore, combined his passion for people with the expertise of the Hay Organization to produce a successful outcome. As a direct result of this event, one of the Hay Group executives became the first director of human resources for Jack Morton Worldwide – a further example of sustainable event outcomes.

Leaders of large organizations such as Bill Morton, as well as the small yet equally complex organizations and producers of both large and small events, can consistently produce successful and sustainable outcomes if they integrate these eight powerful factors.

The Athens Olympic Games Opening Ceremony was an event that produced a successful and sustainable outcome for the Athens Committee for the Olympic Games and the entire Greek nation. Table 4 demonstrates the six phase process used by Morton to produce a successful and sustainable outcome.

Phases	Special Events	Your Organization
1. Research	Identify the purpose, audience(s), and strategic goals/objectives.	Identify (purpose) mission/vision, (audience) market, and strategic goals/objectives
2. Design	Creative process to brainstorm possible solutions to achieve the event's strategic goals/objectives.	Creative process to brainstorm (solutions) approaches to achieve the organization's strategic goals/objectives.
3. Planning	Linking the design ideas with the appropriate tactics to align the audience with the event.	Linking the various (solutions) approaches to align the (audience) market with the product/service (event).
4. Coordination	Flawlessly executing every element to precisely achieve the strategic goals/objectives.	Flawlessly executing every element to precisely achieve the strategic goals/objectives.
5. Evaluation	Comprehensive review and analysis of the entire event process to promote continuous improvement.	Comprehensive review and analysis of the entire development and delivery (event) process to promote continuous improvement.
6. Re-invention	Continuous monitoring of trends and audience (market) needs to insure refreshment and currency of event (product/service).	Continuous monitoring of trends and audience (market) needs to insure refreshment and currency of event (product/service).

Table 5: Phases of event and organizational production

The language may be slightly different, but the outcomes are the same: successful, sustainable and current events/products/services and organizations. Currency is an important goal for every event and organization as it insures that the event or product/service is meeting the needs of today and tomorrow's audience (market).

3.   Finding a Universal Language

The International Olympic Committee (IOC) recognizes the critical importance of a universal language and has historically recognized the critical values of the Olympic Games Movement as Citius (swifter), Altius (higher), and Fortius (stronger). Both athletic champions and championship organizations embrace these values to sustain and grow their success throughout the future.

For example, research processes and projects must be conducted swiftly to meet profit expectations for stockholders. The brand promise and the people who live the brand's core values must aim higher and higher to continuously earn the loyalty of their customers. The product and resulting profits must grow stronger over time to ensure a fair return for the investors.

Whether you are competing for an Olympic Games gold medal or a competing to build a financial empire, your ability to aim higher, move more swiftly, and strengthen your next performance will ultimately determine your level of success. Furthermore, your ability to thoroughly implement the Olympic Achievement will ultimately determine how long you can sustain your success in the future.

Legendary event producers such as Jack Morton Worldwide, great athletes such as Tiger Woods and respected business leaders such as General Electric's Jack Welch each recognize that a useful system is essential for long term success. The Six Sigma® system that was successfully implemented by Welch at General Electric has now evolved to the next level through the Olympic Achievement.

According to Welch and other successful leaders, the ability to develop candor within organizations is one of the key elements that supports a culture of openness, respect, and profitability.

The uniqueness of the Olympic Achievement is its intrinsic relationship to the Olympic Movement itself. Therefore, The Olympic Achievement does use the same proven theories, strategies, and tactics of the planners of the world's most complex sports event to drive your organizations future success.

This book transcends Six Sigma® and, therefore, will help your organization reach a higher level of sustainable performance.

4. Storm Systems & Solutions

From the Coca Cola Company's re-branding debacle with "New" Coke to the recent stockholders revolt within the Walt Disney Company, organizations continually encounter storm systems comprised of weakening economies, internal challenges, and exogenous shocks. Successful organizational leaders practice what Bill Morton describes as a "steady as you go" mentality to demonstrate to the stakeholders that the leader will indeed help get them through the storm. The implementation and widespread adoption of a leadership system is the paramount way that organizations achieve the stability and agility they need to not only survive but also thrive during stormy weather.

4.1 Research

Research and evaluation are intrinsically related. The evaluation of the last product or event becomes the first research that is collected for future developments. Research requires the commitment of the Olympic Games value of Altius (higher) to continually strive to improve the quality of research and evaluation to produce sustainable events and organizations.

In 1993 SAMSUNG Corporation re-branded its organization with a new logo/identity. The purposes of the new identity were "to strengthen competitiveness by bringing the attitudes and behavior of all employees in line with SAMSUNG's desired perception by the public. SAMSUNG's corporate logo was redefined to project SAMSUNG's firm determination to become a world leader." (SAMSUNG Corporate Identity, 2005)

The research for this brand promise aligns the attitudes and behavior of all employees with the desired perception by the public. Furthermore, the brand promise must also express the aspirations of the organization and is similar to the vision statement.

The International Olympic Committee (IOC) brand promise is best expressed through the values of Olympism, which is described by the IOC as a "state of mind", (IOC, 2005). According to IOC leaders, both hardware and sportsmanship are part of this state of mind.

One of the greatest and most rare medals in the Olympic Movement is not made of gold, but rather is a simple metal bolt. On a bitter cold afternoon at the 1964 Olympic Winter Games, during the two man bobsled competition, the British team completed its first race and was now in second place. Upon finishing the race they discovered that they had broken the key bolt on their rear axle, which in essence eliminated them from the competition.

The Italian team leader discovered the plight of the British bobsled team and removed a bolt from his sled and sent it to them so they could continue in the competition. The British competed again and went on to win the gold medal while the Italians took the bronze.

When asked if his unselfish act helped the British team to win the gold medal the Italian team leader said, "The bolt did not win the race. The British won because today they are the best in the world."

This genuine act of unselfish sportsmanship prompted the creation of a new Olympic Games medal that was named after the founder of the modern Olympic Games, Baron DeCoubetin.

The DeCoubertin medal is the noblest honor an Olympian may earn, and the Italians were the first to receive this honor. And it is the most precious medal/hardware any Olympian may possess. (IOC, 2005)

The use of the PRISM analogy is useful when conducting comprehensive research. A prism is designed to refract or disperse a beam of light. Comprehensive research should also result in refraction (break open) and dispersion (scattering) of valid information that may be transformed into knowledge.

One way to achieve this is through the use of a *PRISM* (*Precise Response Insures Successful Measurement*) process as shown in Figure 15. Through the use of the *PRISM,* the event producer or organizational leader is able to conduct a 360 degree analysis of the problem to identify a wide range of potential solutions.

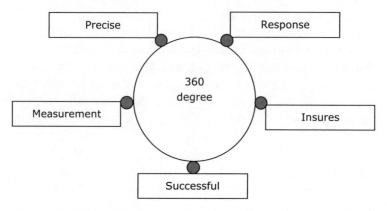

Figure 22: P R I S M

This is an example of higher performance through improved research and evaluation. Whether racing to win the event or to bring your product to market, careful evaluation and research will help your organization move to a higher level.

4.2 Design

Design and reinvention both require a creative process. Leading organizations such as the Olympic Games value creativity and innovation as a core competency. Therefore, the design process for your event, as exemplified by the brand promise, is ultimately the result of the passion and commitment people have for their organization's mission, vision, and values. Events often are driven by both professional staff and volunteers. Each group of stakeholders is motivated by different ideals. The 50,000 volunteers of the 2000 Sydney, Australia, Olympic Games were primarily motivated by a sense of pride that the Olympic Games were returning to Australia and in fact, many of the volunteers were alumni from the previous Summer Games in Melbourne. Through careful recruitment, passionate orientation sessions, detailed training, and ample rewards, the people of the 2000 Sydney Summer Olympic Games exemplified and extended the brand promise during and beyond the games themselves. Ultimately their creativity reinvented the games, which were later hailed by the media as, "the best games ever."

4.3 Planning

Planning and coordination are linked just as research and evaluation are. The coordination of the event or organization tasks must track with the strategic plan. Without a strategic planning process, the event or organization will not have central guidance and therefore may never achieve their goals. Conversely, if the coordination process does not follow the plan, errors or omissions may occur that will prevent flawless execution of the plan.

Therefore, every organization requires a process to insure that progress is achieved. In fact, the term process is derived from the Latin word procedure that means "forward and to go." Policies and procedures should not be inhibitors; rather, they should provide momentum to help the organization advance forward in an efficient manner.

In the case of the International Olympic Committee, the Olympic Games Knowledge Management System (OGKS) provides a process that organizers of the Olympic Games may use to develop the projects they are tasked with leading. The OGKS was developed by the Australians in the late 1990s as a systematic process to document the tasks required for developing and delivering the Sydney Games. This documentation enabled Sydney to transmit their knowledge to Greece so that they could benefit from the accumulated wisdom of collected in Australia.

Similarly, Dr. Clark Hu of Temple University in Philadelphia, Pennsylvania, in collaboration with the International Festivals and Events Association (IFEA), has developed an online knowledge management system to promote safety at festivals and events. The eSAFE system provides event organizers with access to expert knowledge and content experts to advise them in how to increase the safety and risk management factors for their events.

4.4 Coordination

Coordination of millions of tasks performed by thousands of personnel is just one of the many challenges of producing the Olympic Games. A system is required for this massive undertaking and that system is based upon a relatively new science: Project Management.

Project management has become, in the past 25 years, an accepted practice for leading organizations throughout the world. The thousands of members of the Project Management Institute and those who are Certified Associates in Project Management (CAPM) will testify to the necessity and widespread acceptance of this in hundreds of different business operations.

From the identification of the project leader to the closeout of the project, there are specific steps that the members of the project team must follow to successfully complete the scope of work. The following eight steps in Project Management are generally accepted as the pathway that is followed to generate successful project outcomes.

1. Appointment of project leader
2. Draft and acceptance of project charter
3. Definition of scope of work
4. Initiation of project
5. Tasks and sub-tasks needed for completion
6. Identification of milestones recognizing completion of a series of tasks and subtasks
7. Close-out of project
8. Endpoint of project

The Athens Opening and Closing Ceremonies utilized a Project Management system similar to the eight steps enumerated above to manage this complex series of events. Whether constructing a new building, designing a new product or service, or producing the world's most complex sports event, Project Management provides a control system that enables the project team to arrive at their final destination on time and within budget.

4.5 Evaluation

As the partner of research, careful and systematic evaluation enables the event or organization leader to collect and analyze the outcome of the goods and services they have produced.

Goods and services are both products in the mind of the consumer. Whether you are providing consulting services or manufacturing widgets for mass consumption, both are seen by the customer as end products of the brand promise, people, process, and project management. To ensure consistent quality of service and product development, the organization's leader must monitor the creation and delivery to guarantee the customers' expectations are not only satisfied but exceeded.

Fred Stein, president of The Creative Group, was the producer of the Bi-Centennial of the U.S. Constitution Celebration. Stein states that his product is "emotion." "My reason for being is to create emotional responses from the audience. During the event, I monitor the emotional triggers or cues I have embedded in the script to ensure the audience is reacting appropriately."

David Wolper, producer of the 1984 Summer Olympic Games in Los Angeles, concurs with Stein and adds, "As a producer, my product is the reaction of the audience. I must deliver that response."

The Jack Morton Worldwide slogan is "The experience to inspire."

According to Chairman Bill Morton, "Our slogan informs future customers that we have sufficient experience to inspire their audience to perform the action they desire."

In today's cluttered media environment, a product may only break through when it connects on a visceral level with a consumer. In fact, Pine and Gilmore state in The Experience Economy (2000) "commodities become increasingly more valuable when they are layered with experiences." They further state that "you are what you charge for." This suggests that manufacturers and service providers may charge a premium for their products and services if they provide an experience or in some measurable way transform the customer's life.

4.6 Reinvention

The best way to continually grow profits is through continuous event or product/service development. The former president of The Walt Disney Company Cruise Line was asked, "What comes first, people or profits?" Nick Rago, now president of Consultants to Management in Scottsdale, Arizona answered bluntly: "Profits. For if there are no profits, there will be no hope, and if there is no hope, soon there will be no people." The brand promise, the people, the process, projects, and products should naturally result in a strong profit for the organization that masters the Olympic Achievement.

In fact, the Olympic Achievement is in actuality inverted. As the author Stephen Covey suggests, highly effective people and the organizations they lead always begin with "the end in mind." Therefore, if your goal is to drive profits through reinvention, the outcomes derived from research, design, planning, coordination, and evaluation are both natural and normal.

Reinvention is best achieved through maintaining strong focus. The term focus may appear to be restrictive to creative entrepreneurs or other organization leaders. However, creative firms such as Jack Morton Worldwide and The Walt Disney Company maintain strong focus to achieve the strategic goals and objectives. Disney, for instance, is one of the few global corporations to have an appointed a Vice President for Synergy. This leader's sole business function is to synergize all of the Disney business units to strengthen the brand when a new product is developed or launched. An entertainment property such as The Lion King® may produce greater profits if all of the revenue centers work together. Therefore, this property is designed to not only produce profits from ticket sales but also licensing fees, retail sales, amusement park gate admissions, and many other revenue streams.

Firms such as Jack Morton Worldwide have continually reinvented themselves while at the same time maintaining strong internal and external focus. This process of **FOCUS** is best described as *Future Opportunities Cultivate Unlimited Success*. Every producer and organizational leader must continually ask, "How can I best leverage this event, product, or service to maximize revenue through continuous reinvention?"

The process of focused reinvention enables the brand, the product and indeed the company to remain current by anticipating and monitoring the current and future needs of the marketplace. The currency of your event or organization will ultimately determine its sustainability. Through aligning continuous reinvention with a strong internal and external focus, you are better able to anticipate and meet the ever-changing needs of the global marketplace.

When all six phases are carefully aligned with the Olympic Games values of Altius, Fortius, and Citius, successful organizations profit not only financially but also in a more spiritually compelling manner. Our research has proven over and over again, those organizations that cultivate and transmit these values are the ones that not only succeed but also endure. Furthermore, the pathway to this success is paved with events or outcomes from your research, planning, coordination, evaluation, and reinvention.

When asked why she agreed to join Jack Morton Worldwide after they acquired her firm (Caribener), the international President who supervised the Athens's Olympic Games Opening and Closing Ceremonies, stated, "I believed in Bill Morton. I had known him for many years and he consistently demonstrated the business acumen and creative passion to lead the business." She further stated that, in her opinion, leadership is not only about hope, it is also about performance. "Bill and his team performed day after day, year after year in a stable and yet forward moving manner and I suppose that cultivates a sense of hope within those who choose to follow him."

5. How Eight Ovals Made the Olympic Games Rings Burn Even Brighter

During the opening ceremonies of the Athens Olympic Games, the producers created a fiery image of the Olympic Games rings in the center of a large body of water. The heat from the five rings could be felt throughout the Olympic Stadium. However, this image and hundreds more were the result of the power of eight ovals that reflected strategic planning and management, facilitation of human resources, financial control and management, strategic marketing, creation of the event, orchestration of the event and continuous professional development.

For over 100 years the modern Olympic Games have featured opening and closing ceremonies. The producers at Jack Morton Worldwide carefully analyzed these ceremonies as well as the values of the Olympic Movement prior to producing the events for Athens. The design process included inputs from not only the artistic staff, but also from a wide variety of stakeholders. The planning required precise timing so the production would be delivered on time and within budget. The coordination was extremely complex and included rehearsals in Great Britain for effects that would later be produced in Athens. The various elements of the production were evaluated during the rehearsal process as well as at the conclusion of the ceremonies to transfer the lessons learned to their next major event. Finally, the Athens Olympic Games not only reinvented the staging practices for the opening ceremonies, but also reinvented the overall perception of the client, the nation of Greece. Described in a public poll as "the most memorable ceremonies ever produced," the producers achieved their goal of creating new and enduringly positive images of Greece. They accomplished this lofty goal through application of the eight rings and a process known as triangulation.

6.   Triangulation Creates Motivation

The cast (employees), company (community), and audience (customers) comprise a triangle that transmits the core values of the organization. Without triangulation, the organization cannot prosper. For example, Jack Morton Worldwide's values of passion, agility, and respect are transmitted to each of their employees, the community at large and to their current and future customers. This is achieved through a strategically designed human resource development process and a visceral communications plan.

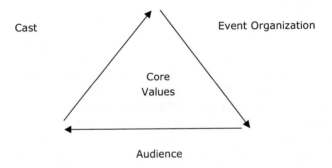

Figure 23: Triangulation: cast, company and audience

When you implement the six phases and transmit core values to your cast, community, and audience, you can lead your organization from one championship outcome to another. Whether you aspire to produce the Olympic Games or to manage any successful business venture, now, for the first time, you are about to discover the Olympic Parallel that will enable you to move more swiftly (Citius), go higher (Altius), and ultimately to produce stronger outcomes (Fortius).

7.   SWATCH® Goes Swifter, Higher and Stronger

During the Athens Olympic Games, SWATCH® created a unique museum in the center of Athens on a busy street. This streetscape generated hundreds of thousands of potential SWATCH®

customers as they explored the numerous ways SWATCH® products have been integrated into popular culture. This street marketing approach created millions of photo opportunities and impressions and perhaps most importantly, millions of dollars of future new sales for SWATCH®.

8. Disney's America in Search of a PRISM

When conducting research for a new amusement park entitled "Disney's America" in Prince William County, a suburb of Washington DC, the Disney

Organization conducted extensive research. However, because they failed to use the PRISM research approach, their project ultimately failed. Disney had intended to build a new park that would promote American history. Disney conducted quantitative research such as real estate studies; however, they failed to get the precise results that would insure their success. The precise results would have come from ethnographic (participant/observer) research methodology to determine the level of resistance by the local citizenry to the new project. By missing this refraction from their research, they were not able to disseminate the precise results that would insure their success.

9. Producing Your Future

The perfect storm that earlier enveloped the co-author of this book in dark clouds, ultimately revealed a fundamental truth that now provides you with a powerful and essential navigational tool to promote future success. Through any storm, you can overcome the economic forces, internal changes, and external shocks by adopting and adapting the power of the six phases to create the outcome you desire.

Your stable and consistent performance during times of turbulence demonstrates not only confidence but also, and most importantly, provides hope for those who join your voyage.

Rotterdam – Maximizing City Event Partnership

Johan Moerman

1.   Rotterdam

Rotterdam was never a typical tourist destination. It's not like Paris; it doesn't look like Venice or Seville. Above all Rotterdam has always been a port city with people that are straightforward. Not interested in building palaces but in quays, warehouses and ships. Quays where you could smell the sea and the rest of the world: spices from Bombay or Batavia. Lemons and bananas from Africa, coal from Germany, leaven, oil, jute …..

Sixty years ago the centre of Rotterdam became a wasteland. Like so many other cities in Europe Rotterdam suffered deeply from the Second World War. The inner city was bombed and completely destroyed. After this war there were no more houses left, no shops, no cinemas, no theatres and only one museum.

From this wasteland a new city emerged. Had to emerge, for there was no time to waste and because it was and is the Rotterdam mentality to move fast. In the 1950s the city council concentrated on rebuilding the port and building houses for the people that worked there. Rotterdam became the biggest port in the world in 1960, but only after the housing problems were solved – at the end of the 60s – the city started to invest in a new concert hall. A temporary theatre, built with bricks that were found in the streets of the destroyed inner city, remained to function until the 80s of the last century.

2. Festivals and Events

In a city with an incomplete cultural infrastructure festivals were able to flourish. In a city without palaces the tents were brought in. Like ships that only need a quay to enter the port, do what they have to do and leave again. Flexible and full of energy.

The first post-war festivals were not only important because there was so little else to do in the rest of the year, but also as experimenting spaces for the development of the cultural sector. They successfully explored and developed new forms of presenting culture and drew the attention of the public to new developed areas.

Later in the 1970s when quality of life became more and more important, festivals were the first examples of the expansion of cultural life. Many festivals that are still around today have their origin in that decade, often with an international perspective like critically acclaimed festivals like Film International Rotterdam and Poetry International Rotterdam.

The city, although very supportive, was not getting the best out of its festivals; there was no event policy, no coordination. No real idea of what could be possible. Funds were divided across different departments and this restricted further growth. Above all it was difficult for festival and event organizers to deal with all those different institutions and unclear conditions. This could be organized better, in order to get better results than so far.

This was not an uncommon situation in the rest of the world either...

3. A Sideline: the Industry, Fragmented but Full of Opportunities

In many large cities, government policy for events was and is non-existing or at least fragmented.

It is a hassle for organizers who complain about the many different agencies they have to deal with and the unclear criteria for getting permits. Of course growth is limited by this fragmentation; in Rotterdam we realized that more was possible than was being done.

We should all realize that I am talking about a young, fragmented industry. Many events are organized by small, vulnerable organizations operating at the limits of their abilities, without staff and financial reserves. Subsidized agencies, volunteer organizations that get things off the ground with much dedication and enthusiasm, small town tourism boards and private businesspeople that try to earn a living producing events.

Due to their scale, and I'm afraid also their origins, they have not always been able to develop sound marketing knowledge or business savvy. And the lack of it thwarts the growth of the industry and the businesspeople working in it. It's evident that the demands placed on private organizers by the unavoidable commercialization and scale expansion are changing drastically.

Simply calling for scale expansion is too easy. A different scale would, it is true, create more space for professionalisation, but it also has several inherent hazards. The vitality and spirit of the industry are also contained in the origin of all these little clubs. It comes from the grass roots, it has a clear link of what is going on in the city, and it has enthusiasm and popular support.

Many important and big events have emerged from the sheer will of a small group of volunteers, or – even more limited – one lonely pioneer who followed his own dream. And the power that exudes from those people's enthusiasm cannot be simply replaced by the first marketing manager to come along.

We cannot simply do a survey, ask tourists their wishes and develop an event that is successful on the tourist market. Most successful festivals have their origin in another goal.

Most of them started as local parties. Cleverly 'used' their economic effects and slowly grew bigger and better. As a result of that they became important for people from other cities as well. When we are talking about the development of our industry we have to realize that the soul, the power and the success of most events has its origin in the culture, in the close connection with the people of a town or even a village.

The most significant challenge for the industry is to maintain the enthusiasm of the local festival organizers, their vitality, their connection with their origin, with their city and the culture of a country, and at the same time see to it that the best initiators, with the best opportunities, grow to become effective, professional, market-oriented organizations that work on a national or even international scale.

4. And Back to Rotterdam...

Rotterdam had the luck of a small disaster that speeded up the developments. In 1990 the city celebrated its 650th birthday. It was not a success. Many civil servants threw themselves enthusiastically into this attractive subject, did not take the wishes of their audience as a starting point, but their own dreams and hobbies. They acted as event organizers and realized too late that organizing events had become a real profession.

But it was the start of something else, something better. Several government agencies saw it as a chance, broke down the walls between them and drafted a common festival-policy with clear targets. In order to achieve that policy a clear distinction between the makers of city policy and event organizers was needed. Rotterdam Festivals was set up at some distance from the government to gain speed and strength.

Rotterdam Festivals: FACTS & FIGURES (from 2006)

Rotterdam Festivals co-ordinates the city's events policy and facilitates a number of audience development activities in the cultural sector. Working for the municipality of Rotterdam, but operating between government, audiences and organisers, it brings together the interests of the city, initiatives by organisers and institutions and the wishes of a continually changing public.

Average government support	EUR 3,500,000
Average total budget	EUR 5,000,000
Festival costs	80%
Marketing	10%
Office, indirect costs	10%
Estimated amount of visitor's	2,400,000
Average Number of Events	50

Table 6: Overview on Rotterdam Festivals

Rotterdam Festivals is responsible for the city's event policy, with the exception of sport events. Operating somewhere between the market and the government, RF tries not to produce too many events itself. We think the best way of realizing good events is to use the initiative of the knowledge of all the institutions and producers in town. Rotterdam Festivals encourages people, organise courses, analyse audiences, contribute to marketing experiments, threaten and, if there is no choice, guide using its funds. At the same time it aims to get the most out of it for the city as a whole. This coordination centre is also the collective memory of the festival city Rotterdam.

Now what does that mean for the way we work in every day life? Basically we operate like an intermediate bringing together:
- the goals of the city,
- people with ideas and initiative: festival producers, cultural institutions
- and audiences.

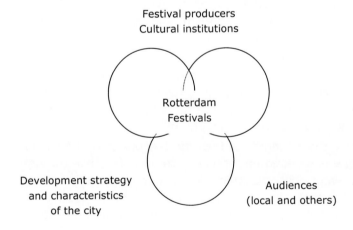

Festival producers
Cultural institutions

Rotterdam
Festivals

Development strategy
and characteristics
of the city

Audiences
(local and others)

Figure 24: Elements

4.1 Events and the City

We strongly believe that events should be connected with the goals and characteristics of the city they are held in. It is good for the city but it can also provide an answer to the increasing growth of events that are without identity, literally senseless and thus superfluous.

As long as a city can organize the Olympics or successfully claims to have one of the top marathons or film festivals in the world (like Rotterdam does), it is not all that bad. But what about the 34th country and western festival of the year or the umpteenth French day? Has it not become a bit much and, especially, a bit much of the same?

Given the internationalization we are facing today there is a risk that festivals will follow the example of television in the western world. There are hundreds of channels, but they all look the same. If festivals develop in the same direction the result will be an enormous 'entertainment inflation', with negative ramifications in the not-too-distant future for both the cultural and economic effect of festivals. That would not benefit the public, or the level of culture, or the development of tourism, and so we all have an interest in making room in policy for concepts such as originality, authenticity and uniqueness.

If, in doing so, we put the city or the country itself first, as the jumping-off point for our thinking, a common denominator emerges so that events can be more than pig-fries and can make an actual contribution to the development and profile of the city.

We look for the strengths of the city, the places and developments the city is working on, and call attention to those through events. The events become more closely tied to the city and acquire a special character that makes them more appealing not only to the city population but also to people outside of the city.

For Rotterdam it means that we prefer festivals with a young, modern and international atmosphere. We choose a tropical Summer Carnival above a tulip parade, an international event about modern architecture above events about the history of the city and a dance parade, where ten thousands of young people dance in the streets, above traditional clog dancing.

4.2   Festivals and Their Audiences

A lot of things have already been said about the importance of events for tourism. Many cities develop events with foreign tourists as the first target group in mind. Many cities copy successful events from somewhere else. They won't be very loyal customers.

Not taking the local people into account would be a great mistake. Most locals don't like the idea that their city is taken over by foreigners that look for some entertainment, but are not really interested in their city and their culture. And if the locals don't like the event it will be a lot harder to be successful: when the taxi driver or the maid in the hotel room doesn't like it – why should tourists?

We have concentrated on Rotterdam and the 'Rotterdammers' in the first place and discovered that precisely that makes us different and interesting for people from other places.

4.3   Events and Initiative

A lot of event coordinators, tourist boards or mayor' offices develop their own events from idea to evaluation.

Rotterdam Festivals never aimed to do all the work. We want to be better then we are and use all the available ideas and energy in the city. The most important question we have to ask ourselves is how we can link the enormous potential and expertise in the city with the objectives the city has formulated for itself.

We believe in the power of the creative class: artists, cultural institutions, festival organizers. They know what's going on, have the ideas and can mobilize the power that is needed to realize a successful event.

It can be useful to have help from the outside the city – we do it often – but we should not forget that in every city there are local organizers who know what the city is about and who have ideas that are connected with the city. We don't tell them what to do, we give them an overview of the areas and the subjects we want to draw attention to. They come with ideas and plans. Often they surprise us in a very positive way by bringing in new, unexpected ideas.

In many ways we try to support the innovation process. One of the examples is an innovation-contest in 2005. For this contest we asked the young creatives in the city, like artists, advertising companies and students, for new innovative ideas. Within a timeframe of five weeks we received 226 new plans, including plans for gaming in the open air, using the skyscrapers of the city as projection screens, a campy 'pet and passion' parade, several ideas for bringing the different ethnic groups in the city together, a festival about nothing (a tour to desolated areas where absolutely nothing happens) ands many, many other crazy but inspiring ideas. Naturally not every idea was brilliant, but it was a wonderful experience to see that every plan was created with a deep involvement with the city, with the people of the city and the way we have to shape our own future.

5. How Can the City Get the Most Out of it?

Then the next question comes in: how can the city get the most out of it.

You can have the money and the ideas. The hardware and the software, but if they don't work together it won't work.

It is one of the most important crucial factors for success. If the police, the shop-owners, the tourism department, the politicians, the event organizers, the cab drivers, understand that they are part of a collective effort and work together the result will be fantastic.

Collaboration means a lot of hard work and we have experienced our moments of frustration, but thanks to the way we work, not engaging in production ourselves but seeking out energy and expertise in the city, co-operative ties are created which would not otherwise have been accomplished, or at least at a much lower rate.

The result visible to the outside world is a greater cohesion between the activities, a more pronounced expression of the unique character and special features of our city, and, as our results reveal, more visitors.

Ten years of Rotterdam Summer festivals

Visitors: x 2
Economic impact: x 3
National Media-attention: x 10

The Rotterdam Summer festivals are a collection of separate festivals each catering to another group in society, organized by different festival organizers. They are planned on 14 succeeding weekends and are nationally marketed as a group.

The Rotterdam Summer festivals include a tropical summer carnival, a dance parade where 300,000 young people are dancing in the streets of Rotterdam, a weekend where people can visit the city's most famous architecture, a world music festival, rock concerts, a street-theatre festival and the world Port festival in which Rotterdam celebrates its port.

Since 1994 it has been developed and promoted as a group with great success.
- The number of visitors has increased from 1,1 million to 2,1 million
- The amount of money spent in the city rose 200%
- Thanks to a special devoted press officer the media attention on national level is now ten times the amount of 1994
- And, harder to measure, but just as important: events are better connected with the character of and development in the city. There are an increasing number of organizers that have become stronger and more professional organizations.

Table 7: Ten years of Rotterdam Summer festivals

But what is more and most important, we have created memories for all those people. Great memories that will always remain and be connected with the city where they took place: Rotterdam, where today you cannot only smell the wonderful aromas of spices and fruits, but increasingly creativity, celebration, art and passion.

Stockholm Water Festival: The Phoenix of Festivals

Charlotte J. DeWitt

Greek mythology tells the tale of the phoenix, a magical bird which lives five hundred years, builds its own funeral pyre, and dies in flames, only to arise symbolically from the ashes and regenerate itself.

Sweden has its own version of the phoenix: the legendary Stockholm Water Festival, which ran from 1991-1999 before self-destructing. At its peak, the Water Festival attracted an estimated four million visitors during ten days in August each year and was Northern Europe's largest outdoor festival.

1. A Legend in its Own Time

Looking back nearly a decade, the festival industry saw the Stockholm Water Festival as the case study of the perfect festival. Research began in late 1989 on the heels of a previously failed attempt by a private entrepreneur, but this time, organizers were determined to succeed. The financial model was unusual for socialist Sweden: a for-profit festival whose start-up costs were funded by private business partners with a vested interest in the tourism/hospitality business... and, unlike most European festivals, no cash investment by the government. Profits were to go to fund the endowment of an environmental initiative of the festival, the Stockholm Water Prize for clean water, awarded by King Carl XVI Gustav annually. It was quickly labeled "The Festival with the Good Cause".

The first *Water Festival* in 1991 was an instant success, with approximately one million visitors, and a profit of SEK 56,000 (approximately US$ 10,000) By 1994, the ten-day festival had grown to be the largest festival in Northern Europe, with nearly four million visitors and a net profit of SEK 2.5 million (US$ 350,000) – *after* an SEK 1.7 million contribution to the Stockholm Water Prize.

In 1994, its annual operating budget was US$10 million; two years later the budget had grown to US$18 million (SEK120 million).

A survey that year by KPMG Bohlins shows that 98% of all Swedes knew of the Stockholm Water Festival, and that 45% had visited at least once since the first festival. Hotel occupancy was at an unprecedented high and the festival generated an economic impact of US$ 5.5 million.

It was enough to make an events professional green with envy, and then, just as quickly, it was gone, a victim of its own success, coupled with inexperience, politics, and what some might label hubris on the part of those who succeeded the original founders. Any one of these elements would have been enough to cause failure, but perhaps the biggest short-coming was that after enormous research and networking efforts by its founders, festival employees simply stopped attending industry conferences, principally due to two successively swift changes in management, neither with any experience in running festivals. Because the Water Festival was the only festival of its type in Sweden, and because of Sweden's geographic isolation, suddenly there was no inflow of knowledge, no exchange of ideas with others in the same line of business. The results were disastrous... and predictable. The festival was clearly an idea before its time in Sweden.

Today, two new festivals have arisen from the ashes of the Stockholm Water Festival, targeting two diverse audiences and sharing, by design, the same dates each year: UNG08 and the Stockholm Cultural Festival (Stockholms Kulturfestival). The two festivals also subcontract work, not coincidentally, to many former Water Festival staff members and utilize many of the same venues of the now defunct festival, yet they each present a fresh perspective of the city via celebration.

Stockholm is one of the world's most beautiful capital cities. Built on 14 islands with another 22,000 islands in its outlying archipelago, it is synonymous with pure waters, clean living, and incredibly unspoiled, natural vistas. But where the Stockholm Water Festival positioned the city as an ecological gem perched on the Baltic, the two new festivals take a different tack. (No pun intended.) The shift is from destination marketing to niche marketing. The focus is on cultural tourism and experiential tourism, in the latter case, to adolescents.

Ultimately, in five years or so, the end result will be the same: more people will discover this Venice of the North, but for different reasons than those of the Stockholm Water Festival.

2.   UNG08

Social responsibility and Sweden have long gone hand in hand: the Nobel Prizes, HM Queen Silvia's World Childhood Foundation and the Stockholm Water Prize initiated by the Stockholm Water Festival all attest to this.

Now, something new is on the horizon in the land of Abba and Absolute, Volvos and Vikings: a festival linking personal responsibility with cause-related programming. UNG08 is the latest effort to reach 13-19 year-olds in Sweden's capital city of Stockholm and teach them to care about more than just themselves.

The festival name is a hybrid of two Swedish words, "*ung,*" meaning "young," and "*08,*" which is the city telephone code for Stockholm— to many Swedes, the most prestigious area code in the country because it symbolizes what many consider to be Sweden's most beautiful, upscale, hip and historic city. But *UNG08* is a festival that is anything BUT elitist, a product of a troubled past.

3.   From Gang Wars to Star Wars

In the summer of 1987, waves of violence and property damage in the suburbs both perplexed and paralyzed ordinary Stockholmers. For six tense days, gangs of teenagers roamed through the streets, smashing windows and destroying whatever lay in their path. This was not an ordinary gang war in the sense of disenfranchised, ethnically motivated groups of illiterate young men fighting each other for neighborhood supremacy. Rather, it was an outburst by twitchy, bored, middleclass suburban teenagers striking out at their own affluent establishment in some sort of negative thrill-seeking. It was a social malaise that totally mystified Swedes, who normally are reserved, polite, and if anything, self-controlled to a fault.

According to *UNG08* festival director Roger Ticoalu, the riots were stopped when other groups of young people – peaceful "gangs," if you will – drove trucks mounted with sound systems out into the streets and staged a big street party, concert and dance. The next year, in 1988, another concert was held... and every year thereafter, always during the last ten days of the summer, which in Stockholm means the ten days in early August just before school starts. By 1994, the street party was welcomed under the umbrella of the *Stockholm Water Festival*, then in its fourth year, itself concerned with this same urban unrest.

4. Easy Street

That year, the *Stockholm Water Festival* featured an entire area of youth activities called "Easy Street" (*Lugnagatan* in Swedish), a walled fortress with a reverse admission policy: only those under the age of 19 were allowed admittance. Non-violence was openly themed, using imagery of the UN's sculpture of a twisted pistol barrel.

Youths voluntarily submitted to a weapons' screening prior to entering the "Easy Street" area which, ironically, is the same venue today for UNG08: a former royal garden called Kungsträdgården, a lovely park smack in the middle of the city with views of the castle just over the bridge. Yet, to equate those suburban Swedish teens with pistol-packing hooligans, even then, was a bit of a stretch. Nonetheless, the point was made: only calm behavior would be tolerated.

"Can you imagine," exclaims Ticoalu, "we went from pacifying gangs of angry suburban teenagers in 1987 to staging an all-night disco in central Stockholm's largest shopping mall, with no protection or barricades for any of the storefront windows throughout the mall!" And indeed, it was incredible—a three-level, multi-tenant mall was transformed into the country's largest indoor disco, all for teens between 15- 19 years old. The year was 1998, and it was yet one more innovative aspect of the Stockholm Water Festival. Today, a decade later, the disco is a part of UNG08 and has been moved to a nearby public parking garage. It represents the festival's only major cost—about SEK400,000 (US$62,000/ EUR42,275) for build-outs.

5. "Tingeltangel"

Meanwhile, on the cultural scene, Claes Karlsson, former director for cultural programming of the *Stockholm Water Festival*, had moved closer to his personal goal of creating a festival with a lot less *"tingeltangel"*, an onomatopoeic Swedish word that is self-explanatory—no commercialized booths, no beer tents, no plastic duck races. No tingle. No tangle of huge crowds swarming on congested, closed streets.

Stockholm had been the *Cultural Capital of Europe*, a European Commission designation, in 1998. For an entire year, the city showcased its cultural offerings to the world as the official representative city within the European Union. This was followed, in relatively quick succession, by the city's Millennium celebration in 2000 and Stockholm's 750th anniversary celebration in 2002. These events laid the groundwork for a new festival based on cultural marketing, rather than destination marketing, and Karlsson played an increasingly major role in all of these.

By 2005, he was given his first opportunity to produce a pilot project for a new cultural festival. Dubbed "Under Construction", this hastily composed test of the future *Stockholm Cultural Festival* featured 80 cultural events on three stages over a three-day period, funded with the blessings of the city. Its success confirmed Karlsson's theory: once having experienced the *Cultural Capital* programming in 1998 and the 750th anniversary in 2002,

Stockholmers were hungry for quality programming. Exit *tingel-tangel*.

6. Faith, Hope and Finances

By 2006, the city of Stockholm was fully behind funding a festival themed around culture. Based on the success of 2005's "Under Construction," it gave some SEK 12.4 million (US$ 1.84 million in 2006 rates) to the first *Cultural Festival*, understanding, as expressed by Cultural Department head Eva Schöld, that it was a reasonable, but not a gigantic sum, and as the festival grew, additional revenue sources would have to be identified... but carefully, so as not to over-commercialize the festival, and with participation from various cultural institutions, as well as trade and industry.

Meanwhile, from an office under the same city umbrella, *UNG08* has been operating a separate organization with its own staff, budget and board since 2000, but with some cross-over. Director Ticoalu handles all the permitting and security for both festivals... and also produces Sweden's National Day celebration in June. He finds a certain wry humor in the fact that he, as an immigrant of Polish/Italian/Indonesian heritage, would be producing a Swedish national holiday, claiming that Swedes are too self-effacing to embrace the concept of celebrating national pride themselves.

In 2007, UNG08's total cash budget was SEK10.55 million (approximately US$ 1.66 million or EUR 1.12 million) and included SEK 2.85 million from the City for National Day expenses. This cash income came from three sources:

- City Culture Department SEK 5.0 million (for UNG08)
- City Culture Department SEK 2.85 million (for National Day)
- Sponsorship (cash) SEK 2.2 million
- Self-generated income SEK 0.5 million

In-kind sponsorships, such as barter deals with media, TV, radio, main stage projection screens, and artists, amounted to another SEK 7.0 million for the organization, bringing its total budget, cash and in-kind, to SEK 17.55 million (US$ 2.75 million/ EUR 1.87 million).

Its governance is unique, in that it is one of the few festivals that allow teenagers to decide what programming they want. There are two advisory boards, each with a maximum of fifty people, and between 600 and 1000 applicants for the 100 slots. Planning begins in January each year, with the youth boards meeting six or seven times a year. Four, full-time permanent staff are hired by the city, augmented by other four seasonal, full-time employees who work six or seven months.

UNG08 uses around 50 volunteers; the Cultural Festival, 100, 60% of whom are new each year. While these numbers may seem low to Americans, Australians and Asians, Sweden's value system has greater belief in paid employment than volunteer work. To many, volunteers take away jobs that people desperately need by doing it for free.

7. Adults: Keep Out!

UNG08 featured over 250 programs in fashion, design, sports, music and culture, attracting some 160,000 active participants aged 13-19, known as "guests," and 600,000 other visitors over a four-day period in 2006, and about the same number (760,000) over a five-day period in 2007. Keep in mind that while most events except the nighttime disco (SEK 80/ US$14) are free, active participation is generally restricted to those between 13 and 19 years of age (15-19 for evening events)—a reverse discrimination policy that works well, say the organizers. Adults are given their own tented lounge area in which to wait while their teenagers enjoy the festival activities on their own. They are not encouraged to mingle with the young people. A special link on the festival's website is dedicated solely to answering FAQ (Frequently Asked Questions) typical of parents.

By comparison, the Stockholm Cultural Festival drew approximately 300,000 visitors to some 600 events over a six-day period in 2007, an increase of some 50,000 people from 2006, which featured 400 events over seven days. However, since both festivals take place "next door" to each other during the exact same time period in early August, and since almost 99% of all activities at both festivals are free, it is difficult to attribute attendance statistics purely to one festival or the other.

Unlike *UNG08*, the *Cultural Festival's* target audience is people between five and 85 years old, with a 60:40 ratio of women to men. As for marketing, the *Cultural Festival* does heavy local promotion, in this case via direct delivery of some 500,000 printed programs to households and boutiques in the greater Stockholm area. By comparison, *UNG08* consciously decreased its PR efforts beginning in 2004, eliminating TV and national newspapers – more consistent with its "08" area code. Both festivals have newspaper sponsors, one local, one national. But where *UNG08* draws kids *in* from the suburbs, the *Cultural Festival* takes the festival *out* to the suburbs – five outlying areas – with a bus to bring curious Stockholmers out to see performances in little-visited areas predominantly inhabited by immigrants.

8. Hands On and Classless

Two innovative, if not revolutionary principles come together in the programming of *UNG08*: everything is interactive or touchable; and everything is inclusive or non-segregated, by design. And everything, but *everything*, is what *kids* want to see and do, not what adults have decided they can do.

Ironically, one whole section of the festival contributes to both the festival's PR and its safety. *Stockholm City* newspaper gives kids a chance to be a journalist for a day, with coaching provided on how to write news stories and how to become a professional blogger. Rows of computers are available for kids yearning to be Clark Kent and Lois Lane – those showing up by 11 a.m. can be published in the day's newspaper.

One tent over, kids can learn how to make a radio program or get tips on how to produce videos—either as a camera person or a performer. Costumes and equipment are available, with appropriate lighting and backdrops. Aspiring DJs can burn a CD demo of their "air time", and actors/camera operators can walk away with a DVD of their work. The tent is run by Fanzingo, a casting company that shoots commercials in the Stockholm area. Nearby, language school EF coaches kids on how to become an *au pair* overseas, and how to study abroad, such as taking a junior year abroad.

Not to be outdone, the Stockholm Police Department operates its own information tent, where kids can ask questions about police work, as well as sign up to "walk a beat" with a police officer to see if they might like police work as a career choice. Only in Sweden—known for its non-violent approach to life—could this be so successful.

9. Zoning Out / Zoning In

UNG08's landscape is divided into numerous zones, most of which are tented. In "Game Zone", participants can try out all the latest high-tech X-box, video, and computer-animated games like FIFA 08, NHL 08, *Burnout simulator*, *Guitar Hero* and more. *Kids* can play a virtual golf match against Tiger Woods (who is married to a Swede and lives in Stockholm part of the year), try out sports car racing, or clamber around an on-site military attack vehicle and use a simulated rocket launcher, courtesy of the Swedish military.

The "MIX Cup" (*MixCupen* in Swedish) zone features competitive matches of American football (known to Europeans as "American" football, European football (known to Americans as "soccer"), and street basket, a more intense three-on-three version of basketball, during the festival. All teams are comprised of players from a mixture of different residential areas (hence, "*Mix-Cupen*"), so that affluent suburban kids play alongside those from the low-income areas populated predominantly by immigrants.

"There are over 50-60% immigrant populations in many of these low-income suburbs," says Ticoalu. The challenge becomes how one audience—the festival participants-- can help another. In 2008, the festival's goal is to "create a totally new concept regarding education and information about the situation in third-world (sic) countries, poverty, etc., and to try to inspire our youth to contribute and help other children," he says.

One idea under discussion for 2009 is to build a huge "camp" with three to four different scenarios (refugee camp, war, famine, etc.) where the youth will spend at least 24 hours and be "refugees" or victims of famine, war etc. The idea is to give the participants not only a mental but also a physical "journey".

They will not be able to eat or drink; they will experience a harsh and tough time, everything to get a small idea of the life of millions of people in the third world. "We are still working on the idea," says Ticoalu, "and there are a lot of obstacles to tackle before we can launch it."

10. Sex in the (08) City, Pimpmobiles and More

"Shout Out" features main-stage appearances by popular, "hip" Swedish broadcasters answering teens' pre-recorded questions dealing with sex ("Ask Olle," a Swedish version of America's Dr. Ruth, on stage), and in the official RFSU government-sponsored tent, teens can learn how to protect themselves sexually and more importantly, how to be responsible for their own choices. RFSU is a government agency disseminating information about sexuality and sex-related issues. And yes, although it is a bit "tongue-in-cheek" for such a serious subject, there is a condom race with a pink trophy, more akin to a Boy Scout merit badge. But that one you'll have to figure out for yourself.

In the "Pimpmobile" tent, if it has wheels or is mobile, teens can decorate it—"low-rider" cars, skateboards, wheelchairs, mobile phones—and an area called Molins (after its sponsor) features a *bling-bling* tent called "Sneaker Lab", where kids can glitz up new high-top canvas shoes with anything that sparkles.

Circus Normal, Stockholm's resident alternative circus company, even teaches participants how to walk a tightrope – a great party trick if there ever was one, and certainly something useful later in life. Another tent dealt with climate change... perhaps an early indication that former U.S. Vice President Al Gore was on his way to winning the Nobel Prize.

11. From the 750th Forward

Claes Karlsson planted the seeds of the *Cultural Festival* in 2002 when, working with Berit Svedberg, Director of *Stockholm's 750thAnniversary Celebration*, he demonstrated that cultural activities were a great visitor magnet and gave added value to the quality of life in Stockholm.

In 2007, the *Stockholm Cultural Festival* featured eight themes based around music, literature, fashion and design, a kids' tent, art, food, Stockholm and its history, and film and theatre – quite a menu. Some thirty venues throughout the city and its suburbs were utilized, with six hundred performances and events. Japanese Wadaiko drums, a Lithuanian version of "Romeo and Juliet," a poetry slam, guided historical city walks, Medieval knights and salsa nights -- like a fine chef, Karlsson assembled an array of cultural offerings that merged both the populist and the artistic, and pulled it off with finesse.

"Stockholm needs more inspiration," he says. "We need more street theatre, more international guest performers, more unknown artists... We need a cultural meeting place with no niche or elitism, an inclusive place where participants in the city's cultural life can exchange experiences and take part in international culture. The festival will contribute to establishing Stockholm as an attractive tourist destination, but that is not our foremost concern, and it will take four or five years."

12. Out of the Ashes

Like the mythical phoenix, Stockholm as a festival city has arisen from the ashes of the *Stockholm Water Festival*. It has taken nearly eight years. Two festivals now exist instead of one, using the same dates, the same venues, and some of the same staff as the *Water Festival*.

Both festivals continue the efforts of the Water Festival to give restless local young people—and adults-- something to do at the end of summer vacation, before school starts. Their combined second-year budgets are comparable to the second-year budget of the Water Festival (around SEK29 million in 1992) – but unlike the Water Festival, they are heavily supported by government money, which allows them to be less commercialized and to focus more on pure content.

The *Stockholm Water Prize*, once the raison d'être of the *Stockholm Water Festival* until taken over by the City in 1996, continues its annual Nobel-inspired award for clean water under the patronage of HM King Carl XVI Gustaf. A new prize, the *Stockholm Junior Water Prize*, was added in 1997 under the patronage of HRH Crown Princess Victoria. While not affiliated with either the *Cultural Festival* or *UNG08*, these prizes live on, again in the same time space as before, in August, during what is now known as *World Water Week*.

The repositioning of Stockholm as a cultural destination and a socially responsive city of substance rings true to the hearts of those who live there. As a tourist destination, Stockholm will "sell" itself effortlessly once this new branding is in place. To those who see festivals as a tourism generator, it is important to remember that the first target market is always local. If residents are happy, the rest of the world will come.

UNG08 and the *Stockholm Cultural Festival* have succeeded in achieving this goal.

Deni Ute Muster

Tracy Hull, William J. O´Toole

1. The Problem

The rapid growth of a festival or event can be the very cause of its decline. Success can bring the new unforeseen problems. This is particularly true of a festival organised by volunteers. The event team are highly focussed on the success of their event and often do not have the time to study the progress of other similar events or recognise the changes required within their own event. This problem was recognised by the Case study. Their solution was to seek assistance from event professionals.

2. Background

Deni: short for Deniliquin, a country town in Australia

Ute: a shortened form of 'utility vehicle'. It is a car with a tray area that can carry up to one tonne. They are common in rural areas of Australia. As in many other countries such as India and Mexico, this work vehicle has become a piece of folk art. The Australian Ute may be decorated with painted designs, extra size tyres, aerials and stickers. The Ute is similar to the American 'pickup truck'.

Muster: comes from mustering cattle i.e. rounding up (gathering) cattle. A group of livestock is often called a 'muster'. In this case it is use to mean 'gathering'

2.1 Description

The Deni Ute Muster takes place over two days, although the audience can arrive a number of days beforehand.

According to their Web site:

"It's about an affinity with the land, about having a great time, about utes that just keep coming, ute after ute, after ute. It's about catching up with old mates and making new ones. It's about the biggest artists in the Australian music industry performing under the Southern Cross out on the largest, flattest open plains on Earth.

It's about patriotism, about the Australian way of life, about being who we are."

The event comprised a meeting place for owners of Utes. The entertainment, food, accommodation and beverage are all geared to satisfy this highly targeted audience.

2.2 Program

The official program of events at the festival includes:

- Two music concerts on Friday and Saturday night including numerous Country music groups Figure 1 shows the program for Saturday.
- Bull Riding in a main arena
- Numerous 'world first' competitions including the greatest number of blue singlets – called the Blue Singlets Muster.
- Tractor races
- Lawn mower races
- Carnival rides
- Army displays
- Whip Cracking
- Best Ute competitions ; such as Best Workman's Ute and Furthest Travelled Ute

There is a trade site that includes clothing and other stalls as well as displays of vehicles and a Ute museum.

However a large part of the entertainment is the attendees walking the site admiring each other's Utes.

2.3 Type of audience

The key to the phenomenal success of this event is the highly targeted audience. The audience, the Ute owners and friends, are also part the entertainment. They are not a passive audience. They take part in the competitions and provide their own entertainment. The Utes and their owners are part of the show. The demographics of the core audience are: young men between ages of 18 – 35. Many are working on farms in the Murray Darling Basin region. However a significant number travel from the cities. The Ute Muster is so popular with this audience that they have a competition as to who drove the furthest to come to the muster (it is often that is more that 2,000 km).

2.4 History

The town of Deniliquin lies in rural Australia. It has a population of 8000 and in Australian terms is a significant town in the rural region. It lies on one of the flattest areas on earth at the beginning of the famous Australian outback. Average rainfall is around 100 mm per year and temperature can easily reach 30C in summer. The town is within the region called the Murray Darling Basin with a population density of less than 5 people per square kilometre. The main agricultural production includes rice, winter cereals including wheat, barley and canola, dairying and livestock products including beef, lamb and wool. All of these facts help to explain the uniqueness and success of the Festival. The utility vehicle is central to the logistics of this rural region.

The Festival began in 1999 as a music event. Some locals wanted to create a country music festival. It attracted about 8000 people. The attendance of the 2005 event was approximately 20,000 people and over 6,000 Utes. That represents an average growth rate of 17% per event. However, it has been in the last few years that the numbers have accelerated.

2.5 Organisation Structure

The Festival was primarily organised by local volunteers. Figure 22 illustrates the path of the development of similar events.

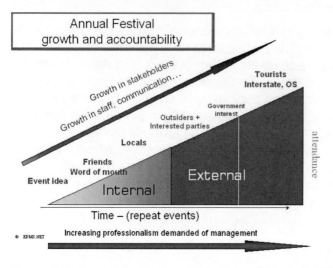

Figure 25: Annual festival growth (from O'Toole 2006)

For the first few years the annual event is organised by a group of friends and interested parties. The organisation structure is level and loose. Any problems can be solved informally. However, as the annual event grows with success, the informal structure can lead to significant risks. A new structure takes over with committees and a formal division of the work. In 2005 the Ute Muster had a President, Executive, Committee and a full time paid 'festival coordinator'. A part-time administration coordinator was appointed and a Public Relations coordinator and Sponsorship coordinator (contractor) joined the team in 2005.

The Festival organisers and the State government recognised that the rapid growth of the event produced new conditions for the organising committee. From a volunteer beginning, the event was turning into a very significant 'rural industry'. The event impacted on the local economy. Its growth meant that outside help was required to review the Ute Muster and compare it to events around the world. In 2005, event management consultants were hired to review the management, marketing and operations and suggest a strategic plan for the event.

3. Impact

The Deni Ute Muster has significant economic, social and cultural impacts on the Deniliquin and surrounding communities. Managing these impacts as the festival has grown has been essential for the on-going success of the event.

3.1 Community Impacts

The Festival plays a significant community strengthening role. Nearly 500 people from within the community are involved in a volunteer capacity with the event, providing opportunities for social interaction, community fundraising and skill development. The Festival has helped build a sense of community spirit and pride among residents. It has also helped to strengthen the sense of identity and belonging of local residents.

With the growth of the festival, organisers have been required to face the challenge of increasing the skills of the community volunteers and getting the right balance between the use of professionals and the volunteers within community. Whereas community volunteers were able to undertake a number of tasks in the first few years, a transition plan was required to transfer some tasks over to professionals. Not alienating the community in this process was important to ensure the communities on-going support of the Festival.

Developing new projects to involve a variety of community members has also been important. A project in 2005 involved bringing in artists to transform a ute into a beautiful piece of artwork.

Bringing thousands of people into a small community has created a number of challenges for organisers. The festival has been required to respond by developing more sophisticated traffic management plans, waste management plans and environmental im-

impact plans. A greater involvement of the local council, police, other emergency services and the road traffic authority has been necessary to ensure the negative impacts on the community are minimised.

3.2 Tourism and Economic Impacts

The Muster has become one of the most recognizable features of Deniliquin. It has helped brand Deniliquin as the Ute capital of Australia. While research is not available, anecdotally, the event has resulted in greater levels of visitation to Deniliquin. People come to visit the location of this famous Ute Muster throughout the year, not just at festival time.

The marketing effort in the lead up to the festival, as well as the clever year round marketing activities (stickers on utes, singlets, etc.) means the Deni Ute Muster is in people's minds year round rather than just at event time. Given the uniqueness of the festival (the gathering of thousands of utes) and the inclusion of high profile musicians, national and, on occasions international media attention is achieved.

The economic impact of the festival was estimated to be around $4.5 million (2004 festival, quoted by festival organisers in 2005). This impact is both on Deniliquin and the neighboring towns. Hospitality businesses in the nearby towns indicate the muster weekend is their best weekend of the year.

To maximize the direct economic impact on the region, the organisers seek to use local services and contractors where available, rather than importing these services from outside of the region. Where ever possible local plumbers, electricians, caterers, equipment hire companies and other services will be used. This continued support and use of local businesses is vital given the reliance of the festival on the financial and in-kind support of local businesses as sponsors.

Analysing the tourism and economic impacts has been important in order to obtain government funding and to attract and maintain sponsors.

The Muster provides direct employment – initially employing one staff member and now employing 5 full-time staff along with other part-time and casual staff and contractors.

4. Marketing the Event

The marketing of the Deni Ute muster is highly creative and can be seen as one of the secrets to their success. Promotional ideas include:

1. Muster launch in a nearby state capital.
2. Guinness book records in the number of Utes in any one place
3. World record for the number of blue singlets (which led to an increase in the sales of the singlets with the Deni Ute muster logo)
4. Creative programming with the performers
5. House boat river cruise for the media representatives and VIP's

Each of these elements is exploited to the full by the event's promotional team. Even the risks – as outlined below – make it into the national press.

The marketing of the event is fully evaluated by the event team. The press coverage is listed. The marketing for the next event begins during the event.

5. Risk Management

During the early stages of a festival the risk management is regarded as on-site risks. What may be called operational risk. The Deni Ute Muster with its mix of cars, young men and alcohol has plenty of those risks. The event team were admirable in their work in minimising these risks. It is not everyone who can successfully handle the potential volatility of this mix. There were numerous stories arising from the mix that the reader will find amusing. They may not have been so amusing at the time and it is a tribute to the event organisers that they were able to manage the risks.

5.1   Risk One – the Early Days

When the festival began it attracted a large rural audience. At first the festival was seen as a music event. Its name was "Play on the Plains". However it was obvious that the car park was filled with a certain type car. It was also obvious to the volunteer organisers that here was an opportunity to rebrand the event as a gathering of a type of car – the Ute. Gradually, the branding has changed as the festival grew and developed. In this case the risk was turned into an opportunity and became the theme of the festival.

5.2   Risk Two – the Map

One problem that arose was from the attempt to create a map of Australia with the Utes. 2000 Utes were driven into the field of a farm to create the map. The 'map' would be photographed from a hot air balloon suspended above the field. A creative idea that would bring plenty of publicity. However, the time it took to get the cars in place was phenomenal and the drivers had to wait a long time for the map to be completed. While they waited for many hours they drank beer. The result was that once most of the map was completed, many of the drivers were over the alcohol limit for driving. Therefore they had to stay until their alcohol content was reduced. The map took a lot longer to create and disband than was first thought.

5.3   Risk Three – Dogs

Another risk arose from the numerous dogs brought to the event by the attendees. Most Ute owners also own a dog. The back tray of the Ute is a favourite spot for a dog. Many of the dogs are working dogs from the farms. The Ute owners brought their dogs to the Muster. Over 2,000 dogs at an event is a major problem. In particular, their waste is a health hazard. Two to three tonnes of "doggy do" can be 'produced' per day. After much discussion, the only solution available to the Festival team was to ban the dogs. The public thought that this would be the end to the Ute Musters – as it is near impossible to separate a Ute owner from his dog. The next year attendance dropped – but the year after it picked up again.

5.4 Making the Risk Management Process Visible

These three risks are examples of the festival management successfully employing the risk management process. Part of the consultancy (outlined below) included demonstrating this process to the event team so it may be used in all areas of the event. It was obvious the event team were already using the process, but it was hidden and needed to be formalised. Risk management can be used in every functional area of the event. The functional areas of an event are Administration, Marketing, Operations and Program design. The risk management standard in Australia – and now in many other countries – stresses that it must be embedded in management. Every aspect of event or festival management must contain a risk management process. Put simply, this means asking 'what can go wrong?'.

Two risks often overlooked in the rapid growth of a festival are:

1. Marketing risk – such as exaggerating the claims for the event. The enthusiasm of event organisers can sometimes lead to promotion that embellishes the truth. In some countries this will come under 'unfair trade practices'.

2. Contract risk – contracts can be complex documents that need specialised knowledge of a particular field. Volunteers, no matter how well meaning, may not be able to understand contracts designed by professionals.

6. Management system and consultancy

A consultant company was engaged to overview and provide advice concerning the management and direction of the Festival. The risk management used by the event was an example of the hidden processes already successfully employed by the Deni event team. A large part of the consultant's work was to 'make visible' the management system. Once the system can be described, it can be evaluated and improved.

Figure 23 illustrates the consultation methodology. The process included working on each of the objectives of the event and providing a best practice strategy to reach those objectives. The objectives of the event were distilled from the consultations with the event staff and an understanding of the history of the event. The best practice strategy was derived from the standards in the event industry and the trends affecting the industry.

Consultancy Methodology

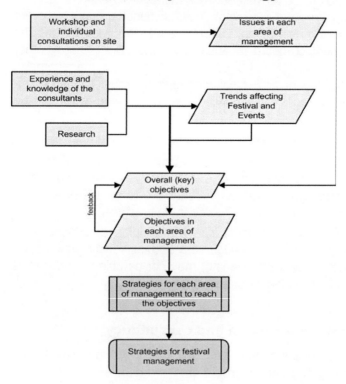

Figure 26: Consultancy Methodology (from O'Toole 2006)

The consultants recommended that the management system change to be project management based. The festival was well on its way to this type of system. It was committee based and the various functional units had tasks and schedules. Their current system had developed organically – responding to problems as they arose. It was robust and obviously very successful. However, once an event develops to a certain size the event management system has to be acknowledged and described. This means that every festival will improve the management of the festival. Often events mistakenly only evaluate the event. For an event to be sustainable, the event management must also be evaluated.

7. Conclusion

The Deni Ute Muster is a typical example of a festival created by volunteers, run on enthusiasm and passion. Its success brought new pressures to the organisation. The impact of the Festival placed it as a major rural industry in the region. The local council and the state government recognised this impact. The response was to call in consultants to a three year strategy. The core of the consultancy was to suggest building on their project based structure and to introduce an embedded risk management process. The project risk management approach allows all the best in the Festival, such as the marketing and operations, to continue. It enables the Festival to control its growth and at the same time facilitate changes that will benefit the strategic direction of the Deni Ute Muster.

References:

O'Toole W. J. (2006) EPMS CDROM – www.epms.net
Deni Ute Muster website: www.deniutemuster.com.au/

Managing the "Unmanageable" – Producing New York's Greenwich Village Halloween Parade

Lewis Siris

On every October 31 (for the last 30 years) the streets of New York City's famed Greenwich Village transform into a stage for one of the United States' most unique and fantastic celebrations – New York's Village Halloween Parade.

Originally founded by a small group of neighborhood artists and puppeteers, the Parade has grown over the last 30 years into a truly participatory spectacle with over 35,000 costumed marchers, hundreds of Halloween characters, giant masks and puppets, hundreds of musicians playing a variety of music from around the world, stilt walkers, jugglers, break dancers and other street performers all walking, dancing, marching, riding and performing in front of an estimated audience of 1.3 million along the route.

The Parade is a truly multicultural event expressing the diversity, traditions and creativity of the people of New York City. It is an event which has a positive impact on the economic life of New York City, bringing hundreds of thousands of visitors to the city, providing Greenwich Village businesses and restaurants their most successful night of the year. The estimated economic impact on the local economy on the day of the Parade is over $60 million (USD.)

The Village Halloween Parade is at heart a mobile artistic event. It is not a traditional parade by any stretch of the imagination and doesn't fit the mold of military-style or ethnic heritage parades. Current political events are portrayed and satirized, alternate lifestyles are celebrated and the amazing creativity of regular citizens, both New Yorkers and visitors from around the globe is on display.

While the Parade is televised in entirety by a local news station it is not designed nor choreographed specifically for TV. This is a live event and everything we do is for the enjoyment of the spectators and for the parade participants.

The Parade is produced on an extremely minimal budget due to the generous pro-bono and reduced rate participation of hundreds of volunteers and artists. The Parade's puppeteers and mask-makers, choreographers, visual artists and hundreds of musicians all give of their time and creativity to mount this remarkable celebration.

It is astonishing how we produce this event without major sponsorship or funding, Event Marketers, as they consider our sponsorship solicitations, seem unable to understand the tremendous opportunity that exists for them with so many people from every demographic of society involved or viewing. They look for "targeted" demographics to the point of being oblivious to the million plus potential "targets" The alternative lifestyle marketers feel the event is not targeted to their demographic. The traditional marketers feel the event is too targeted to the alternative lifestyle demographic. These event marketers do not rise to the creative challenge and business opportunity afforded to them through sponsorship and participation in this one-of-a kind event.

1.   Planning

Each year's planning begins with the Parade's Artistic Director developing a theme and presenting it to her creative team. The theme often comes from mythology or traditional Halloween themes. Sometimes it has a subtext related to social issues (i.e. the environment) or in most cases just pure celebration.

Once the theme is decided on, our team of puppeteers, mask makers and choreographers begin working on the oversized elements (puppets and masks) that are the signature of the Parade. On a lovely farm overlooking the Hudson River in upstate New York, old puppets are refurbished and new ones brought to life. Hundreds of volunteers arrive during the late summer and early fall to help build, decorate and test out the puppets and to rehearse the choreography and puppet operation.

Twice in the last five years we have reacted to specific tragedies that have taken place in our country. The 2001 Parade came only six weeks after the attacks of September 11th and was one of the first major events to take place in New York City after that tragedy. Through an inclusive process with all the various stakeholders we explored if (in the light of what just happened) it was appropriate that we undertake the production of the parade.

The consensus was that it was important for a variety of reasons to continue with this grand New York City tradition. Our Mayor also encouraged all New Yorkers to continue living our lives as proof that we will not be broken. The theme changed to the "Phoenix Rising" as a way to focus on our emergence from this tragedy demonstrating that our city (and our country) could rise out of the ashes of that terrible day.

Tragedy struck again in 2005 with Hurricane Katrina devastating the Gulf Coast and laying waste to the great city of New Orleans. It was clear that we needed to dedicate the parade to the victims and evacuees of Hurricane Katrina and the rebirth of the City of New Orleans. We brought in (and replicated) elements of a Mardi Gras Parade and "flew" the Phoenix once again.

2. Setting the Stage

Imagine inviting over 30,000 strangers (all in costumes or masks) to participate in your event without knowing in advance who (or how many) will show up. At New York's Greenwich Village Halloween Parade anyone who comes in costume gets in the lineup. That's one of the unique and exciting aspects of the event. Consider also that they all have different reasons for being in the parade, different costumes and makeup, different levels of energy and you want them to proceed past an audience of over a million people in some kind of "organized" fashion while meeting some time-critical arrivals at key areas.

Add in several thousand police officers, traffic jams on parallel streets due to the re-routing of traffic, over two dozen news crews from around the world in addition to hundreds of amateur photographers, videographers and bloggers encouraging people to "pose" in the middle of the parade flow and you have a small idea of what our Parade Operations Team goes through each year. Let's not forget about the occasional protest march, wedding celebration, spontaneous performance art piece, product launches and other "guerilla" marketing initiatives taking place inside the parade at unexpected times and in the most inappropriate locations.

3. Parade Operations

"Please follow the directions of the parade marshals. Ok, move to your designated sections now. Wait, move on our signal, and don't walk ahead of the group in front of you. Don't throw anything into the crowd please. There are too many of you on this parade float. Turn here, turn here! No, don't turn there. Move out of the broadcast area your turn is over and let the next group in. Where did that vehicle come from? Sorry, no simulated weapons fire, and please put your clothes back on."

It certainly would be nice if the parade participants would always follow our direction but that is often not the case. There are times when our experience tells us to just stand back and let the parade unfold in its own way and watch for any situations that require our intervention. Other times we gently guide the action back to where we need it to be and once in a while we jump in to take more decisive and proactive charge. We keep things flowing, remove any impediments and obstructions, and gently guide this powerful river of color, energy sound and creativity through the streets of New York City.

3.1 Understanding is the Key

In most crowd management scenarios it is important to understand (to the extent you can) the dynamics of your crowd, their expectations, the nature of the event and any other influencing factors on their behavior. The weather, geography and site considerations, time of day and length of the event, visibility of cameras and lights, behavior of surrounding and sub-groups and their various interactions, and even the name and theme of the event all affect how crowds behave. We also need to take into consideration what their motivation, goals and energy levels are.

There are different dynamics and behaviors for different type of parades. An ethnic parade differs from a military style parade, a strike parade differs from a carnival-style parade, and religious processions and coronation parades have their own demeanor. Where other parades limit interaction and social distance between elements – and between elements and spectators – the Halloween Parade fosters the opposite. Part of the excitement is this interplay amongst all the elements and the interaction with the spectators.

In this event we need to understand that the participants in the Halloween Parade are essentially "actors" appearing on a mile-long stage (many for the first time) who can easily be caught up by the excitement and enthusiasm of participating in such a festive and boisterous event. The transformative nature of masking and costuming also needs to be taken into account in dealing with the participants.

JC Crocker, in Victor Turner's Celebration: *Studies in Ritual and Festivity*; informs us in his essay on *Ceremonial Masks* that "masks are more than a painless way of changing identity: just because they completely hide the wearers they (also) transform. By donning a mask one becomes what otherwise one could never be. Men into women, old into young, human into animal, mortals into gods, dead into living (and vice versa)." As parade organizers we need to recognize this transformative power and how it affects the participant's attitude and behavior.

The overwhelming amount of visual and auditory stimuli in combination with the length of the route can render some people to become temporarily disoriented as to time and space and unable to follow the direction of our parade marshals. Now imagine trying to get them all to disperse at the end of the parade route in an organized manner, utilizing the designated streets for their particular group, while we separate our "curated" elements from the thousands of general public in costume, floats and other vehicles.

It can be challenging at times (and even counterproductive) to try to impose regulations or structure on a crowd this large and spontaneous. The few rules we have are generally regarding vehicle entry and safety, the throwing anything into the crowd (even sponsor products) and any behavior that interferes with the safety of the participants or the enjoyment of the spectators.

As the parade is considered a "free speech" event it is difficult, and in most cases not advisable, to try and edit or control the way the participants look or the content of their messages (if they have one.) We have been surprised once in a while by something extraordinary taking place and in some cases have to negotiate with the police to keep some parade element from being removed from the route.

The Parade Committee has an excellent working relationship with the NYC Police Department, who does a remarkable job in keeping this event the safest place to be in New York City on Halloween. They manage emergency access and egress, direct traffic, provide enforcement of drug and alcohol restrictions and keep the spectator areas from getting too overcrowded and provide general assistance to everyone who needs it.

3.2. How We Do It

When I introduce myself as an organizer of the Parade the response I usually hear back is "I love that Parade but I didn't know anyone actually organized it." While this amuses me it actually reinforces that our behind-the-scenes approach works – yet is not readily apparent to the spectators.

Two Phases

The Village Halloween Parade is basically organized into two phases. Phase One includes the elements produced by the parade team; puppets, masks, special lighting, music and dance ensembles. This is the lead section with specialized choreography and it is important to maintain the integrity of this section. It establishes the theme of the event and has iconic elements that the spectators expect.

Phase One is set up on two streets adjacent to the general lineup and is sent out just ahead of the other sections. One challenge is to try and keep the other elements from moving up too fast and overrunning this phase diluting the performance.

Phase Two includes all of the costumed thousands, sponsor elements and a few dozen bands interspersed throughout. While we give assigned areas to large or invited groups anyone can stand anywhere, usually near a band that they like. The lineup is a party unto itself. People wander around checking each other's costumes out, participating in impromptu dancing in the streets, listening to band rehearsals, and watching or participating in media interviews. The energy and enthusiasm builds and then is released at the start line and explodes throughout the parade route.

3.3. Management "Musts"

Staffing

If I am asked which is one of the most important areas in event and festival management, my answer inevitably is staffing. Site layout with proper flow and ingress and egress is obviously critical, the choice of talent is important but as tastes vary who is to say one show is better than another. You can have a great looking event with terrific talent, but if the staffing is weak the success of the event and the enjoyment of the spectators and/or attendees can be compromised. The quality and experience of your staff, opportunities for event-specific training and overall staffing levels are important to maintain.

While there may be some basic default requirements in terms of event staffing please remember that different events (and different functional areas in events) may require variations in the default profile. All events are "event-specific" and "site –specific". There is not one template for event management and staffing.

Every event has some unique element, opportunity, special need and challenge.

In an idiosyncratic event like the Halloween Parade it is advisable to keep as many of the same key staff and volunteers as possible since many aspects of the event cannot accurately be reduced to a standard production plan. One has to work the event to truly understand it and we rely on the staff's institutional knowledge of the event and their creative solutions to lessons learned from previous events. Of course we have detailed assembly and dispersal maps, spreadsheets telling us where the beginning of the parade needs to be at a certain time and other calculations on how to pace and structure the flow of the participants.

Handing someone the "production book", going on a walk-through and even participating in a tabletop exercise theoretically should prepare them for the event but once they are on the street we usually throw the book out and rely on our experience and instinct. The internalization of knowledge gained in a university level event management program is invaluable as it gives one a bedrock foundation to rely on in the middle of an event, but there is no substitute for real-time on-site experience.

I liken the study and practice of event management to the journey of a jazz musician (which at one point in my life I was). After years of practicing their scales, harmonies, various riffs, studying jazz theory and history, listening to historical recordings and studying and emulating great solos: once on the bandstand performing and improvising with their fellow musicians they operate on a more spontaneous and intuitive manner. In festival and event management it is often the same. Nothing can really prepare you for every eventuality but through listening, communicating, looking, remembering, being flexible, spontaneous and keeping a good attitude, success is fostered.

I believe in creating a "360 degree" training experience. Reviewing footage and photos of previous events, analyzing after-action reports, processing attendee surveys, imagining next year's event, participating in tabletop exercises, reviewing each aspect of the event in terms of its nature, special needs, past problems or desired activities all help in rounding out the knowledge base needed to successfully manage the event.

Communication

I cannot stress enough the necessity of strong, on-going communication between all the relevant entities, staff and general public in any kind of festival or event. Issuing two-way radios to your staff and instructing them not to use it unless there is some kind of problem is not "communication".

Communication begins with event naming and promotion. It ends with the post-event evaluation and public thank yous. Event communication includes signage, staff attire, event credentials, site maps, color scheme, public announcements and private conversations. Event communication needs to be a dynamic system where constant monitoring of event status, audience ingress and egress, adherence to (or deviation from) the schedule, is done by everyone on staff. All of the festival and event stakeholders should be in this system. Police and other local authorities, media and sponsors all need accurate, timely and relevant information.

In the Village Halloween Parade communication is ongoing between the parade marshals and parade management, between parade management and police, between parade marshals and parade participants and between all parties and the public. We need to know where the front and back of the parade is at all times. We monitor if there are any "gaps" between elements leaving stretches where the spectators are waiting too long to see something. We keep track of the on-air performance schedule and sponsored element visibility on camera. Float and vehicle activity is monitored for safety and pace. Does the lighting look ok, are the puppeteers interacting with the spectators, and do the police have any issues with anything? Are any of the elements out of order so we can inform broadcast personnel as well as the dispersal team who is waiting to send them to their designated spots?

We have to communicate with the 30,000 parade participants letting them know where and when to turn to leave the route. We need to closely communicate with the police so they are up to date on what is happening or what changes have been made. We communicate with the spectators prior to stepping off through sending out our "money grubbers" to collect change from the crowd giving them an opportunity to feel that they are "sponsors" of the festivities to come creating a closer relationship with us.

Point of view

If one plans or manages a festival or event from only a single point of view one may do disservice to the event and to the various stakeholders. I like to look at the design and management from as many different points of view as I can. Look at the festival or event from the point of view of the host city and relevant event-related department's, i.e. police, fire, emergency medical services, sanitation, transportation, and public works.

Please don't overlook your artists and other participants' needs and desires (other than what's it the contract "rider"). Get into the heads of your audience and spectators, plan for the needs of the staff and volunteers; understand the point of view of the venue management and venue staff. Basic questions to start this process are simple and could include "what do they need" and "how does this work (or not) work for them" can help inform your planning and decision-making.

4.   Grace under Pressure

As previously described, the Village Halloween Parade is a high-profile, creative, colorful and exciting event. Being on the street amongst the sea of humanity trying to manage with out controlling, directing without suppressing, giving and responding to directions while at times unable to even hear yourself speak due to the "roar" of the crowd and the wonderful musical cacophony taking place is an high pressure yet amazing experience.

Once you understand that (in reality) you can control what you can and you can't what you can't, it is easier to relax to some degree and enjoy the parade. Everyone in the parade has their own idea of what the parade is and how they fit in so once the parade is released it takes on a life of its own and we do what we can to allow it to unfold in a spontaneous and creative manner while maintaining some default degree of order. Keeping everything flowing, looking good, preserving the integrity of our special elements, and interacting with law enforcement is what we ultimately do. Nothing is a problem until it becomes one, and once it does, there are a myriad of possible solutions. Remembering, as discussed earlier, the festive dynamic and the transformative nature of the event informs how we "manage" it, and ourselves.

5. Why We Do It

The Halloween Parade is truly a labor of love on the part of the hundreds of artists and volunteers who put it on year after year. There is a recognition of the importance of this (and other celebrations) to our city specifically and society in general. "The idea in back of the Parade is not only to give the holiday meaning, but to reveal the City to itself" wrote E.B Mero, a public recreation advocate, in the early 20th century. Bringing people together in a festival atmosphere where barriers of race, class, religion and age are temporarily broken down and traditional roles may be reversed is a humanizing opportunity that we are grateful to have. The parade not only reveals the city to itself, but to many actually transforms individual experience.

Turner writes, in the introduction to his book that "Just as the capacity to dream and fantasize, though not immoderately, is considered by psychologists to be indispensable for mental health, so, likewise, exposure to these objectified dreams and fantasies which are thrown up by celebratory enthusiasm may be necessary for social health. Perhaps, paradoxically, we confront our own personal, singular depths more fully in these collective forms than we do through introspection for they arise from a heightened sense of our shared humanity, even if they clothe themselves in the guises of a thousand different cultures. Whether laid down or crystallized in durable images and structures or expressed in the immediacy of social "peak experience," a celebratory performance rejoices in the key values and virtues of the society that produces it, and has a history whose high points of success and conquest (or even noble failure) exemplify qualities of moral and aesthetic excellence."

The beating of the drums, the fanfare of the brass, the thousands of feet dancing in the street, a river of creativity flowing through our streets, from costumed poodles to twenty foot tall stilt walkers, grandmothers with their grandchildren, friends, lovers, people of all ages, religions and races delighting in the "celebratory enthusiasm" of New York's Greenwich Halloween Parade make it clear to all of us involved why we do this.

Harry Potter is Coming! – Deutsche Post and Weltbild at the Controls of the Hogwarts Express

Corinna Geimer, Christiane Legler, Carolin Maluck, Julia Seehausen

In the summer of 2005, the German publication of the sixth book in the Harry Potter series, "Harry Potter and the Half-Blood Prince", was imminent.

In 2003, when the fifth Harry Potter novel appeared, the Weltbild publishing group had already initiated a major marketing activity in conjunction with the Deutsche Post. On that occasion, the main focus of the activity was on the special service where the Harry Potter books were delivered hot-off-the-press at midnight on the day of publication. In 2005 too, this was to be the core focus of the large-scale Harry Potter marketing campaign staged by Weltbild and the Deutsche Post. As with the previous volume, both companies wished to put their joint efforts into offering all Harry Potter fans the extra service of having the much sought-after book brought to them by "night express delivery" within the first few hours after sales began at midnight – so to speak, right to their armchair.

1. Task and Target Group

Naturally speaking, in the case of Volume 6, the aim was to make even better use of the fans' enthusiasm, reaching and "infecting" an even wider audience.

The sales launch and the night-delivery service were to be accompanied by a prelude event for a wide audience. Not only for Potter fans, but for the general public at large, awareness of the flexible and personal service was to be highlighted, and the image of both companies associated with the likeable and young product "Harry Potter". In June 2005, the event unit of PLEON Bonn, then still known as BOB BOMLIZ GROUP Bonn, was therefore called on by its longstanding customer, the Deutsche Post, to draw up a concept for an appropriate large-scale event.

2. The Choice of the Event Location

Initially, a number of large and well-known locations such as the Europa-Park Rust and the Rosenau Stadium in Augsburg were looked at. Parallel to the creation of a multi-facetted event concept, a first step for the agency was to examine the envisaged locations and to research possible alternatives. Listing the crucial working parameters, Carolin Maluck, the project manager in charge, said, "This was not particularly easy, as we had no indication whatsoever of how many Potter fans to expect. At the same time, the question arose as to where we could find the best conditions for as Potter-oriented a setting as possible with logistics structures suitable for a large-scale event. And we had to take into account on an equal basis the wishes of both customers – the Deutsche Post and the Weltbild publishing group – with regard, for example, to the proximity to their respective group headquarters. And finally, the run-up time of just under four months was quite a sporting challenge. At that juncture, many event locations were already fully booked."

Burg Satzvey in Metternich quickly emerged as an event location capable of ideally meeting the various requirements:

- The Medieval castle atmosphere offers a stylistic match for the Potter scenery and free creative space for the visitors' imagination.
- The castle is conveniently located with good traffic accessibility in one of the most densely populated regions of Germany.
- The castle complex offers space for approximately 10,000 visitors, and the surrounding castle grounds can readily accommodate stages, special effects and atmospheric decoration and lighting.

- The annual Medieval Tournament held at the castle regularly attracts an audience of around 10,000, so that Burg Satzvey is in possession of the necessary experience with regard to traffic and logistics – while still managing to exude a far greater charm than a stadium or fun park can, both of which are directly designed as mass-audience venues.

The decisive criterion which ultimately tipped the balance in favour of Burg Satzvey, however, was the railway track which runs across the castle grounds – and which was envisaged as enabling a "big bang" to be staged surrounding the actual arrival of the books.

3. The Event Concept

The content and the legal parameters necessitated the drafting of an event concept consisting of two parts. For families and young Potter fans, an afternoon programme was drawn up under the heading of "fun and games". In order to facilitate a continuous build-up of tension up until 24:00 hours, the earliest deadline for selling the new Potter book, and with the aim of addressing a wide audience, the programme and atmosphere from 18:00 hours onwards were put under the working title of "party and music".

The question of visitor management was a particular challenge in the case of this project. The special aspects of the remit lay not only in the large numbers of visitors involved and in the uncertainty as to the actual public response, but also in the question of how to distribute tickets and in the specific legal parameters involved.

3.1 Parameters: Ticket Handling and Visitor Management

"Initially we had plans to distribute the tickets on a sales basis. The reason for this was not one of refinancing the event. It was simply a matter of obtaining calculable statistics for catering, security, traffic and parking management, etc.", is how Corinna

Geimer, in charge of the project on behalf of the Deutsche Post, described the point of departure. "However, this proved impossible from a legal standpoint, since the author, J. K. Rowling, has placed her veto on admission charges being made for any Harry Potter events."

One option was to allocate the tickets via branches of Weltbild plus and the Deutsche Post. "But arbitrary distribution of free admission tickets could have resulted in the recipients regarding the tickets as being of lesser value. It was likely that customers at the various branches would each pocket three or four more tickets than they would require for themselves and their families. The difference between the number of tickets distributed and the actual number of persons planning to attend the event would have been enormous", explained Julia Seehausen, Event Manager for the Weltbild publishing group. "We restricted ourselves to issuing personal invitations to our best and most important customers in the region. Response feedback from the persons invited provided us with a good overview of the public echo." The Deutsche Post also issued personal invitations to its most important customers and contacts.

In addition, large batches of tickets were dispersed as competition prizes. A call to enter the competition was issued by means of a nationwide direct mailing with information flyers for the event, in the context of media cooperation with various newspapers, online sites and a broadcasting group in the immediate regional vicinity, as well as via regionally distributed information posters.

Entries for the competition were registered by postcard, fax and telephone hotline. Each entrant had the chance of winning a maximum of five tickets with a single entry, the aim being especially to allow families to take part together in the event.

Since a degree of visitor fluctuation was to be expected between the afternoon and the evening, and since neither the agency nor its clients anticipated all ticket holders actually turning up for the event, a total of 20,000 tickets were issued via the channels listed. Within two-and-a-half weeks of the competition's launch on 1 September 2005, all the tickets had been allotted.

The media involved were inundated with requests for additional tickets; and a number of ticket holders successfully sold the tickets they had won via eBay.

Even in view of this positive echo prior to the event, the actual numbers of those attending on the day itself surpassed all expectations. Over the course of the day, just short of 19,000 guests celebrated together at Burg Satzvey in joint anticipation of "Harry Potter and the Half-Blood Prince". The event organised by Weltbild and the Deutsche Post was thus the biggest party worldwide in conjunction with the appearance of the sixth volume in the Harry Potter series.

Children's homes

In addition to the competition prize winners, a second group of persons was admitted to the Harry Potter party. Children and youngsters from various children's homes in Cologne were invited by the sponsors to the event at Burg Satzvey. In order to ensure the children and youngsters could attend, the invitation included a bus shuttle service to take the guests to the party and back home after the event. This charitable involvement was very well received by the children's homes, by the 250 children and youngsters from the homes and by the regional press.

VIPs

The event was given an additional highlight in the form of prominent Cologne TV personalities. RTL comedy star Janine Kunze and the "Verbotene Liebe" soap actor Ron Holzschuh were two early arrivals at the castle, coming in the afternoon with their respective partners and children. With a view to making their stay at the Harry Potter party as harmonious and peaceable as possible, a VIP area was erected at the outskirts of the event where the local personalities dropped in periodically throughout the entire party to enjoy the exclusive catering or spend a few quiet moments away from the bustle of the party atmosphere itself.

3.2 Basic Prerequisite: Atmospheric Decoration

One of the most important components of the concept was that of consistent and stringent decoration. The aim was to utilise the medieval atmosphere of Burg Satzvey without this taking the overhand; at the same time, care had to be taken to avoid direct allusion to the scenery of the Harry Potter films, since these were understandably independent of the book copyrights, and therefore not in the ownership of the clients.

Numerous walking acts – characters from the books such as Harry Potter, Hermine Granger, Ron Weasley, Albus Dumbledore and Hagrid, but also other magical and mythical creatures, castle ghosts, woodland spirits, and water sprites, a unicorn and a variety of owls and birds of prey – peopled the scenery and were at the ready to interact with the visitors. Artists on stilts with fantasy costumes illuminated from within took care of special spine-chilling effects, especially after dusk had set in. Mystic woodland creatures from Hogwarts' "forbidden forest" mingled with the guests, surprising them with weird sounds and acoustic effects.

Market and gastronomy stands were used to recreate the sensation of Diagon Alley, the wares on offer including magic wands, witches' cauldrons, amulets, flying broomsticks, and further magicians' utensils and attributes as well as, of course, original Harry Potter merchandising articles.

The range of culinary offers extended from magic potions and dishes all the way to a whole spit-roasted ox. And, floating overhead throughout the entire event, another feature was the "flying car", an inflatable, detailed copy of Arthur Weasley's flying vehicle.

All hostesses and promoters on duty at the event were outfitted with college uniforms styled on the Hogwarts clothing. Those parts of the castle interior used for the event were decorated in the proper style with satin, candelabras, bats and alternating lighting effects.

Fireplaces, cobwebs, magic brooms, large-scale portraits, and crates and canvas sacks printed with wording such as "flea powder", "dragons' hair", and "elves' dust" were distributed throughout the entire castle complex. A water sprite patiently paddled round the castle pond in a boat.

Once darkness had set in, the castle was illuminated from various directions and bathed in a multitude of colours. The castle courtyard and grounds were lit with fiery torches, furnaces and candles. A number of the walking acts, such as the water sprite and the unicorn, were picked out with spotlights. Fire acts and flame jugglers performed at various points throughout the castle grounds creating a special atmosphere there.

Low-key, yet readily identifiable branding for the event's sponsors was achieved by positioning five-by-five meter red and yellow Weltbild and Deutsche Post pagoda-style tents throughout the entire castle complex. The tents offered space for a variety of audience activities and for the sales counters where the much longed-for Harry Potter, Volume 6, was offered for sale starting at midnight.

In addition, flags bearing the logos of the two companies were hoisted on flagpoles around the Burg Satzvey jousting grounds and at the main castle entrance gate. This logo presence was supplemented by the use of classic banners in the area outside the castle.

It was possible to use the Deutsche Post mobile show truck for the central stage programme. Two roofed-over grandstands and two marquee tents, the latter with transparent, foldable side walls and furnished with long tables and benches, were erected in case of rain or showers.

3.3 The Afternoon Programme

The afternoon stage programme – held on a main stage and a side stage – was closely oriented on the school lessons which play such a major role in the J. K. Rowling novels. The contents of the various quizzes and guessing games were, for example, the ingredients for the magic potions and the magic spells and their meaning. The game of "Quidditch" was the theme behind a variety of dexterity contests held on-stage for members of the audience. By varying the ability levels of the contests and offering different prizes, young members of the audience and older Potter fans were both actively involved in the event programming. The stage shows were complemented by the performance acts of various magicians, quick-change artists and acrobats. Bernd Fuchs, TV presenter with the German channel RTL and an experienced event professional, emceed the show on the central stage.

In addition to the two main stages and the non-stop accessibility of the offers presented by the stalls in the Diagon Alley, decentralised audience participation activities were available at numerous points throughout the entire castle complex. These included short magic courses for children at hourly intervals, a children's face-painting and fancy-dress stand, a tunnel experience with spine-chill stations, a photo activity whereby children could send the resulting photo straightaway as a postcard, etc., etc.

One of the special highlights of the afternoon was a series of Potter readings from Volumes 1-5 of the books in the castle's Bourbon Hall. It had been hoped to have Rufus Beck – the narrator of the German Potter audio books – as the personality for the readings, but he was unavailable, since travelling abroad at the time. However, TV's GZSZ soap opera star Daniel Fehlow, who was enlisted as an alternative, turned out to be a major attraction, not only for the female section of the audience.

Young and old alike were further impressed by a grand bird-of-prey show held on three occasions during the afternoon at the Burg Satzvey jousting grounds. The star of the show was a huge owl which brought letters to its trainer, just as the owl Hedwig delivers letters to Harry in the Potter books.

3.4 The Evening Programme

Since the actual launch deadline for the book had, due to legal stipulations, been set for midnight, it was necessary to keep interest up between the afternoon programme and midnight itself. Anastasia, presenter on the MTV music channel and outside reporter for the "Wetten, dass … ?" wager show was successfully enlisted as emcee.

The central show programme got off to a start with the appearance of the cover band JCB. This multicultural professional ensemble consisting of two singers and four instrumentalists performed songs that were well suited to the needs and tastes of such a mixed and varied audience.

The first highlight of the programme was the finale of the grand Potter costume competition. In the course of the afternoon, all Potter fans in fancy dress who wished to enter the competition had the opportunity of being photographed by a promotion team. This was followed by the awards for the best costumes witnessed by an audience of, at this point, around 15,000 spectators. The first prize winner received a detailed Märklin scale model of the Hogwarts Express, and further high-quality Potter prizes were awarded to those placed second and third. On the whole, the competition attracted a vast number of visitors, since many of the guests had turned up wearing costumes, a good deal of them highly imaginative, and some of them almost professional.

After the costume competition prizes had been awarded, Patrick Nuo drew the audience's attention to the main stage. This Swiss artist, a number of whose singles have already made their way into the German charts, began by attracting mainly the younger members of the Potter audience. His catchy, well-performed pop soon caught the ear of the remainder of the audience, in the course of his almost 60-minute appearance.

After the concert, Anastasia prepared the Potter fans for the long-awaited highlight of the evening – the delivery of the new Potter book.

3.5   Midnight – The Arrival of the Books

30 minutes before midnight, presenter Anastasia led an "entourage" of almost 10,000 Potter friends from the main stage to the railway track where a further surprise awaited the audience – a meadow, a clearing and a stage, all of them invisible from the castle itself. Artificial fog, stroboscopic lighting in the trees, and mystical music from hidden loudspeakers lent the location a mysterious and suspense-packed atmosphere. The visitors crossed

over the nocturnal meadow and gathered on the clearing in front of the stage, directly next to the railway tracks.

In order to give the hosts the opportunity of presenting their involvement, the Deutsche Post and the Weltbild publishing group were called on to speak immediately before the countdown. Representatives of both companies addressed the audience with brief, emotional statements, thus presenting themselves memorably and long-term as hosts of this unique event.

Following the hosts' words, the mood of excitement and suspense had to be maintained till midnight. Bernd Fuchs and Anastasia announced the magicians' show. The Gebrüder Ehrlich, a famous, award-winning magic duo ("Magicians of the Year 2004"), gave a demonstration of their paramount artistry. Just before midnight, the magicians distributed to the audience a magic potion they had mixed during their act. The energy the potion gave them enabled the audience to "conjure up" the train containing the new Harry Potter book.

3.6 Hogwarts Express

The objective was to make the delivery of the books as suspense-filled and imaginative as possible. With this in mind, the arrival of the Hogwarts Express on the tracks at Burg Satzvey had been planned as the "big bang" of the evening. The train was loaded with copies of Volume 6 straight off the press.

A nostalgic locomotive had been chosen to serve as the Hogwarts Express which, in its form and construction, very closely resembled the original Express. Decorated with an eye for detail and equipped with magical light effects, the arrival of the train was to be the absolute highlight and a unique sensational surprise. Not even the media had been informed in detail of this highlight, so that they too tensely awaited the arrival of the Express.

The locomotive had undergone a comprehensive maintenance check before the event and then been driven to the nearest possible waiting position. Since the Burg Satzvey segment is part of the German railway's public track network, the nearest railway station situated ten kilometres from the Burg had to be used as the waiting position.

Just before it arrived at the castle, the locomotive came to a halt with engine damage. The mechanics in charge set to work immediately and were able to repair the damage and get the locomotive moving again within an extremely short space of time. Since the locomotive was a unique specimen, it was impossible to have a back-up engine available as might otherwise have been the case. In order to ensure the best possible back-up service, however, specialist mechanics had been hired for the full railway assignment, and they finally succeeded in repairing the breakdown within the space of 45 minutes.

Operating alone on the main stage – his co-presenter had to catch a flight urgently and was unable to stay on – Bernd Fuchs managed to resolve the precarious situation very professionally. He invited members of the audience onto the stage and read scenes from the last volume with them. By thus integrating them in the stage programme, Fuchs held the attention of the eagerly waiting audience, and prevented them going home disappointed.

Just before 1 a.m., the Express finally arrived at the castle, puffing steam, bathed in fairytale lighting and bearing the sixth volume in the Harry Potter series, much to the delight of the visitors.

Visitors to the event also had the opportunity of purchasing the book on site, starting at midnight. Sealed crates containing the books had been delivered in the course of the afternoon and had been guarded throughout the entire event by security personnel. At the stroke of midnight, the crates were opened and sales commenced at the many sales counters in the castle, so that the Potter fans present could begin reading the book at once.

Despite the brief hiccup caused by the breakdown of the steam engine, the event was nevertheless blessed with good fortune insofar as the weather remained stable throughout the entire party, much of which took place in the open air. It did not begin to rain until roughly half an hour after the official end of the event.

4. Feedback

The huge impression the book-launch party had made on audience and media alike became clear after the event. Media coverage of this, the largest event marking the book's publication, was comprehensive, nationwide and highly satisfactory. Thanks to the cooperation with regional radio stations, the wide distribution of the admission tickets, and persistent press relations, media interest was already high in advance of the event.

Coverage of the event itself was given not only by regional channels, but also by ZDF, Sat.1 and RTL in their News & People formats.

Public interest in the event was overwhelming, with innumerable requests for additional admission tickets beforehand, and a final toll of 19,000 attending the event.

Weeks after it took place, the event was still vividly present for those who had attended, as testified by numerous letters and cards of thanks sent to the hosts and to media editors by visitors to the party, enthusiastically expressing what a wonderful day they had experienced at the castle.

The children and youngsters from the Cologne children's homes will also have long-lasting positive memories of the party – one week after the super party, they were sent parcels by the sponsors containing original merchandising articles and the original college uniforms from the Potter party.

For them and for all the other fans, there has only been one burning question, right since the day after the biggest-ever Harry Potter party. – Will the Deutsche Post and the Weltbild publishing group be extending an invitation again to another party to mark the appearance of the seventh, presumably the last, Harry Potter book in the summer of 2007?

Communicating a Country – Denmark's HCA Event Viewed from the PR Side

Lars Blicher-Hansen, Christian Have

"We do not have too much to brag about in a small country like Denmark but we have one world famous person – Hans Christian Andersen – and it would be a miss for us if we did not take the opportunity to make a world-wide cultural celebration and some cultural profiling of Denmark on the occasion of his 200th birthday.

My involvement with the project is two fold – I am a member of the Board of Directors of the Hans Christian Andersen 2005 Foundation, while also being responsible for cultural event tourism in Denmark in the national tourism organization VisitDemark.

The program of Hans Christian Andersen 2005 started on April 2, the birthday of Hans Christian Andersen, and concluded on December 6. We had three main purposes with the celebration: to ensure that as many people as possible world-wide would attain a greater and more nuanced familiarity with Hans Christian Andersen – we wanted to inform people that Andersen was not only a fairy-tale writer, but also a travel writer, poet, playwright, artist and, to a high degree, a philosopher. Our second – and secondary – purpose was to create awareness about Denmark as Andersen's homeland and as an interesting cultural destination. Today we can say that we were successful with these two objectives. One third purpose was to make the Danes proud of "their" Han Christian Andersen and the fact that a small country could do a grand international celebration. Did we succeed in that? The answer is no.

The Hans Christian Andersen 2005 Foundation was established by the Bikuben Foundation, the City of Odense, the County of Funen, the Danish Ministry of Culture and the Danish Ministry of Economic and Business Affairs. The foundation was an interesting mix of private and public funding. The contribution of approximately 11 million EUR by the Bikuben Foundation is by far the largest private donation given to a European cultural event. In total, the foundation was financed with approximately 31 million EUR. We wished to make a multicultural event crossing borders, languages, cultures and politics. Instead of the initially planned 35 countries, the foundation has given financial support to independent activities in almost 50 countries world-wide. The supported activities include ballet, modern dance, classical music, theatre, TV, radio, film, conferences, art exhibitions, tourist attractions, etc.

Our strategic partner has been a network consisting of the official representatives of Denmark: Danish embassies and consulates, Danish Cultural Institutes, market offices of VisitDenmark and selected communication agencies. In addition, we announced Hans Christian Andersen Ambassadors. In total 180 high-profile personalities – statesmen, actors, singers, writers, sportsmen, etc – acted as Hans Christian Andersen Ambassadors in key markets, creating visibility and media coverage and immediate interest in the celebration.

We started with a warm-up for the celebration during 2003 and 2004. We have done a lot of web-based promotion; also to promote Hans Christian Andersen related tourisms. In Denmark, we have had a lot of different activities, probably a few too many. However, some of the initiatives that began in 2005 will stay there in the future (for example, new museums). In one of our projects called "Andersen was here" we located different places in Denmark which inspired the writer. We made a special website, HCA2005.com, in different languages, published e-mail newsletters and various publications, including an 18-volume collection of Andersen's works. There was even Hans Christian Andersen beer and wine.

The results so far are great: we have had 50,000 – 60,000 registered press clippings, which mean publicity worth at least 100 million EUR. We made 12 video news releases, i.e. sent out live footage via satellite for free usage by television stations, which got about 500 million viewers. Around a hundred tour operators have made their Denmark programmes.

Of course, we hope that the most important result of the project will be the long-term value. We do a survey of tourists every year, asking them a number of questions, including their motivation for the visit. In the second and third quarter of 2005, 72% of all hotel guests were aware of the Hans Christian Andersen celebrations and 9% of those guests (6% in total) mentioned Hans Christian Andersen as a main or partial reason for their coming to Denmark.

As I already mentioned, we achieved two of our three main objectives, but some things also went wrong. We had very high ambitions. When the taxpayer's money is involved, it makes the issue very sensible and a slightest mistake can cause negative press. So, while the press outside Denmark has been fabulous, in Denmark we have also had problems. The budget of the opening show was exceeded (because of including a performance by Tina Turner), resulting in the change of the Chairman and the Secretary General of the Hans Christian Andersen 2005 Foundation, which caused as scandal in the Danish media.

The lesson to be learned from our project is: prepare the home base. This was something that we also experienced when Copenhagen was the European Capital of Culture in 1996. However, we are still glad that we did the celebration and are looking forward to the future. The year 2006 is the Mozart year and in Austria there has already been criticism of the people running the celebration. Everybody has his or her vision of how the celebration should be done. We, however, will be looking forward to the 300th anniversary of Hans Christian Andersen." (*Speech held by Lars Blicher-Hansen in Estonia, 2006*)

1. Background and General Objective

In 2005, Denmark celebrated the bicentennial of the birth of storyteller Hans Christian Andersen with an international arts year. The aim was to encourage a wider and deeper understanding of

Hans Christian Andersen's life and work, a unique opportunity to take a closer look at the man and the poet.

Most people are familiar with works like *The Ugly Duckling, The Emperor's New Clothes* and *Clumsy Hans*, but there was a feeling that the image of the Danish author had become narrow and constrained – too idealised and simplistic – and part of the mission became to excavate the writer and view his work and its contemporary relevance anew.

Andersen was a storyteller for children of all ages, but he was also a knowledgeable critical journalist with great enthusiasm for science, an existential thinker, an observant travel book writer, a passionate novelist, a deft paper clip artist, a neurotic hypochondriac and a sex-fixated eccentric. He was a man of demons, dreams, yearnings and visions. He was a man of flesh and blood.

Education was crucial to Hans Christian Andersen's authorship. Had it not been for education – there would have been no Hans Christian Andersen. The same lessons apply today.

Consequently, two of the central issues highlighting the celebration were education and research. The hope was that inspirational material for primary school teachers, research publications and projects, conferences and prize papers would contribute to the opening up of new aspects and interpretations of Hans Christian Andersen's life and work.

Hans Christian Andersen 2005 was launched as a celebration of Denmark and a rediscovery of the perhaps most famous Dane ever. And in all aspects of communication, special emphasis was given to associating Hans Christian Andersen with Odense, Copenhagen and Denmark. It was necessary to bring the modern and timeless Andersen into play when showing to the world that Denmark was in the forefront within art, culture, design, technology and ethics.

The fact that the organisation and the funding of the project was made up by both of political, public and private parties meant a great variety of stakeholders and resulted in that project work and communication was challenged on a daily basis.

2.   The Overall Strategy

The Hans Christian Andersen 2005 Foundation came into being through a historic agreement between the Danish State, spearheaded by the Ministry of Culture and the Ministry of Economic and Business Affairs, and Odense Municipality, Funen County and Bikuben Foundation. The backers contributed a total of DKR 200 million for this national and international celebration, making HCA2005 Denmark's biggest cultural effort ever, a national campaign aimed at catching world-wide attention for Hans Christian Andersen.

To achieve The Hans Christian Andersen 2005 Foundation's general objectives, the Foundation focused on two main areas:

- Project/production
- Communication

Hans Christian Andersen 2005 acted as co-producer but productions were generally considered to be the responsibility of collaboration partners. The Foundation took initiatives, but rarely assumed direct control of productions, and entered into contractual agreements and partnerships with professional organisations.

The partnerships were mostly co-productions with one or more contributing funding partners, with the producing organisations raising the majority of funds needed and with Hans Christian Andersen 2005 contributing additional funds to make extraordinary achievements possible. This strategy ensured full and responsible involvement from all partners and Hans Christian Andersen 2005 made it part of its terms and conditions for entering into co-producing partnerships that the productions in question be shown in a minimum of three countries: the country where the production originated from, as well as Denmark and one other destination. Projects and productions were planned in three main areas:

- Art and entertainment
- Education
- Tourism

Projects were categorised to facilitate an understanding of the opportunities involved. There were four general categories:

- Major international projects to be launched worldwide
- Projects with international partners primarily of interest to the national media in the respective countries
- Nationwide projects
- Local projects

Projects were also categorised according to the commercial aspects of the individual projects. Research related projects were launched differently compared to tourism related projects. What all these projects had in common was that they were communicated as widely as possible without compromising quality.

A decision had been made to disregard the age-group aspect when defining project related target group segments. Instead of targeting selected age groups, as has been the tradition for several decades within the world of communication, emphasis was given to the current and more efficient trend of addressing groups of people with common interests. Planning was divided into three phases:

- 2002/03 Preparation and Planning
- Production
- Presentation

3. Overview of Projects and Involvement

Throughout 2003, the Foundation planned programs within the three main areas that were to constitute Hans Christian Andersen 2005. Negotiations took place with artists and organisations in Denmark and abroad and all proposals were evaluated by the Foundation's artistic council before the Foundation started looking for additional partners or entered into agreements. News of project partnerships was released continuously. Subsequently, the role of Hans Christian Andersen 2005 was primarily one of coordination between co-producers and international communication and promotion as well as following up on the projects in question. It goes without saying that although Hans Christian Andersen 2005 was not actually producing projects, the Foundation followed all collaborations closely, based on regular reports that all partners were contractually obliged to submit.

A number of educational projects were planned within kindergartens as well as primary and secondary schools. Hans Christian Andersen was used as a lever for exploring new paths within pedagogies. A number of pilot projects were initiated in educational institutions.

"Hans Christian Andersen for the Sixth Grade" was a project where all Danish schools received a new illustrated edition of Hans Christian Andersen's best-known fairy tales. The book was introduced to sixth graders. In cooperation with the Danish Centre for Children's Literature, The Hans Christian Andersen 2005 Foundation provided inspirational material about Hans Christian Andersen for schoolteachers that worked with children approximately age 6 – 16. This material was also translated into multiple languages and was made available free of charge on the Internet for download. Many of Hans Christian Andersen's fairy tales were translated into new languages and old stories were published in new editions. Among others, the complete work of Hans Christian Andersen has been republished in Danish in 18 volumes and more than 9,000 pages.

The book has been published into the following languages for the first time: Chinese, English, French, Polish, Russian, Spanish, Italian, Turkish, Arabic, Japanese and Hungarian.

The lasting legacy of the bicentenary was also secured through the establishing of a humanitarian foundation: The Hans Christian Andersen abc Foundation. It was established to make a worldwide contribution to combating illiteracy.

Prior to the bicentenary, a number of activities contributed in spurring Danish and international interest in the celebration:

- In Denmark Hans Christian Andersen's birthday was celebrated in Odense in 2004 with a number of performances relating to the author, and with an award ceremony for Odense Municipality's great Andersen Award presented to a number of artists designated to create new works during the bicentenary.

- A number of pilot projects were initiated in Education and Tourism.
- The celebration portal www.HCA2005.dk was established in collaboration with the Odense Municipality Museums, the University of Southern Denmark and the Royal Danish Library. The portal provided access to the collaborating partners' collections and news about HCA2005.
- A number of books were published from 2003 onwards, including Andersen's Collected Works, all of which generated interested and qualified the general audience to appreciate the celebrations.
- A number of Hans Christian Andersen 2005 launches abroad, organised in collaboration with the offices of the Danish Tourist Board, local PR agencies, consulates and embassies generated continuous interest.
- The first press conference announcing the appointment of Andersen Goodwill Ambassadors took place in September 2002. Another events launch followed on Ellis Island, USA in 2004.

A number of the international co-productions opened and toured from the summer 2004 onwards – usually receiving their world premieres in the towns and cities where they were originally produced before moving on to festivals like the Lincoln Festival, Festival d'Automne and Barbican's BITE and before being presented in Denmark during the main celebrations. A number of projects continued to tour internationally beyond 2005.

In Denmark, the celebration period was limited to 2nd April (Andersen's birthday) – 6th December 2005 (the day Andersen was received in Odense, the city of his birth, as an honorary citizen).

4.   PR and Information – Locally, Nationally and Internationally

The PR and information related approach to Hans Christian Andersen 2005 was to build the project continuously over years –

and not simply start a few weeks before the grand opening in Denmark on 2 April 2005. This strategy was based on the argument that the many international launches of Hans Christian Andersen 2005 projects all over the world were a time consuming task, which demanded a much longer timeframe.

The first phase of the celebrations started in year 2003 and was dealing with the widening of public awareness of Hans Christian Andersen and his bicentennial in 2005. Phase one lasted approximately one year. Phase two aimed at enhancing the awareness of the content and vision of the celebration while phase three involved the launching of the entire Hans Christian Andersen 2005 project.

In 2003, the first phase and kick-off of the Hans Christian Andersen 2005 celebrations began on three levels: locally, nationally and internationally.

4.1 Locally

First and foremost, the project and secretariat of the Hans Christian Andersen 2005 Foundation were locally based in Funen, Denmark with a very high level of information and could actively involve the relevant institutions.

4.2 Nationally

Simultaneously, the project was launched nationwide. Partnership had been forged with, among others, Wonderful Copenhagen and the Danish Tourist Board. Also, press conferences were held on the launch of the hca2005.com portal and on the framework agreement with the Danish Broadcasting Corporation, DR, and in connection with the awarding of the Odense City Hans Christian Andersen Award.

4.3 Internationally

Parallel to the national efforts, an international network of selected PR platforms was established – i.e. PR agencies and/or PR consultants, embassies, consulates and key market representatives of the Danish Tourist Board – to ensure global media coverage.

Hans Christian Andersen 2005 was widely represented at international travel fairs, cultural expos and other international events suitable for project exposure.

5. The General Communication Task – International Perspective

The primary and most important communication task of the project was no doubt to convey to the whole world, including Denmark, what Hans Christian Andersen stood for. Naturally, the project was Danish but the general aim was global – just as it was for Andersen himself. This is why this catch phrase was devised to emphasise this:

Hans Christian Andersen 2005 – Join the world-wide celebration

This catch phrase set out 2005 as a worldwide Hans Christian Andersen Year. The communication strategy was specifically targeted at generating global awareness of Hans Christian Andersen and, through him, Denmark and its values.

A sure basis for such ra strategy was predicted since contacts had clearly shown an intenational interest in participating in the celebration, and the Hans Christian Andersen 2005 Foundation had reason to believe that large, important cultural institutions and public figures within the arts were willing to back Hans Christian Andersen 2005.

The catch phrase followed the marketing title 'Hans Christian Andersen 2005' and was featured on all logo material where possible – posters, cloth banners and advertisement, animations, printed matter, etc.

6.   Criteria for Success

Comprehensive documentation of the whole project was, of course, planned to ensure proper reporting and to be able to document and pass on experiences from a very vast project.

The project was to be measured by a large number of qualitative/quantitative success criteria.

6.1   Qualitative Targets

- Benefiting parties and artistic partners: satisfaction with the project
- Other stakeholders
- Local audience satisfaction
- National audience satisfaction
- International audience satisfaction
- The financial stakeholders: satisfaction with the project
- Communication partners: satisfaction with the project

6.2   Quantitative Targets

- Project target
- Media target – TV potential
- Press response target
- Audience target
- Target for increase in tourism and conventions

7.   Hans Christian Andersen 2005 Ambassadors

A committee of Hans Christian Andersen 2005 Ambassadors was established to create international awareness of Hans Christian Andersen 2005. This was done simply by the presence of an ambassador at different events related to the Andersen bicentenary or an ambassador sharing his or hers view of Andersen with the world. Hans Christian Andersen Ambassadors endeavoured to promote awareness and the wider appreciation of Hans Christian Andersen, his life, his work and his enduring message of human- ism, magic and imagination. Hans Christian Andersen Ambassa- dors were furthermore to help create awareness of the bicenten- nial celebrations in their home countries as well as the humanitar- ian purpose of the Hans Christian Andersen celebration.

2004 Hans Christian Andersen Ambassadors plus Honorary Ambassadors were selected among public figures and celebrities within the fields of literature, television, film, theatre, dance, mu- sic, business, sports, education, philanthropy, entertainment and politics.

Hans Christian Andersen Ambassadors in Denmark were se- lected by the Hans Christian Andersen 2005 Foundation. Hans Christian Andersen Ambassadors from other countries were se- lected by the Hans Christian Andersen 2005 Foundation in consul- tation with partners from the country in question, i.e. the Royal Danish Embassy in conjunction with the marketing department of the Danish Tourist Board and/or a local communication agency. Foreign representatives within Denmark also offered suggestions and facilitated contact with potential Hans Christian Andersen Ambassadors.

A celebrated Dane or an official representative from Denmark preferably, appointed the ambassador and thus marked the open- ing of Hans Christian Andersen 2005 in the country in question. A letter was issued to the Hans Christian Andersen 2005 Ambassa- dors relating the vision behind the ambassador concept, the role and tasks they were to undertake and what H.C. Andersen 2005 had to offer the ambassadors. All of the Hans Christian Andersen 2005 Ambassadors were invited to the grand opening on 1-3 April 2005.

8. The Primary Media Platforms

Experience from similar very large manifestations shows that in- ternational communication should be based on the following three main media areas:

- Newspaper and magazine articles
- TV/Radio
- Digital Communications e.g. HCA2005 Portal

8.1 TV, Film and Radio

TV, film and radio were the most powerful media with which to convey Hans Christian Andersen. The TV media was a key partner in promoting Hans Christian Andersen 2005.

An extensive TV and radio coverage of the entire project was desirable. As already mentioned, an agreement was made with the Danish Broadcasting Corporation (DR).

The TV media has great and wide-reaching international impact, especially – as the case was – if programmes are syndicated. Programmes on Hans Christian Andersen fell into several categories ranging from documentary, drama and children's programmes. This is why setting precise targets for media impact was manageable – and the impact was immense!

Hans Christian Andersen programmes contained most of the ingredients necessary to ensure TV success:

- Universal human condition
- Humour
- Concerns everyone universally
- He is a universal household name
- Represents many aspects and layers
- Can be told in many ways
- Can be treated on an intellectual as well as entertaining level

DR (Danish Broadcasting Corporation), as official Hans Christian Andersen 2005 media partner, contributed enormously to the visibility of Hans Christian Andersen 2005. Among their many projects was the TV-series "Young Andersen", which won an Emmy for "Best Foreign Miniseries" in November 2005. The two episodes were broadcast in February 2005 on DR1, Sunday evening at 8 p.m. (primetime) and were watched by 1.3 million viewers. [42]

China – Europe Interact Culture & Communication Co, Ltd. was behind the TV-series "Hans Christian Andersen – the Fairytale-like Life of the Fairytale Writer". This Chinese TV-series regarding the life of Hans Christian Andersen was shown 1 – 3 April 2005 in three episodes on CCTV.

CCTV reaches 90 percent of the Chinese population and part of South East Asia and has a potential of 1.1 billion viewers.

A Hans Christian Andersen DAB radio channel was established and Hans Christian Andersen was the centre of the Danish National Choir and the Danish Nationals Girls Choir's 2005 programme.

The programme – for the Thursday concerts in Copenhagen and for the tours to Europe and the Far East – had three agendas: new compositions; well-known works, which took their points of departure in the poet's life and writing; and music by Hans Christian Andersen's many composer friends. The programme was thereby a reflection of the music surrounding Hans Christian Andersen, as well as his life and work.

In the period from 2 April to 12 December 2005, 183 short radio pictures of three to seven minutes duration was broadcasted daily on Danish Broadcasting Corporation's P2. The broadcast was a daily greeting from Hans Christian Andersen on one of his countless journeys. Hans Christian Andersen's diaries and travel letters was the founding texts and as a rule they were performed in chronological order. The music was especially composed for the series and performed by The Danish Radio Sinfonietta.

9. Information Matters

Information was the basis of communication with the local, national and international networks. Information was disseminated through newsletters and through a small number of strategic press conferences.

---

42 *The Danish population counts 5.4 million people year 2005 – Statistics Denmark*

9.1 Press Conferences

Press conferences were held within each key market area when Hans Christian Andersen 2005 was launched. Additionally, infrequent press conferences were held when deemed sufficiently necessary. The partners took part in the press conferences when necessary. An average of one press conference a month was normal in 2003, 2004 and 2005 with the exception of Hans Christian Andersen's birthday and other special events. Additionally, regular press briefings were given in either Odense or Copenhagen, which naturally were of more informal nature.

International press conferences in key markets were held separately.

9.2 Event Catalogue

In early 2005, an illustrated event catalogue was issued with a full list of all Hans Christian Andersen 2005 events world-wide. The event catalogue was published in Danish, English, German and Japanese.

9.3 The HCA2005.COM Portal

All headings on the hca2005.com pages featured three pulsating threads in the colours of the partners. The threads symbolise the interconnecting of the world through the project with the portal as the main instrumental asset.

Hans Christian Andersen 2005 was a project with great, worldwide demand for information in relation to the general public and – on a more confidential level – project partners. Information was available from a single source only to ensure correct dissemination of information to all parties.

The hca2005.com portal mirrored the entire Hans Christian Andersen 2005 project and was pivotal in the overall objective of providing information on the Danish fairytale author.

This portal was one of the most important communication tools during the Hans Christian Andersen 2005 celebrations. Since

January 2003 internet users were able to surf the informative and interactive sites on the portal. There was a complete Danish and English edition as well as 14 minor editions translated into other languages.

Since January 2003 and until September 2005 the portal has had 1.090.257 unique users[43] and 3.872.683 page references. The traffic was heaviest in the period from February – May 2005, which were the months just before and after the 200th birthday of Hans Christian Andersen.

10. Grand Opening: The Fairy Tale Weekend

On Friday, 1 April 2005 The Royal Danish Theatre opened the bi-centennial celebration of the birth of Hans Christian Andersen with a performance entitled *"Horseradish Soup and Stuffed Cabbage"* that united drama, mime, singing, dancing, music and artistry – the quintessence of Andersen's art.

This was not a performance about Hans Christian Andersen, but a tribute to him.

On Saturday 2 April the festivities continued in the city of Odense. It was a day with fabulous variations on Hans Christian Andersen's many fairy tales and characters. There were concerts, readings and presentation of the city's main Hans Christian Andersen Award.

During the evening the whole world was entertained by a two-hour, live TV broadcast from Copenhagen, Denmark. The show was called "Once upon a Time".

The broadcast was a magical performance incorporating some of Hans Christian Andersen's most popular fairy tales and inter-preting them through narration, song, and dance as well as short dramatic films, giving a taste of the writer's life story. More than a 100 million viewers around the world[44] watched sequences from

---

43 *Unique users are different users which have visited the homepage in a given pe-riod of time. The information's are based on a registration of the users IP-address as well as placement of cookies in the browser (Source: Google).*
44 *EBU, Reuters, APTN and Wonderful Copenhagen*

the show, which was showed by more than 60 international TV-stations.

The three day long opening event ended on Sunday, 3 April 2005 with a reception held at the City Hall of Copenhagen.

These events were all attended by the Danish Royal family as well as Danish and foreign Hans Christian Andersen Ambassadors from all over the world.

11. Some Highlight Events

Hans Christian Andersen 2005 was a project that widely embraced very large productions with a popular appeal as well as more marginal productions with narrow appeal. For this reason, the communication task involved segmenting the areas covered by Hans Christian Andersen 2005.

Below are three major projects and events, which have had great impact on the visibility of Hans Christian Andersen 2005.

"The Andersen Project" of Robert Lepage visiting the Danish Royal Theater May 2005, followed by a world tour until June 2006.

The "Berliner Märchentage" from 3 – 20 November 2005. (Annual Fairytale Festival in Berlin and Northern Germany) In 2005 the festival was dedicated completely to the celebration of Hans Christian Andersen. More than 150,000 people visited the festival, which had 1,300 Hans Christian Andersen projects in 330 different places. "Berliner Märchentage" was one of the greatest Hans Christian Andersen projects through the celebration year.

The Travelling Exhibition about Hans Christian Andersen made by Odense City Museums. The exhibition has now been shown in 43 countries and more than 250 locations around the world. The Travelling Exhibition has been translated into: Dutch, English, Japanese, French, German, Chinese, Spanish, Czech, Polish and Portuguese. [45]

---

45 *Odense City Museums*

12. Media Monitor

Since 1 January 2003, The Hans Christian Andersen 2005 has received weekly batches of press clippings about Hans Christian Andersen 2005 from the printed media in 35 countries. During this timeframe 36,360 press clippings have been registered in total.

With reference to materials collected from international partners and Danish embassies around the world until 1 November 2005, two reports have been made to estimate the worldwide visibility of Hans Christian Andersen 2005.

This is based on programmes from radio, television and video news releases as well as 14,903 press clippings from print media outside of Denmark. The media value and therefore visibility of Hans Christian Andersen 2005 internationally has been estimated at 3.12 billions DKK. (Approx. 413,000,000 EUR Jan. 2006) – it is considered to be an extremely conservative estimate.

13. Results at a Glance

- The Hans Christian Andersen 2005 has resulted in 250 projects getting financial support and an additional 130 projects were given the Hans Christian Andersen 2005 logo collaboration. Only 10 of the planned projects were cancelled due to different causes – economic and artistic. Besides the official projects, local initiatives helped bringing the total of Hans Christian Andersen projects up to more than 2000 worldwide.
- The humanitarian initiative has resulted in the establishment of the Hans Christian Andersen abc Foundation. The Hans Christian Andersen abc Foundation has joined UNICEF and UNESCO on their existing literacy-programmes. Three programmes have already been targeted and more will follow in the future.
- In total 204 Hans Christian Andersen Ambassadors and Honorary Ambassadors were appointed.
- The Hans Christian Andersen celebration abroad has given Denmark a lot of positive interest and attention, which is to

be considered priceless – also in the long run. The Hans Christian Andersen celebration 2005 has given Denmark an image as a culture and event destination, which was very much needed. 72 percent of American visitors in Denmark and 58 percent of Japanese visitors knew about the Hans Christian Andersen celebration before their journey to Denmark during the celebration year.[46]

- The H. C. Andersen celebrations achieved a level of visibility that far exceeded what was expected: among other things monitoring services returned 14,903 press cuttings from 35 countries – a number estimated to have a monetary, commercial value in the area of DKR 3,120,000,000[47].

- The opening weekend events 1 – 3 April 2005 peaked with the show on April 2nd which was broadcast to a potential 593,000,000 viewers in 29 countries.

- H. C. Andersen Paraden in Copenhagen in September had potential viewer ratings of 56,700,000 world-wide, and an estimated commercial value of DKR 5,600,000.[48]

- The appointment of football legend Pelé as Hans Christian Andersen Ambassador was potentially viewed by 53,000,000 with an estimated monetary value of DKR 5,300,000.[49]

- The Copenhagen city walks "In the Footsteps of H. C. Andersen" -potential viewers came to 40 million and the programme had an estimated monetary value of DKR 5,600,000.[50]

- A total of DKR 102,000,000 was allocated to artistic and cultural initiatives both in Denmark and abroad. This includes the translation of the collected works of H.C. Andersen, permanent museum exhibitions and other initiatives that will give Andersen visibility for a long time into the future.

---

46 Report on tourisms impact on economic and employment – for VisitDenmark autumn 2005
47 1 Danish Crown (DKR) equals 0.15 EUR or 0.17 $US – status: August 2006
48 Report from Wonderful Copenhagen
49 Report from Wonderful Copenhagen
50 Report from Wonderful Copenhagen

- DKR 15,000,000 was allocated in subvention of educational projects, including the translation of educational material into 20 languages. This material has been available for download from the internet, for free.
- According to the search engine Google, H.C. Andersen broke all records for a Danish name with no fewer than 772,000 page references that are three times the number he had had 1 ½ years before 2005.
- DKR 24,000,000 was invested in H.C. Andersen projects related to tourism. This has given a focus on H.C. Andersen as a draw for tourists. On top, a number of tourism related press trips were organised for 67 reporters and photographers. H.C. Andersen has been visible in various tourism trade fairs in the years 2003-2005.

TOYOTA – The Cologne City Grand Prix

Kay Dallmann

The Toyota Motor Co. Ltd (Toyota) was established in 1937 by Kiichiro Toyoda as a spin-off from Toyoda Automatic Loom Works. Today Toyota is one of the leading car manufacturers of the world, known for quality, reliability, durability and sociability. Customer perceptions vary widely throughout the world. Next to vehicles produced for the mass market Toyota has built a long history of success in the motor-sport world. As for the success in manufacturing of vehicles, Toyota's success in motor-sport is rooted in the "Toyota Way", which stands on two main pillars: Respect for People and Continuous Improvement. The Toyota way is a very subtle accumulation of best practices, philosophy and innovative processes.

The Toyota Way

Two Pillars: Continuous Improvement, and Respect for People.

Challenge

We form a long-term vision, meeting challenges with courage and creativity to realize our dreams.
- Creating value through manufacturing and delivery of products and services
- Spirit of challenge
- Long-range perspective
- Thorough consideration in decision making

Kaizen

We improve our business operations continuously, always driving for innovation and evolution.
- Kaizen mind and innovative thinking
- Building lean systems and structure
- Promoting organization learning

Genchi Genbutsu

We practice Genchi Genbutsu... go to the source to find the facts to make correct decisions, build consensus and achieve goals at our best speed.
- Genchi Genbutsu
- Effective consensus building
- Commitment to achievement

Respect
We respect others, make every effort to understand each other, take respon-
sibility and do our best to build mutual trust.
- Respect for Stakeholders
- Mutual Trust and Mutual responsibility
- Sincere Communication

Team work
We stimulate personal and professional Growth, share the opportunities of
development and maximize individual and team performance.
- Commitment to education and development
- Respect for the individual; realizing consolidated power as a team

Table 8: The Toyota Way[51]

Toyota has captured many WRC and CART titles, and made a significant impact at the 24 Hours of Le Mans. Toyota is one of the
top manufacturers in terms of different racing categories and
sheer number of race entries – a presence that has supported the
development of the motor-sport itself over the years.

The motto has been, and continues to be, taking on new challenges in new areas. Having completed all of the groundwork,
perhaps it was inevitable that Toyota would challenge the pinna-
cle of motor-sport, the F1 Series. Next to the internal challenge,
the platform offered high media-value and can possibly lead to a
change in customer perception towards a more emotional, dynamic and technologically advanced perception.

To build a competitive Formula 1 racing-car, Toyota decided to
use its existing motor-sports facilities in Cologne, Germany. Since
its foundation the Toyota Motorsport GmbH (TMG from now on)
has been the breeding place of many success stories, ranging
from several World Rally Championships to a successful entry into
Le Mans. The heritage and knowledge provided by TMG were the
basis for a start into the Formula 1 with the Panasonic Toyota
Racing Team. As of today, TMG is the only Formula 1 race car
manufacturer to build in Germany.

The Toyota Deutschland GmbH (TDG from now on) is located just opposite to the TMG. TDG is embedded in the
structure of Toyota Motor Europe (TME from now on) as a
National Marketing and Service Company. TDG is responsible

51 Source: TMC

for the sales and the marketing of Toyota products in Germany. In 2005, TDG employed 336 people and sold a total of 132,000 vehicles. The vehicles sold places TDG among the largest importers in Germany.

For TDG the superior quality of its products and services resulted in a real value proposition in terms of customer satisfaction. Throughout the German media landscape Toyota vehicles are known for their reliability and price to quality ratio. However, buying decisions are not solely driven by human rational. Selling a superior product in mature market conditions is possible only when people perceive more than pure product value. TDG is needed to make people become aware of the products' emotional dimension.

In 2003 a new CEO took position at TDG. One of the objectives of TDG became to emotionalise brand perception. Some of the early guiding questions were: how to utilize the possibilities given by the geographical closeness of TMG and TDG? How to integrate the Panasonic Toyota Racing Team beyond the official media and race calendar? How to reinforce the awareness of Toyota constructing its Formula 1 race-car in Cologne, Germany? How to bring Formula 1 closer to the people to create a unique experience benefiting TDG? How to thank Cologne and its citizens for their support?

An idea was born: The Toyota City Grand Prix

The answer was to generate a genuine city Formula 1 feeling for the citizens of Cologne. Together with the citizens, the media and VIPs were considered to share in the excitement created by the sound and speed of the Toyota Formula 1 racing-cars. This triggered a link that created interest towards the Toyota brand, reinforcing its values plus creating additional emotional connections. In short: motorsport on a friendly but sophisticated level; offers a customer experience that enables contact with the evolution of the Toyota brand and its products.

1. The Goals and Objectives

Deducted from the idea, several goals and objectives were established:

1. To move closer to Cologne and its people, demonstrating the area of motorsport while presenting itself as a sympathetic brand
2. To strengthen and emotionalize the tie between Toyota and F1 in Germany
3. To emotionalize the brand
4. To strengthen the ties between Cologne and Toyota
5. To combine a public event with a media event and to explain the brand Toyota in a comprehensive, more personal and experimental mode.

The convergence of interest was only overcome by diligent preparation. One of the first tasks was to identify all of the parties involved, collect all the relevant information and create a common understanding of the goals and objectives. The Toyota Way's principles were guiding in that process.

2. Internal Resources

Before approaching outside parties a good understanding of the use and availability of internal resources was developed. A review of the goals and objectives was inevitable. Key-words such as: Cologne, Germany, media-event, personal, comprehensive and demonstration, triggered a feeling about the scope of the project. The scope of the project and TDG's company structure meant that several departments had to be involved. It was anticipated that working across departments would make coordination and communication more complex. Therefore, communication was key, right from the start.

For this project two departments, the marketing and the press department, worked jointly from the beginning. Both departments ensured the necessary links to advertising agencies, media agencies, TV-stations, VIPs and last but not least the event agency. To guide and monitor progress of the project a project manager was selected right at the beginning. The structure applied for coordination was a project structure being able to exchange resources on demand.

In this project, the buy-in from the CEO and the empowerment of the project manager allowed for fast progression when dealing with other parties. During the project it appeared that a guiding coalition at the top management level and a shared vision across all parties eased reaction time and decision making.

3. The Parties Involved

Next to the obvious parties of TDG, TME, TMG and the City of Cologne, several other external parties needed to be involved: the first being the event-agency. Therefore a briefing was set up and circulated to event agencies with a record of public events of similar size. The briefing included a short description of the initial situation, the defined goals and objectives, the target group, the task and a timeline. A budget was not given to increase the level of possible inputs. After the agency was selected a common understanding was developed on the basis of a rough draft. At the same time a timeline with milestones and a date of no return was established. The timeline was drawn up using a backward approach. Milestones and the point of no return were given by physical processes and experience such as printing of invitations, booking of advertising space, development of key visual and consent with media and the city authorities. From the day onwards, the concept of the event was presented, three month were left until the execution.

Booking of advertising space and key visuals involved other parties as an advertising agency and a media agency. As the agencies were already in daily contact with the marketing department as part of their contract, no additional briefings needed to be written. Media broadcast was one of the most critical milestones, as the 2nd objective could not have been met without the reach and frequency popular television channels offer.

Timeline until Event

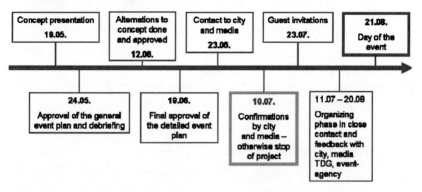

Figure 27: Timeline until event

4.   The Target Group(s)

The target group could not be divided according to demographics. The event was planned to be in the city centre and was targeted at young and old and families and singles alike. The challenge was to find activities that were entertaining to the very young, the dynamic and the elderly at the same time. The common basis for targeting was that the activities should respect TDG fundamentals such as safety first and contribute to the sophisticated "high-touch" and friendly atmosphere.

5.   Status and Facts before the Event

A powerful guiding coalition was formed – TDG, TME, TMG and the mayor of the City of Cologne. Objectives and goals were shared and understood among the coalition. Availability of internal and external resources was checked. The project manager was empowered to act. An event agency was specified with the task. A state of urgency was created through the timeline. Finding a suitable day was difficult as various variables needed to be considered, e.g. vacation, regional fairs and other events. A project structure whereby resources were exchanged on demand was used to coordinate the project. A guiding spirit towards the fulfilment of the objectives and goals was created.

Furthermore, possible race-tracks for the demo-run were researched. The involvement of media was given high priority to secure a return on investment. Media involvement meant to secure favourable pictures – Toyota in combination with as many happy people as possible. The number of possible VIPs depended on the agreed location but was also limited by budget. Security and protection for the public was given top priority during planning and execution.

6.   The Structure: Stakeholders

The main stakeholders in this project with high interest and power were TDG, TME, TMG and the City of Cologne. Should either one of them withdraw at any point in time, the project would have been terminated. Stakeholders with less interest but high power were those holding property in the immediate environment of the event location and bureaucratic machineries as the public affairs office and the traffic regulations office.

Stakeholders that had less power but high interest were the local police office and the fire brigade to ensure emergency planning. People living in the immediate environment of the event were likewise categorized. Every entity in the immediate environment that could prove an impact on turnover for the time of the event was to be considered a stakeholder of less power but high interest but was treated as a stakeholder of high power.

The development of a stakeholder-power matrix helped to identify the risk involved when dealing with the various stakeholders. Especially stakeholders with less interest but high power need to be carefully checked and approached early to secure involvement.

7. Idea and Solution

Apart from the technical requirements imposed by TMG, such as street conditions and drain covers, environmental legislations such as noise and pollution were fundamental in the choice of the event location. Among the possible alternatives the third proposal bared the least future conflict, because it was not in the immediate city centre.

Reinforced through its modern buildings and spacious environment, the location seemed appropriate. In addition it had good traffic connections, which would ease accessibility from outside Cologne. A drawback of the location was the missing proximity to crucial points ensuring sufficient number of pedestrians passing by without prior notice of the event.

8. Concept

To attract as many people as possible and to start creating early media suspense a media and promotion campaign was launched. The media campaigns as well as the promotion were developed within four weeks time. Both campaigns were linked to the race and carried two advantages: to spread the word and to underline the uniqueness of the event. For that purpose a key visual was developed. The key visual was used stringently through all means of media and highlighted the theme, the place and the time.

Figure 28: Key visual

A very important instrument installed at that point of time was the event Web page. The Web page was used to monitor the success of the promotion and media campaign.

The promotion was built around a narcissistic concept. Everybody who wanted to promote himself or herself as a good race commentator was given a platform. People were invited to comment for two minutes on a TMG Formula 1 test-drive. Presentation ceremony was scheduled for the event date. The prize to win: tickets for a Formula 1 race. The casting box used for the promotion was located on a crucial point in Cologne. The location was branded with the key visuals, flags and other means. Four promoters dressed in racing overalls were used for a total duration of ten days. The promotion took place during the weekends before the event weekend. The promoters were also used to distribute flyers around the point of activity. A positive side-effect of the promotion was the generation of film footage to be displayed at the event.

An issue that needed to be tackled was media. To attract as many journalists and TV-channels as possible, a media-event was done. As most members of the Formula 1 team were to be present for the day, the force of attraction was converted into a press conference and one-to-one interviews.

Thus the final concept was a combination of a promotion, a media event and a public event.

9. The Budget

Budget composition City-Grand-Prix

Total cost	100%
City miscellaneous (police, trellises, city authorities, etc.)	9%
Motorsport service TMG (cars, drivers, pit-stop, incl. handling)	5%
Pit Stop truck Michelin	4%
F1 Merchandise booth	6%
Location	3%
Catering	6%
Software / media production	1%
Technical equipment	13%
Decoration / stage setting	10%
Tents / scaffold	5%
Entertainment program	5%

Invitation procedure	2%
Logistics	0%
Manpower	8%
Traveling costs	1%
Concept costs	14%
Administration	2%
Miscellaneous (media, co-operations, etc.)	4%

Table 9: Budget composition City-Grand-Prix

10. Marketing and Communication Insights

Next to the cooperation's with press and media highlighted previously an interesting concept was developed with the local public transportation system. At the day of the event, all tram stations on the tram lines to the event used their displays to make people aware of the event. In this sense every pedestrian moving along the lines has been reached.

11. The Location

The location was subdivided into several fields of activities. The modules allowing for product experience and brand exposure were the following: Hybrid contact area, Land Cruiser Off-road simulation, exhibition of the product range, ADAC child-safety, F1 merchandising, Prius shuttle service for VIPs, the Michelin pit stop truck, the Formula 1 simulator and last but not least the Paddock area. Next to those modules, a climbing garden, a children's playground, a centre stage, a public viewing screen and several catering facilities were placed. Importance was placed on the center stage, for its location to allow for optimal sound and exposure to the public.

When planning for the location, security and safety played an important role. Emergency exists were considered and influenced the position of the modules. Access roads needed to be kept free and clear. The VIP-area was above a garage allowing for secure ways to escape the public when requested. As the foundation of the pace was hollow the buckling load was limited.

12. Design and Decoration

Next to hundreds of meters of banners, the buildings in the immediate environment were used for banners. A skyscraper highlighting a Toyota product was hung from one of the surrounding buildings. Additional space was given to sponsors of the racing team to create an authentic racing atmosphere.

The VIP area was located in a bar and also partly divided into the media area where the press conference took place. Room decoration was kept simple but sophisticated. Due to the high ceilings, several TV-screens were installed to show demo-videos, the promotion film footage and the actual city-run. A one-to-one scale Formula 1 race-car was put up with pit-walling allowing for pictures. In the VIP as well as in the Dealer area, Formula 1 merchandise material was used to underline the theme.

According to the colour-coding the stage was also in red and white.

13. Messages

Raw emotions were the theme created by the sound and smell of running and performing race engines. The first value emphasised: customers first. Except for the VIP area, spectators could touch and see everything that they wanted to. There were almost no limitations and admission was free, except for catering.

The hybrid area transported the image of ecology and sustainability. Spectators could ask questions to the people at the display and inform themselves about Toyota's approach towards the environmental road-crash that could lie ahead should energy consumption continue to rise.

The technological proposition was underlined by the hybrid competence displayed and by the Formula 1 paddock club. The Formula 1 cars and the LeMans provided examples of technological competence.

14. The Process

The way from idea to execution was short – three month time – and intense in terms of meetings. After the draft concept was agreed on, a detailed run down was prepared. Several inspections of the event-location were necessary to check the street conditions and meet the technical specifications. Basically the whole infrastructure needed to be checked, number of power plugs available, voltage needed for modules, water possibility to set up toilets, etc.

Moreover, agreements from the owners of surrounding restaurants to be used for dealers, VIPs and the PR conference were to be established. It was a political game trying to satisfy the various stakeholders and creating a common spirit. Fortunately the location was used regularly for big events. In that light stakeholders could relate to the preparations necessary.

The event-agency had to work on the documents needed to run the event until the last minute. Bureaucratic machineries were a hurdle not easy to jump, especially when time was short. Anticipation and consideration of what might be valuable for stakeholders proved a solid ground for bargaining. A ticket for the VIP area, paddock access or being co-pilot during the demo-run proved powerful.

Location visits became regular with varying specialist for sound, visuals, stage setting and safety. Details for catering and timing were considered, for instance the time to move from the VIP-Area to the stage or to the paddock was taken and contingency plans were drawn.

Planning the availability of in-house resources was also a challenge. Vehicles for various purposes, such as the VIP-Shuttle, exposition and pace car, needed to be allocated and prepared. The budget needed to be presented and approved by senior management and presentations were prepared to update the various stakeholders (TME, TDG, TMG and the City of Cologne) on a continuous basis.

Invitations to the VIPs needed to be sent out and tracked constantly. Tact was very important in dealing with VIPs.

Finally, the budget needed to be reviewed several times to ensure compliance with the estimate. Reviewing the budget was done at three levels: the direct supervisor, the department controller and finally the Board.

15. The Event as Such

Raw Emotions – on August 21st, the first Toyota City-Grand-Prix took place in Cologne. For the first time in Cologne's history, a car manufacturer displayed its strengths in motorsports to the public, attracting 50,000 spectators during the day.

For a day, TDG turned the heart of Cologne into Germany's third race track, enabling Ricardo Zonta and Olivier Panis to show what the Toyota Formula 1 race-cars are capable of in an exiting show-race.

The event started with a spectacular motor show parade from TDG's headquarters, through the city streets and into the event location. Amongst the racing cars on show were three world Rally Cars, two Yaris-Cup Cars and the legendary Toyota 2000 GT. The two Formula 1 racing-cars and the Le Mans GT1 were carried on open trailers, accompanied by a police escort. The parade was topped and tailed by two Prius pace cars.

A range of extra activities were provided to entertain young and old, singles and families alike. To top off the paddock atmosphere, both the race team and the race drivers were involved in activities throughout the day. Several activities, such as the F1-simulators, children's playgrounds and a tire changing competition helped raise the level of excitement to a crescendo just before the show-race. Orchestrated by local entertainers on a large outdoor stage, the event culminated in the show-race around the event location. After the race, local heroes spurred the mood with live-acts and music to die away the summer evening.

Toyota brand power was also supported through other activities such as:

- Hybrid contact area
- Land Cruiser Off-road simulation

- Exhibition of the Toyota and Lexus range
- ADAC child-safety
- F1 merchandising
- Prius shuttle service for VIPs
- Michelin pitstop truck

16. Reactions (Guests, Media)

The event strategy, to use Formula 1 as an anchor to create awareness and to get people in touch with the Toyota brand was successful. The goals and objectives set have been exceeded. TDG has shown that it was possible to leverage its global investment in Formula 1 by arranging a successful national campaign.

After the event the newspaper article headings read as follows and exemplified that the city and its citizens enjoyed the event:

"A breath of Monaco"
"Formula 1 thrilled 50,000 Spectators, Motor Sport at a Touch"
"That was Excellence"
"Motor Sport for Everyone"

Five days after the event, *horizont*, the important German weekly on Marketing, had the following headline on page two:

"The race at the Rhine only knows winners – Toyota-City-Grand-Prix fascinates 50.000 guests in Cologne / image transfer from Formula 1 circus to brand and products works well"

Horizont called the event the happening of the week with four stars out of five maximum. The rating resulted from the following attributes:

- affinity to brand / realization
- PR-effect / target group affinity
- Positive overall impression

In total more than 15 million media contacts were generated. An astonishing 16 TV contributions and 140 media contacts, ranging from daily newspapers to yellow press, were recorded. The media-value of the event had an equivalent of more than EUR 2,000,000.

Media (156 reports)	Contacts
TV	6.160.000
Daily Newspaper	7.793.170
Yellow Press	1.055.966
Trade Press	34.820
Weekly Newspaper	126.790
Advertiser / Freesheets	127.000

Table 10: Media Contacts

17. Evaluation

Evaluation was conducted through on-site surveys and a media survey. The media survey calculated the immediate return in media value and provided the hard facts. The on-site survey was conducted on a basis of a sample size of 2,000. The survey provided important insights into the soft facts of the event and whether objectives and goals had been met.

To conduct the survey a total number of 2,000 people were used using hand-helds.

The final outcome of the surveys proved, that the goal to further emotionalize the Toyota brand was fulfilled. In terms of value dimensions, the event added image value and awareness. The visitors were prepared and willing to get in contact with Toyota which provided a positive opportunity to present the brand. However, not all models seemed to gain: the cross-country vehicles were not among those preferred by a majority of visitors. The mix of fun, race feeling and high-tech worked for the brand. All stakeholders involved won: TMG for getting closer to the people, TDG for adding positive vibrations to the brand, the City of Cologne as enabler and sponsors by being present within a positive image frame. The question of whether the topic of ecology or sustainability is a perfect communication goal might be discussed.

The event deepened the ties between Cologne and Toyota. Comparing the image performance indicators as well as indicators for awareness and liking with those figures obtained at the event one could see that those from the event are significantly higher. Which means that among a group of people not basically attached to Toyota the event raised likebility levels significantly.

There was a high media interest and a possibility for new formats of cooperation with events of this kind.

18. Integration of Communication

The integration of sponsors played an important role to create an authentic racing atmosphere. Spectators should have a real race feeling, for which reason branding opportunities were presented to sponsors of the Panasonic Toyota Racing Team.

In the pre-event phase it was also important that all different media channels provided the same message, place, time and theme. Every point of contact with a Toyota dealer was used. Dealers and various stakeholders were given posters to highlight the event.

EMBOK: A Theoretical and Practical Model for the Event World

Julia Rutherford Silvers

Planned events are gaining increasing recognition and popularity as cultural, celebratory and commercial communication tools. They are also experiencing escalating scrutiny as expectations rise and outcomes are examined in terms of return on investment as well as accountability. These pressures converge in the need for recognition of the management of these events as a legitimate profession, one that relies on a common body of knowledge as a basis for defining the tasks and skills required for practice and the scope of responsibilities associated with event management endeavors. The Event Management Body of Knowledge (EMBOK), as expressed in the International EMBOK Model shown in Figure 20, provides both a theoretical and practical structure to meet the needs of event professionals and achieve the requirements for status as a distinct and genuine profession.

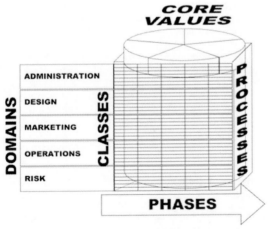

Figure 29: International EMBOK model

341

The International EMBOK Model was developed by the International EMBOK Executive[52], a group of event management practitioner and academic experts. The concept was first suggested by William J. O'Toole in 1999 and an initial domain structure was developed and proposed by this author in 2003, which was based upon an affinity analysis of the knowledge systems supporting the event management industry including numerous occupational standards, certification knowledge domains, academic curriculums and literature review (Silvers, 2004). This domain structure was rearranged and expanded at a retreat in July of 2004 to include phases, processes, and core values, as shown in Table 11.

PHASES	PROCESSES	CORE VALUES
Initiation	Assessment	Continuous Improvement
Planning	Selection	Creativity
Implementation	Monitoring	Ethics
The Event	Communication	Integration
Closure	Documentation	Strategic Thinking

KNOWLEDGE DOMAINS and CLASSES

ADMINISTRATION	DESIGN	MARKETING	OPERATIONS	RISK
Financial Management	Catering Design	Marketing Plan Management	Attendee Management	Compliance Management
Human Resources Management	Content Design	Materials Management	Communications Management	Decision Management
Information Management	Entertainment Design	Merchandise Management	Infrastructure Management	Emergency Management
Procurement Management	Environment Design	Promotion Management	Logistics Management	Health & Safety Management
Stakeholder Management	Production Design	Public Relations Management	Participant Management	Insurance Management
Systems Management	Program Design	Sales Management	Site Management	Legal Management
Time Management	Theme Design	Sponsorship Management	Technical Management	Security Management

Table 11: Scope of the international EMBOK model

---

52 *Members of the International EMBOK Executive include Glenn A J Bowdin, M Phil, ILTM; Joe Goldblatt, Ed.D, CSEP; Matthew D. Gonzalez, MCSE, PMP; Janet Landey, CSEP; Philip Mondor; Kathleen Nelson, Ph.D., CSEP, CMP; William J. O'Toole; and Julia Rutherford Silvers, CSEP.*

1. EMBOK: The Foundation of a Profession

Widely acknowledged as a key characteristic of a profession, a body of knowledge represents the ongoing sum of knowledge related to the tasks, skills, and information amassed through experience by practitioners and research by theoreticians. In order to collect and make this knowledge explicit and transferable, a structure for capturing, categorizing, situating, and retrieving data must be established. Once a body of knowledge is defined, it serves as the foundation for other attributes that signify status as true profession including competency standards, specialized education, jurisdictional authority, and best practice direction. Creation and adoption of the EMBOK sets the stage for accomplishing these facets by serving as the structure for a knowledge system, an assessment system, and a management system.

As a knowledge system, the EMBOK provides an informational architecture that supports data collection and retrieval as well as a classification scheme that describes the nature and scope of event management. Its structure employs several traditional classification systems such as the whole/part nature of a tree approach and the type/instance nature of a faceted analysis approach, which facilitates a flexible and user-based system suitable for managing the often overwhelming amount of information surrounding an individual event project and the true scope of obligations and opportunities of the profession.

As an assessment system, the EMBOK offers a framework for defining, evaluating and enforcing competency and quality standards. Event management practitioners are charged with making decisions that affect individuals and organizations, often with significant economic, political and social implications that impact safety and financial well-being. It is reasonable to expect that controls requiring proof of competency in order to practice, i.e. standards of entry, will emerge so that unqualified or unprepared individuals that do not recognize and understand the scope of their responsibilities are not allowed to perform these functions. It is also reasonable to expect that quality standards will emerge that assist those purchasing event management services, hiring event management personnel and permitting events to occur to make informed decisions, as well as assigning accountability commensurate with the trust and confidence invested in these professionals. Until there are standards of entry into the event management occupation/profession that are based on an agreed-upon set of core competencies (and a rigorous assessment process), all credible credentials suffer. Unless the industry as a whole comes together to establish the parameters for mutual recognition of core competencies and mutual recognition of "valid" credentials, a buyer-beware market will continue, to the detriment of the industry as a whole.

In concert with assessment is the establishment of the curriculum that prepares individuals for the profession. Professions are typically recognized as occupations requiring specialized skills and knowledge that must be acquired through dedicated educational or training programs based on explicit criterion. Credentials are awarded upon completion of a program of study and/or rigorous assessment of performance standards, as well as continuance of professional development education. The EMBOK, due to its holistic and comprehensive nature, provides the definition of tasks and scope of responsibilities that may easily be modularized and standardized for educational programming, as shown in Table 12, as well as job descriptions for personnel.

Major Functions	Performance Elements
Accounting	• Understand the terminology
	• Understand the system
	• Collaborate with accountants and/or bookkeepers to maintain the system
Budget Management	• Determine profit objectives
	• Forecast costs and revenues
	• Allocate financial resources according to priorities
	• Track budget performance
Pricing	• Calculate direct and indirect costs
	• Determine profit requirements
	• Establish pricing structure

Cash Manage-ment	• Establish payment policies and procedures
	• Develop cost controls
	• Manage cash flow
	• Implement cash handling procedures
Reporting	• Establish reporting system
	• Interpret financial information
	• Prepare financial reports
	• Maintain financial records

Table 12: Curriculum model for financial management[53]

As a management system, the EMBOK provides a systematic approach to the complex and often expansive project parameters and responsibilities. It may be used to create budgets, develop work breakdown structures, establish timelines, conduct risk assessments, and pursue continuous improvement through a standardized, predictable process that collects and integrates historical data, as shown in Table 13. Its knowledge domains may serve as an organizational structure delineating divisions, departments or committees that prescribe a structure of authority and accountability, as well as establish the personnel and services to be outsourced and the connected procurement criteria.

Assess	Select	Monitor	Communicate	Document
Initiation				
Goals & objectives; profit philosophy; resource definition; cost estimation; feasibility	Pricing structures; preliminary revenues & expenditures budget; chart of accounts	Interpret financial information; cost & revenue forecasts & estimates	Business plan; budget projections; pricing quotations	Record assumptions & budget projections; cost estimates; set up spreadsheet; business plan
Planning				
Cash flow needs; accounting & banking services; negotiation metrics	Financial procedures; cash flow timetable; credit policies; banking services	Cash flow; budget allocation; bookkeeping	Financial reporting system	Budget performance; calculations; contract negotiations

53 Silvers & Nelson (2005), Reprinted courtesy of speaking of events

Implementation

Cost controls; fixed & variable expenses	Purchasing & change controls; payable & receivable procedures	Cash flow; track budget performance; make appropriate adjustments	Reporting procedures	Maintain budget-to-actual & cash flow records

Event

Cash handling & transaction needs	Cash handling procedures	Process transactions; review & verify master account	Cash transaction reports	Cash reports; transaction records

Closure

Evaluate profitability & budget performance	Make future budget recommendations	Payables & receivables	Final budget performance reports	Budget-to-actual performance; audit; records & reports

Table 13: Planning system for financial management[54]

2. EMBOK: The Practical to the Theoretical and Back Again

A body of knowledge is comprised of theory and best practice heuristics gained through experience. The theory is based and built upon the professional tasks identified by the community of practice performing these tasks, which must then be transformed into a transferable knowledge system that may be continually enhanced. This is the role of both academic institutions and industry associations – formalizing the skills necessary for the professional tasks to proceed as well as clarifying logical, consistent and relevant foundations and the universe of tasks of the profession's jurisdiction (Abbott, 1988).

In addition, both have a role in the pursuit of creating new knowledge through research that will quantify, qualify, verify, or validate commonly held beliefs and practices that industry practitioners have acquired throughout their careers, turning the "school of hard knocks" into hard science. Creating new knowl-

---

54 Silvers & Nelson (2005), Reprinted courtesy of speaking of events

edge through research is a significant link between academia and industry, providing students with learning opportunities and industry practitioners with data that can serve as a foundation for good decision making, event development, and strategies for continuous improvement. This research may be conducted within the academic realm as well as by associations that serve various industry sectors. Research data from both sources will contribute to the body of knowledge and serve current and future practitioners, as well as benefit event consumers through improved standards of practice (Silvers, 2006a).

The practical applications of the EMBOK for event management practitioners are countless. Yet the clear advantage is the ability to elevate the "expert" status of the professional service to be applied to problems that amenable to expert service, determining the best or most likely successful strategy based on specialist knowledge and experience rather than trial and error. As more and more emphasis is placed on Return on Investment (ROI) and Return on Objectives (ROO), event management professionals are moving from mere project managers to strategic executives, or event architects as it were, charged with shaping the event design to strategic goals as they are being developed, thereby conducting brand management not merely managing the logistics (Silvers, 2006b).

The EMBOK framework facilitates the ability to construct and deconstruct an event in the pursuit of these strategic activities. This holds true as an educational exercise such as a case study analysis as well, allowing learners to develop an appreciation for and understanding of interpreting the client's desires and objectives to design the concept or vision for the event and the practicalities of event production within the realities of the resources available. Case studies have long been recognized as a valuable learning tool, providing instructors with methods for promoting mental inquiry (Knowles, Holton, & Swanson, 1998) and students with real life examples to analyze, synthesize and evaluate. The structural delineation expressed in the EMBOK not only provides clear direction on the task requirements of professional event management, it suggests practical exercises in a case study context that will develop the skills necessary for peak performance beyond the academic setting.

3.   Dimensions of the EMBOK

Event management, from conceptualization and execution to final appraisal, is a holistic endeavor requiring a systematic and comprehensive approach. The dimensions of the EMBOK – phases, processes, core values, and domains – categorize the typical functions associated with these endeavors in a broad variety of event genre.

The phases illustrate the overall temporal dimension of event management into which all other functions must be integrated. Although based on traditional project management, the difference is that there is a definitive deadline associated with an event project; the date is fixed, not flexible. Each event project will have a linear timeline that will vary according to the type and scope of the event project, and the tempo will be established by the available time. Typically the initiation and planning phases will be shorter than the implementation phase, but this, too, will depend on the complexity of the event. During these three phases decisions can be made whether or not to proceed with the event, but once the event begins the only no-go possibility is closure (or cancellation of specific elements or activities included in the event). The event itself may only last a short period, but the intensity of the activity and responsibility will increase. Once the event has closed there is still important work to be accomplished, much of which will contribute to the success of the next event – either this event's recurrence or the production of a different event.

The processes represent a widely adopted, proactive and cyclical system capable of responding to the changing nature of event projects. The adoption and implementation of an effective process system is an integral part of creating a Quality Management System that meets the criteria for initiatives such as the ISO Quality Standards. A process may be defined as a set of activities or steps that transforms inputs into outputs. These activities are interrelated and interactive, and in order to be effective, must be systematic. Although many event organizers follow this process system instinctively, they often do not recognize it as a system, one that requires conscious application in order to be effective, efficient and consistent.

The core values represent those paradigms and practices that embody the beliefs, ideals and standards that infuse a fundamental level of quality into decisions made and actions taken throughout an event project and all event management endeavors. They are the attitudes and customs that guide decisions toward choices and behaviors worthy of esteem and replication. In today's demanding and competitive world it is advisable to adopt the core values as one's routine way of thinking so that everything about the event project and its management will be permeated with quality and credibility. They will help establish guidelines and procedures for consistently striving for and achieving excellence. No hierarchy of importance is implied; they are all equally vital to excellence in event management.

The domains of the EMBOK represent the overarching areas of activity or functions within event management. They illustrate the full scope of the responsibilities assigned to event organizers as well as categories suitable for an organizational structure or effective knowledge management. Note that these are organized alphabetically, again without any implied hierarchy or sequential application. However, of prime importance is the illustration of the full scope of the responsibilities and obligations assigned to event organizers. When one looks at the thirty-five elements included in the five domains and then considers the vast number of applications and implications each element represents, as well as the effect each decision regarding each element has on every other element, the scope of responsibilities (and opportunities) may seem overwhelming. However, this magnitude also reveals countless opportunities for specialization.

4. EMBOK Domains: The Backbone of a Diverse Industry

All sectors – meetings and conventions, cause-related and fund-raising events, corporate and live communications events, festivals and civic events, fairs and expositions, social and life-cycle events, entertainment and leisure events, and spectator and participatory sports events – have administrative functions, event design functions, marketing functions, operations functions, and risk management functions that must be performed. The affinity analyses used to formulate the EMBOK Domain facets clearly indicated that the practitioners in each sector are performing the same functions, albeit with different emphasis and different issues per each sector. This commonality of skill sets, as well as similarity to the functions required in other industries, leads the way to career mobility and the ability to integrate and apply a broader field of knowledge within the profession of event management.

The Administration Domain facets represent the functions found in any business or project environment; selecting, allocating and directing financial, human, time, and information resources. These are fundamental workplace skills required of a manager in any business context and, although not necessarily what attracts individuals to the event industry, are critically important to the success of an event project. The policies, procedures and systems developed and utilized here will assure sound business practices are employed to ensure the most effective and efficient use of these always-limited resources to benefit the event project.

The Design Domain facets encompass the creative functions that establish the experience that attendees and guests will encounter at an event, and distinguish the event industry from most other industries. These are typically what attracts many individuals to the profession, yet require just as much due diligence as any other aspect of event management in order to deliver a quality experience that meets expectations of both client and attendee. These facets also represent many of the specialized products and services that are procured from outside resources or developed as areas of specialization for an event organization.

The Marketing Domain facets include the functions that cultivate financial, political and social support for an event project by shaping image and communicating value. An event is a transitory and intangible product with varying target markets capable of providing experiences that enrich and even transform an individual attendee/consumer. Events are also a tool for reaching and teaching consumers in profound ways, reflected in the "live communication" aspect of marketing plans for countless companies and organizations. Managing the marketing aspects of an event project and using events as a marketing tactic require a comprehensive and systematic approach in order to achieve the desired results.

The Operations Domain focuses on all the people, products, and services that converge at the event. Closely associated with the Planning, Implementation and especially the Event phases, the functions included in this domain seek to manage this assembly within a specific place during a specific time period. This requires the application of proper logic, anticipation and balance in order to facilitate a safe, effective, efficient and coherent event experience for all. Competency in these areas is the foundation of most credentials in the event management industry; and for good reason because inexperience or incompetence can cause a plethora of problems or outright failure of an event project.

The Risk Domain facets consist of the legal and moral obligations event management practitioners have regarding the safety and welfare of people and the protection of fiscal assets and physical property. Inattention to these functions can result in unpleasant outcomes, dangerous conditions, and disastrous consequences. Although often mandated by law or policy decree, these are the areas most often misunderstood or ignored by event management practitioners, which jeopardizes not only individual event projects; it also endangers the very efficacy of professionalism throughout the industry.

It is important to recognize that the event industry is a horizontal and vertical industry, encompassing both the event management practitioners in the various sectors and the vendors supplying the goods and services for those events. The EMBOK serves all these role players. Event management practitioners may use the EMBOK to consider all the possibilities to ensure a comprehensive analysis, compelling them to consciously eliminate those responsibilities and opportunities that are not applicable for a single project. Vendors may use the EMBOK to better understand their role within an overall event project as well as adapt their products and services according to a specific sector. For example, the types of security services and their objectives are different for rock concerts and for trade shows.

5. EMBOK: A Practical Point of Reference

The EMBOK serves as a point of reference for a broad spectrum of stakeholders including event organizers, industry associations, educational institutions, sponsors, regulatory agencies, and quality assurance and competency initiatives worldwide.

Event organizers may use the EMBOK as a model to improve quality, efficiency and profitability, measure competency, and create specializations and career mobility. They may use it to identify the gaps in their expertise and experience in order to steer their professional development endeavors or to determine areas of specialization for their career paths or marketing efforts. They may use it to develop checklists, task lists, and numerous other job performance aids, as well as workforce training programs. The EMBOK can be a structure for everything from creating budgets to analyzing insurance requirements, estimating staffing needs to developing sponsorship strategies, establishing site selection criteria to devising procurement plans, conducting feasibility studies to performing risk assessments, and countless other adaptations.

Associations and community of practice organizations may use the EMBOK as a model for benchmarking certification and professional development programs in order to establish the leadership specialties they offer and enhance career portability for their members. They may use it to clarify and communicate their mission to internal and external constituencies, establish and promote their unique value proposition, and develop and position their distinctive brand. They may use it to conduct research into best practices and emerging issues relevant to their members' needs, as well as develop products and services to meet those needs.

Educational institutions may use the EMBOK as a model for creating and refining curriculums that will prepare students for a career in event management. They may use it to benchmark and align the scope of their programs with industry's demands, develop areas of specialization, and adapt existing curricula to the event management context. A significant aspect is the directing and conducting research into the theory and application of event management, which will validate existing knowledge and create the new knowledge that confers the authenticity of the professional jurisdiction.

Sponsors may use the EMBOK as a model for establishing assessment criteria for evaluating competency and quality assurance in order to enhance return on investment. From commercial sponsors contributing to an individual event to destinations bidding on or purchasing a mega event, expectations are established for favorable outcomes for event and sponsor alike. The EMBOK provides a framework for establishing these expectations for both entities, as well as a method for measuring outcomes in a consistent manner.

Governments may use the EMBOK as a model when considering policies and regulatory legislation to protect their citizenry and minimize their liability. They may use to benchmark existing laws and regulations in order to identify gaps or vulnerabilities that require attention. They may use it to establish criteria for authorizing an event to take place, verifying the ability of the organizers to produce a safe event project. They may use it to set standards of performance or limits of event magnitude based on the capabilities of existing infrastructure and public service capacities, as well as determine user-based fees based on demand.

6. Conclusion

The ways in which event management professionals can use the EMBOK framework are plentiful. But, the bottom line is, by using the EMBOK framework one may approach the multifaceted job of event management in a comprehensive manner, ensuring all critical functional responsibilities, possibilities, and opportunities are addressed properly and completely. Using the EMBOK allows one to systematically approach one's duty to perform due diligence, reducing the claims of "I didn't realize" or "I forgot" and increasing the effective use of opportunity management to the benefit of the event host and attendee alike.

The EMBOK, however, has a broader application in the movement toward recognition as a genuine profession, perhaps with standards of entry that create a protected jurisdiction for practitioners. Most certainly it can raise awareness amongst consumers, clients and employers, defining the importance of and respect for the specialized skills and knowledge necessary to perform the complex requirements of competent event management. This, in turn, will enhance public trust and confidence in practitioners, as well as confer autonomy and authority to make the necessary problem solving decisions and have those decisions accepted as credible.

Literature

Abbott, A. (1988). The System of Professions: An Essay on the Division of Expert Labor. The University of Chicago Press.

Knowles, M. S., Holton, E. F., & Swanson, R. A. (1998). The Adult Learner (5th edn.). Butterworth-Heinemann.

Silvers, J. R. (2004). Global Knowledge Domain Structure for Event Management. In Z. Gu (Ed.), Conference Proceedings, Las Vegas International Hospitality and Convention Summit (pp. 228-245). University of Nevada Las Vegas.

Silvers, J. R. & Nelson, K. (2005). Introduction to Financial Management for Meetings & Events. Speaking of Events.

Silvers, J. R. (2006a). An EMBOK Research Menu. The EMBOK Project. Silvers Website.

Silvers, J. R. (2006b) Event Management: Architecture, Engineering, or Project Management?, Mark Sonder Productions Ezine, Summer 2006

Authors

Carina Bauer, Marketing and Operations Director, IMEX. Carina joined IMEX in the autumn of 2002 and is responsible for all aspects of the marketing and communications mix, specifically concentrating on strategic partnerships, sponsorships and press relations. She is also responsible for operating controls. Carina has served on the Board of the MPI UK Chapter and currently serves on MPI's International Multicultural Committee as well as the PEC-E host committee for London 2008. Prior to IMEX Carina held the position of Managing Director of GoodBean Coffee, a family owned chain of coffee shops located throughout the South of England. Carina holds a degree from Oxford University in Politics, Philosophy and Economics.

Tony Carey, CMM, CMP, is now – after 25 years as a professional meeting planner, running his own agency – consultant to the international conference industry. A founder of the UK Chapter of Meeting Professionals International (MPI), he was the first non-North American to chair MPI's International Education Committee. He has been the director of ICCA's 'Forum for the Young Professional' and has presented educational programmes in over 120 different cities, world-wide, is editor of MPI's 'Professional Meeting Management – a European Handbook' and the Convention Industry Council's new international manual. He has also authored two books and received awards for his magazine columns which appear in four international publications.

Kay Sebastian Dallmann is an experienced manager with over seven years of international exposure and a proven track record of five years in the automotive industry with extensive experience in various marketing functions. As a manager for sponsoring, co-operation's and motorsports he successfully established new strategies for new products and launched multiple scorecards to enable better control in the field of sponsoring. His most recent work is in the area of product management, responsible for three product lines (Light Commercial Vehicles, 4x4 and Hybrid).

Charlotte J. DeWitt, CFEE, is President of International Events, Ltd., Boston, USA, and has worked in some 27 countries since 1979. She has designed and produced over 150 waterfront festivals, parades, and international events, including the finale of Singapore's Millennium Chinese New Year's celebration and the opening of the Kuala Lumpur International Buskers' Festival in Malaysia. A highly respected consultant, author and lecturer, she is Past Chairwoman of the International Festivals and Events Association/World (IFEA), today representing some 3000 members in 38 countries on five continents; and founder/ past President/CEO of IFEA Europe. A Certified Festival and Event Executive, she lived in Sweden from 1994-2004.

Tony Erpelding is creative director of Delhi Productions, which designs and builds innovative, experience-based exhibits and themed environments, as well as original media productions, for corporations and museums. For over 25 years Mr. Erpelding has pioneered some of the most creative exhibit and event designs in the industry for companies such as, Sony, Disney, Novellus Systems and Apple Computer. Prior to merging with Delphi, Tony's own design firm created retail and environments for brands such as NutraSweet, Weyerhaeuser, Burger King, Chevron, AT&T and Apple Computer. His interdisciplinary approach to projects provides unique, integrated creative solutions using the latest technologies and story telling techniques.

Sabine Funk has worked in the music industry for nearly 15 years. Since 2000 she is Production Manager of the RhEINKULTUR festival, one of Europe's biggest open-air music festivals. In 2003 she became the RhEINKULTUR GmBH's CEO. In addition, Funk runs her own company – the "Bonn Promotion Dept." and works as a Production Manager for all types of events, with super scale events in public places being her specialty. In 2007 Sabine

Funk created „wissenswerk", a new platform designed to promote the exchange of knowledge and experience within the live music industry. Sabine Funk is certified occupational health and safety engineer and combines a degree in business administration with a professional education as master of event technology.

Corinna Geimer is a Consultant Central Key Account Management at Deutsche Post AG. As responsible project manager she supports the client Verlagsgruppe Weltbild.

Joe Goldblatt, PhD, CSEP, is a Lecturer in the Tourism, Hospitality and Events Group at Queen Margaret University in Edinburgh, Scotland. Prior to this position, he was senior lecturer at Temple University's School of Tourism and Hospitality Management and he also served as executive director for professional development and strategic partnerships for the School. He is the founding president of the International Special Events Society and the developer of the original Certified Special Events Professional program. He is the author, co-author or editor of 19 books and hundreds of scholarly and trade publication articles. He has lectured on five continents in over 50 countries and produced hundreds of events.

Lars Blicher-Hansen is Special Projects Manager at the national tourism organisation VisitDenmark. Journalist by profession, he has worked within the meeting and event industry for more than 20 years. He was Managing Director of the Danish Convention Bureau. Since 1997, Lars Blicher-Hansen has been responsible for special projects at VisitDenmark, i.e. the national Internet portal visitdenmark.com, the tourism promotion of the Hans Christian Andersen 200 Anniversary celebrations, a centre for international event tourism, Event Denmark, and now the development of new meeting concepts, "Meetovation".

Donald Getz, PhD, is a Professor in the Haskayne School of Business, University of Calgary, Canada / Professor, School of Tourism, University of Queensland, Australia and visiting Professor, Göteborg University, Sweden. He is author of several books and many research articles on event management, event tourism and event studies. He was a co-founder of the research journal Event Studies, and he frequently teaches, speaks and consults on event-related topics around the world.

Christian Have is founder and CEO of Have PR & Kommunikation. Since 1983, Christian Have has handled a huge number of various PR and communication projects, both in Denmark and abroad. He published his first book "Visibility Equals Existence" in 2004. Have PR & Kommunikation is a PR and communication company specialising in arts-related and humanitarian projects, both nationally and internationally. The company's exclusive commitment to art and culture has made it one of the leading companies of its kind in Scandinavia. Have PR & Kommunikation has won a European SABRE Awards in the category Entertainment and Culture for their PR/Communication work of Hans Christian Andersen 2005 worldwide.

Tilman Henke worked as a volunteer with the Association of Christian Scouts and Guides and was active in the Protestant Youth Work in Schools programme in the Rhineland. Following training as a bank clerk, he studied economics at the University of Witten/Herdecke. He was employed in the financial management department of German Telecom Ltd in Bonn. Since 1998 he has worked for the German Protestant Kirchentag as Director of administration and finance and as Office Manager for the local Kirchentag offices in Stuttgart, Frankfurt, Berlin, Hannover and Cologne. Since November 2006 Tilman Henke has been a member of the Executive Board with responsibility for the areas of finance, personnel and administration.

Moniek Hover is a senior lecturer in Imagineering at NHTV International University of Applied Sciences, Academy for Leisure, Breda, the Netherlands. She is chair of the Imagineering Competency Group. She is responsible for the research programme on experience (instruments). The Academy for Leisure is the largest programme at NHTV University with some 1,800 students. It focuses on the international leisure industry which has been roughly divided into Event Management, Sports management, Management of Creative Industries and Leisure Project Management. In 2007 the Academy for Leisure has been awarded the Special Quality Mark for Imagineering by the NVAO (Dutch Flemish Accreditation Organisation).

Tracey Hull is an events consultant working with local government and event organisers. Tracey has managed and worked with a large number of events in regional Australia.

Christiane Legler is Senior Consultant in the field of Event + Sponsoring at Pleon (Europe's largest communication agency) and responsible project manager for the conceptual design of the event.

Polo Looser started his career as a tour guide within the tourism industry, working for Kuoni Ltd. for over ten years. Back in Switzerland he completed studies in business administration and changed to the pharmaceutical industry, where he headed the sales unit. In this position he brought a number of new products to the market and hosted a multitude of event. Polo took this experience to the agency, where he consults customers in the area of event management and implementation since ten years. During this time he completed his studies in Change Management as MBA in Switzerland and USA. Today he is Managing Director for the Central European Region of MCI, employing more than 80 talents.

Carolin Maluck is Senior Consultant in the field of Event + Sponsoring at Pleon (Europe's largest communication agency) and responsible project manager on the part of the agency.

Aaron McConnell, MBA, graduated from the University of Calgary with his MBA in 2005. Currently he is the event director of the TransRockies Challenge. He has extensive event management experience as the organizer of three UCI World Cup Mountain Bike Events and eleven "24 Hours of Adrenalin" mountain bike relay events throughout North America, as well as numerous other events.

Johan Moerman is managing director of Rotterdam Festivals Council. Until he founded Rotterdam Festivals in 1993 he was deputy director of the Rotterdam Arts Council. Besides these responsibilities he does some advisory work. He is a Board member of the International Festivals and Events Association, the European Network for Audience development AEN and the Rotterdam Philharmonic Gergiev Festival.

Simon Naudis' background is in financial services and advertising. As Sales Training Manager at Yellow Pages he got his first taste of training and development. After working for General Telephone & Electronics (GTE) he set up a training consultancy the original Answers Training. He has written numerous articles on management and sales related topics and is regularly called to deliver events on behalf of the Association of Exhibition Organisers, Training and Enterprise Councils, Business Links, the Chartered Institute of Training and Development and other national and international government bodies. He has also written two books on selling; Advanced Telesales – The Definitive Guide and The Gentle Art of Firm Persuasion.

Gabriele Nottelmann completed courses in Scandinavian Studies, Roman language Studies and Public Law in Kiel and in Turku (Finland). During and after her studies she worked at North German Radio (NDR) in Kiel as a radio reporter. After a year abroad as an editor with Swedish Radio in Stockholm she became the Press Consultant of the German Protestant Kirchentag in Frankfurt/Main 2001. Following that she worked for Lufthansa in Hamburg and in Frankfurt as adviser for internal communications. At the 31st German Protestant Kirchentag in Cologne she worked as consultant with responsibility for environmental issues.

William J. O'Toole is an internationally known event and festival consultant working with local and city authorities including Dubai Tourism. He trains event and festival managers on developing their management systems. His textbook is used for courses around the world. He is a founding director of the International Event Management Body of Knowledge (EMBOK).

Mike Ribalta is a journalist, media-producer and event-manager. He acts as head of the department for the professional visitors and worked at the Fira de Tàrrega since 2001. He also is responsible for the national and international promotion of Fira. With wide experience in cultural and artistic promoting as well as in media his background includes script writing and film producing for the Catalan TV and communication manager for the town hall of Sant Cugat. He studied history at the Universitat Autonoma de Barcelona.

Francisco Juárez Rubio is director of the department of finance and business administration at the University of Lleida (UdL), Spain.

Julia Seehausen is Event Manager at Verlagsgruppe Weltbild and responsible project manager on the part of Verlagsgruppe Weltbild.

Urs Seiler works as brand experience consultant and journalist in Zurich, Switzerland and Sussex, England. He is the author of the longseller Trade Fair Management – Success lies beyond the m2 (Messen Messbar Machen in German). His forthcoming book "Brand Entertainment. Erlebnismarketing in der Kundenökonomie" is out in the German language.

Julia Rutherford Silvers, a Certified Special Events Professional, is the author of Professional Event Coordination (Wiley, 2004), Risk Management for Meetings and Events (Butterworth-Heinemann, 2007), as well as numerous distance learning courses, instructional videos, booklets, articles, and award-winning research papers on event management topics. She is the originator of The Event Management Body of Knowledge (EMBOK) Project. She serves as an adjunct faculty member of the Tourism and Convention Department at the University of Nevada, Las Vegas, for whom she teaches Meetings and Event Risk Management and Meetings and Event Coordination online.

Lewis Siris (President/Executive Producer) of Public Works Inc., is regularly called upon by government entities, corporations and non-profits to plan and produce a wide variety of public celebrations and events. He has played significant roles in a wide variety public events including: the New York City Marathon, the 1996 Summer Olympics, Ticker-tape Parades for championship sports teams, First Night NYC 2000/2001, New York's Greenwich Village Halloween Parade, Op Sail 2000, and President Clinton's Inauguration, among others. Lewis has given presentations on a variety of event related topics for the International Festivals and Events Association and First Night International.

Ulrich Wünsch, M.A., is professor in Event Communication and head of the Event Management department at the International University of Applied Sciences Bad Honnef · Bonn, lecturing with a focus on events created by corporations. He consults and coaches for the event and hotel industry as well as creating events for clients like Lufthansa Cargo, Postbank, Kaufhof AG, Tropical Island. After having studied German language and literature, linguistics, psychology and marketing in Germany and the USA, he acted as dramaturge and director at various municipal theaters in Germany, worked as a journalist for print, radio and TV and was member of the executive board of an event agency operating Europe-wide.

Brian Wiseman has spent his entire career in the Marketing Communications Industry with particular emphasis on Exhibitions. In the 1980's, Brian launched FHM magazine. He has been a key player in both the exhibition and publishing industries over the last 35 years. Brian sold his exhibition company in 1989 to Blenheim Group PLC, becoming the Deputy Chairman of the UK operating arm. He was with Blenheim for a number of years, and was responsible for organizing a wide range of successful exhibitions. Since leaving his last full time position, Brian has used his experience and knowledge to acquire a number of consultancy projects.

Ana Maria Zumsteg, a native of Peru, Ana Maria completed studies in Hospitality Management in Switzerland and worked for various hotel chains in Australia, New Zealand and Asia. Following further studies in Tourism she joined Griffith University (Brisbane, Australia) where she worked as Senior Teaching Fellow for over four years. Back in Switzerland, Ana Maria joined Zurich Financial Services in 1998. After completing post-graduate studies in Marketing she has held a number of positions in the field of marketing and communications and is currently the Head of Events Strategy for the Group.